DMU 0392788 01 9

KT-451-428

ENDURANCE
START TO FINISH

MARCY PAVORD

ENDURANCE START TO FINISH

J. A. ALLEN · LONDON

British Library Cataloguing-in-Publication Data.
A catalogue record for this book is available
from the British Library.

ISBN 0.85131.648.4

Published in Great Britain in 1996 by
J. A. Allen & Company Limited,
1 Lower Grosvenor Place,
Buckingham Palace Road,
London, SW1W 0EL.

Typeset by Setrite Typesetters Ltd, Hong Kong
Printed by Dah Hua Printing Press Co., Hong Kong

Photographs by Eric Jones & Marcy Pavord
Photograph on page 79 by Bob Langrish
Designed by Paul Saunders

CONTENTS

Aknowledgements

The author would like to thank the many vets, riders, farriers crews and organisers who have unknowingly contributed their knowledge and experience of the sport, without which this book could not have been written. Particular thanks to Rod Fisher MRCVS, for reading the manuscript, to Kerry Ridgway DVM and to my husband, Tony Pavord MRCVS.

INTRODUCTION

'ONE HORSE, one hundred miles, one day' is an oversimplified definition of the aim of endurance riding at championship level. At beginner level, as in many sports, the definition could be 'a nice day out with my horse and a rosette at the end of it'. The satisfaction of having achieved something worthwhile is the factor that is common to both and in this book we shall look at ways of reaching that state of achievement at whatever level you choose.

First, however, let us explain what the sport is all about and try to share the intense experience that comes only from taking the partnership of human and horse to its ultimate limits.

Why do endurance riders feel they have a right to this claim? It is because only in the endurance sport does the rider spend so much time in concerted effort with one horse. The resulting relationship is deep and personal, a one-to-one commitment with its own rules, language of communication and reciprocal understanding. Top endurance riders are usually strongly individualistic, independent, determined people. So are top endurance horses. Many horses which become endurance winners would not be tolerated in other disciplines nor in a more conformist environment, both for reasons of temperament and because of their need for individual treatment and attention. Nowhere is the oft-repeated premise that 'all horses are individuals' felt more strongly. Most endurance riders have only one high-level horse at a time. Those who do have more than one are well aware of the need to give them their appropriate share of attention, just as with children, otherwise jealousies can get out of hand.

This is not to suggest that human characteristics should be attributed to horses. Horses have their own distinctive behaviour patterns and mental processes and learning about these, so that you can communicate effectively with your horse and channel its behaviour in the most desirable way, is just one of the many intricacies of the sport.

It is a sport which encompasses practically every aspect of horsemastership, athletic and mental training, horse psychology, health and veterinary considerations and riding techniques, with the one exception of jumping, and therein lies its endless fascination for those once nudged into entering their first ride.

But why does anyone do it? Show jumpers and event riders often ask this question and the answer is no more satisfactory than the answers to the question 'Why climb mountains?' or 'Why go to the moon?' The sport which the arena-based rider might consider a quick way to get a sore behind, represents the greatest challenge imaginable to the rider who is also a lover of adventure. Endurance riding is an exploration, not only of new territory and the horse's ability to conquer it, but of the self, constantly setting and achieving new personal goals, new levels of confidence and self-reliance and doing it all in communion with a creature from another species, which is, nevertheless, an equal partner in the enterprise and also a friend.

To understand what really makes endurance riders so committed to a sport which, in an era of of commercialism, still generally eschews prize money, you

Young riders and cousins, Linda and Donna Helme, riding Siberia and Bobby, tackling a long hill on the spectacular Red Dragon Ride in Wales.

must understand the power of the relationship between human and horse which has existed since the dawn of time. No other non-human creature has played such an essential part in shaping the course of history and the horse's most vital role has been that of providing a means of communication and transport over vast distances. More remarkable still is the horse's willingness to co-operate with people in their ventures, to show trust and, indeed, the nearest

An enduring partnership depends on the development of trust and co-operation between horse and rider. (Janice Cockley-Adams with Dahook.)

thing that horses know to affection, which is to prefer to be near you rather than not. These two factors are the essence from which the endurance sport is distilled.

With its power and strength, the horse is responsible for carrying the rider. With his or her ability to think and reason, the rider is responsible for maintaining the horse's well being throughout the venture. It is this responsibility which gives the endurance rider the incentive to learn everything he or she can that will help them to achieve a successful outcome to their effort.

If endurance serves to remind the modern equestrian world of the horse's natural abilities and lifestyle, it will perform a great service. By stabling the horse, limiting its exercise and bending its activities to fit a stylised, modern, human ideal, we have created such an artificial environment that the horse's evolutionary heritage as a free-roaming, distance-covering creature is frequently forgotten. We think horses like to be tucked up inside at night and that more than an hour of hard exercise constitutes overworking them. Indeed, endurance riders are sometimes accused of cruelty for making their horses go so far in competition.

This vital point must be cleared up right at the beginning of this book. Going for long distances does not harm horses. Horses with plenty of space to range over may easily cover 20 or 30 miles (32–48 km) in a day with no training whatsoever, so when you start endurance riding at the lower levels of the sport there is no need to fear. You will probably be much more tired after your first 20-mile ride than your horse will!

With training, horses can easily cope with further distances, even up to the championship distance of 100 miles (160 km) in a day. The critical factor in the equation is speed. Horses can run fast – it is their natural means of escape from predators. However, they would not necessarily have to run fast for more than a few miles to escape being caught and eaten. In endurance riding, as they progress through the levels of training, they are expected to maintain progressively higher speeds over the various distances, commensurate with any restrictions imposed by terrain. This is where the skill of the rider and trainer comes in. The horse's athletic ability to perform in this way is enhanced by training, just as its ability to jump or do dressage would be. Correct training enables the rider to conserve the horse's energy, to go faster when speed is needed and to maintain an even pace, which does not overstress the horse, when it is not. Going too fast, for too long certainly will cause problems and although the rider is expected to learn this as their experience grows, the sport also insists on stringent veterinary controls which have the effect of stopping any horse which shows signs of impending trouble. This combination of rider skill and veterinary control ensures that the welfare of the horse is maintained throughout competition.

Endurance is still considered a 'fringe' activity by the majority of competitors in equestrian sport and as its goals are entirely different from those of the

Passing a final vetting when the horse is tired can be a nerve-wracking experience. At an international competition, there is a hug for Mellways Royal Prince from the British team vet.

other disciplines, perhaps this is no bad thing. It is entirely amateur in the truest sense of the word – a thing done purely for the love of it (amateur comes from the Latin *amator*, meaning 'a lover') – but it suffers from modern misinterpretation of the word, which is to suggest doing things in an inexpert, unsophisticated way. Nothing could be further from the truth – it takes a great deal of expertise and knowledge to complete a 100-mile (160 km) ride successfully.

Endurance is a sport for all ages: a dedicated mum with a very young competitor.

This 'amateur' status puts endurance outside the mainstream, where money interests and commercial pressures place more importance on cups, trophies and prize money than on the satisfaction of taking part and achieving the best performance of which you and your horse are capable on the day. The result is that while the sport finds it difficult to obtain sponsorship, publicity and promotion, it remains open, friendly, encouraging to newcomers and will subject you to no pressure except the personal goals you set for yourself. The old ELDRIC (European Long Distance Rides Conference) motto 'To finish is to win' may no longer hold true now that we have international championships, but it is still the basic principle of the vast majority of competitions at the lower levels.

This question of whether you are there to win or simply to make a good show of taking part raises a further question: do we have here two separate sports in one?

The answer is partly yes, in that there are two distinct types of competition. At the higher, international, most challenging level, the aim of being first past the post, as well as passing all the veterinary controls successfully, adds a fiercely competitive edge. At the lower end of the scale, shorter-distance rides are run to set standards, with the aim of testing horse and rider against *competitive conditions*, not against other horses and riders. Somewhere in the middle the two

The amazing Veronica Lott with Caron Gambler. The pair completed their first 100-miler when Veronica was 68 years old. They completed the same ride twice more and, nearly a decade later, are still competing.

aspects meet and it is entirely up to you, as a rider, how far along the competitive road you wish to go. This wide range of levels and groups of competitions attracts many people to the sport as there is considerable recognition of consistently good achievement at the lower-distance levels and there are plenty of goals to aim for without ever reaching the stage of thinking that you have gone as far as you can go with any particular horse. We shall look at all of these later in the book.

It is somewhat ironic that a 'minority' sport should have made such a major contribution to general horse welfare and knowledge. The intense demands which the sport places on the horse's physical ability, coupled with the increasing speeds at which major long-distance competitions have been won over the past decade, have forced those involved in its organisation to pay tremendous attention to these subjects despite a total lack of any funds for scientific research. The result has been a high degree of veterinary and horse management knowledge, developed mainly through observation and experience and making use of whatever scientific input was available from studies of horses engaged in other athletic pursuits, principally racing in its various forms.

The scientific and veterinary aspects have been geared mainly to understanding the problems that occur in endurance competition, how to treat them when they do occur, how to recognise early indications of stress and thus prevent more serious trouble and how to advise riders on minimising risks by improved management. Throughout the endurance riding world, which includes Europe, the Americas, Australia, New Zealand, South Africa and the Middle East, there are experienced, endurance-riding veterinary surgeons who have developed a highly effective system of controls for protecting the horse during competition. This knowledge extends to coping not only with the injuries and metabolic problems which may occur in normal conditions but also those that occur in conditions of extreme heat and humidity. Seven years before the equestrian sporting authorities began to worry about the potential problems facing horses going to compete in the Olympics in Atlanta, British endurance horses were winning World Championship gold medals in Rome, racing 100 miles (160 km) in conditions reported as 'very hot and humid'.

The horse management side has seen the development of a group of riders, aided by their essential back-up crews, who are skilled in producing horses capable of the sustained effort required for success at speed over distance. They also know how to monitor the horse's changing condition during a competition, how to conserve and best utilise the horse's energy reserves and how to present for the veterinary inspections with the best chance of passing 'fit to continue'. These skills are acquired through experience, study and communication and exchange of views with others throughout the sport. The all-pervading concern for the horse's welfare and interest in helping to resolve difficulties ensures that if you, as a newcomer, have any queries or problems, other riders and the officiating vets will always be happy to help and advise.

Sport is the contemporary alternative to exploration and conquest. As the horse aided people in those earlier endeavours, so we can continue to develop the horse/human relationship through equestrian sport. Endurance as a competitive sport began in the 1950s in America, when Wendell Robie set out to prove that horses then were as good as those of the old pioneer days by riding 100 miles (160 km), from Squaw Valley to Auburn, California, over the old

At top level it is the ultimate equestrian challenge. Benedicte Atger and Sunday D'Aurabelle on their way to a team gold medal for France at the World Championships in the Hague.

Australia's top young rider Brook Sample and Sharahd Cavalier.

Pony Express trails, in under 24 hours. That successful attempt founded the world's most famous ride, now familiarly known as the Tevis Cup. The history of the sport since then is well documented elsewhere but the ultimate goal – to complete the distance successfully without detriment to the horse's welfare – remains the same and this book is dedicated to all who share it.

CHAPTER 1

THE RIGHT TYPE OF HORSE

MOST newcomers to endurance riding begin with the horse they already possess. Later, if their ambitions progress, they look for a horse with more natural aptitude for the sport. Most riding horses can achieve a basic level of endurance, just as they can in show jumping or dressage but, beyond that, success requires the right horse for the job. The 'right horse' is not a stereotype but an individual animal possessing a variety of contributory characteristics which will provide the basic material from which an endurance horse can be developed. These characteristics will not be equal or identical in every prospective performer – to take a basic example, they might be of different breeds – but the sum of the characteristics in each case should give a starting point from which you can reasonably hope to work for success.

Before we can decide what kind of horse we need, we must take a look at what we are going to ask it to do. This can be listed as follows:

- Keep going for several hours, possibly up to 24 in one day.
- Maintain an average speed which is high enough either for the set speed of a particular class or to beat the competition in a ride against the clock.
- Cope with varying types of terrain and going.
- Stay sound.
- Recover well, avoiding metabolic problems.
- Pass veterinary inspections in all respects 'fit to continue'.
- Give a comfortable, enjoyable ride that does not overtire the rider.
- Continue to perform well over a lifetime's career.

A steep climb over rough shale in near darkness – just one more challenge to the intrepid.

No horse is going to fulfil all of these criteria all of the time. There will be problems and setbacks, but the pursuit of excellence is a valid goal and we should not make the mistake of thinking that because our particular horse, managed in a traditional way, is incapable of achieving it, the goal must be too tough. There will always be some horses who achieve success in any specific competition and this provides the criteria by which the others should be judged. Were they not fit enough, having an off day, badly managed or simply not the right horse for the job?

The goals are there. The problem is to find horses that can achieve them, through selection and training and, ultimately, through breeding specifically for the sport.

As standards worldwide have been raised through better scientific knowledge, the principal problems inherent in the sport have become more clearly identified. Consequently, it is now easier to define the type of horse which is more likely than another to be successful.

Without doubt, the major cause of failure is lameness. Any horse which goes lame during a competition, or by the time of the final vetting after the finish, is eliminated and more horses are eliminated for lameness than for any other reason. Everything which contributes to the horse's soundness, from its basic conformation to the way it is ridden, is therefore of vital importance.

The second most common cause of failure is elimination for metabolic

Lameness is the major cause of elimination and its prevention is intrinsic to training and management.

reasons, specifically demonstrated by a high heart rate. There are many potential reasons for this to occur. The most usual one is that the horse is not fit enough but there are others, some of which can be taken into account when selecting a suitable horse.

Apart from avoiding the negative aspects of actual elimination, we want to choose a horse which has positive potential for success. In countries where there is a large pool of horses from which to select and where they are more likely to be considered a material resource than part of the family, they will be tested in competition – often with the minimum of preparation – and if they do not make the grade they will be discarded. Although heartless, this is not such a bad means of selection as only the best are retained for competition and future breeding. In Britain, and most other countries where horse riding and ownership is a leisure activity often enjoyed by all the family, such a system would be unacceptable, both morally and on animal welfare grounds, and impractical because of the cost of buying a horse and the smaller selection available.

The result is that there are plenty of unsuitable horses around and very few potentially brilliant ones and this produces a tendency for owners to scale their goals down to suit the horse rather than improve the horse to achieve the goal. Riders who are new to the sport are frequently amazed at how much even mediocre horses can achieve once they begin to take their training and management more seriously. Where standards of training and management are high and horses are treated on an individual basis, it should be possible to take them to their potential limits of achievement without overriding. However, those limits will be much broader if we begin by selecting a horse that is inherently suited to the sport.

First, let us list the attributes that a potential endurance horse should have:

- healthy constitution on which to build training
- hard, tough, well-conformed feet
- a strong skeletal framework, with dense, hard bone
- athletic conformation appropriate to endurance work
- a high percentage of aerobic energy-producing muscle fibres
- a strong and healthy heart
- healthy lungs and respiratory system
- a tough and assertive mind

Healthy Constitution

As with any horse whose future career is to be ridden, it is important that the young endurance prospect should have been well cared for during its formative years. Stories of 'res cue cases' going on to tremendous success are heartwarming, but neglect is more likely to have the effect of permanently damaging a horse's chances of ever reaching the top. A youngster who is undernourished does not develop properly. Apart from failing to realise its full growth potential, it is liable to develop bone and joint abnormalities which will cause problems later on. Failure to attend to regular worming can result in permanent damage to the digestive system. Neglect of the feet will result in uneven growth and, as a consequence, abnormal bone growth because of distorted pressure on the joints. Overfeeding of youngsters can have equally disastrous consequences. It stimulates the bones to grow too fast, without the accompanying development of strength and hardness, so that deformities result.

Young horses need an adequate, balanced diet, regular, routine health care and an environment that gives them the freedom to develop naturally. They should not be 'worked', i.e. lunged, nor backed at too early an age, while living on a hillside or in the old, traditional 'ridge and furrow' field will help them to develop strength and agility. Safe, natural obstacles in the environment are useful, or you can quietly introduce your youngster to simple ground exercises, such as stepping over poles or through tyres and accustom it to things it will meet in later life – flapping washing, water, umbrellas, vehicles (at home, not on

An Arab stallion with an appealing outlook and good basic conformation of the compact, strong type.

the road!) and other animals. Grooming, general handling, picking up feet, loading, walking and trotting out in hand and getting used to wearing tack are all things that the youngster can learn which will save time and trouble later. Such an education will be of far more value in giving it a sensible outlook on life than trying to introduce formal training too soon.

Hard Feet

Lameness is the major cause of elimination in endurance rides and most fore-limb lamenesses are in the foot. These two simple facts emphasise the vital importance of good feet in the endurance horse and yet it is remarkable how often poor feet are overlooked when everything else appears satisfactory. Appearances, however, can be deceptive and it is very likely that problems in the feet will lead to more serious problems elsewhere if they have not already done so.

Consider the weight of the average riding horse (between 360 and 550 kg or 800–1,200 lb), which is transferred to the ground by the very small weight-bearing area of the feet. The horse carries about two-thirds of its weight at the front, so a horse at the lighter end of the scale is taking approximately 120 kg (265 lb) in weight on each front foot – the equivalent of nearly five bags of horse feed! Add to that the weight of the rider and then the additional force created by movement and it is easy to see why both strength and perfect balance are needed in the feet.

The feet cannot be considered in isolation. Whatever happens in the feet has a corresponding effect all the way up through the limbs and the rest of the body as each related area tries to compensate for any defect and thus takes additional strain, which ultimately affects that part of the body's ability to perform.

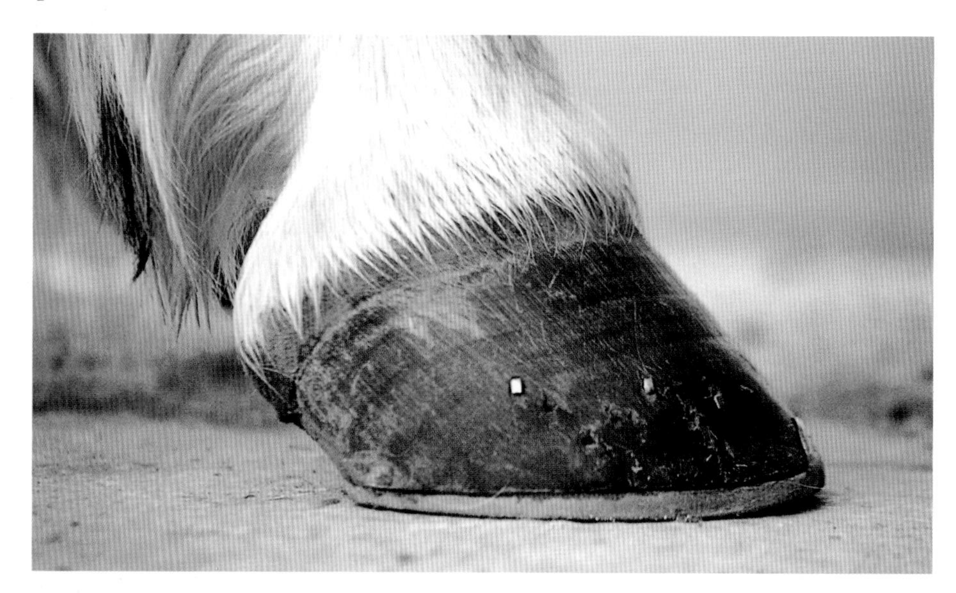

A foot which has overgrown the shoe at the heel. This is a common problem which often leads to corns unless the foot is regularly reshod with sufficient width to give more support to the hoof wall.

Unfortunately for them, perhaps, horses are remarkably forgiving creatures and frequently try to go on performing when there is a chronic problem of which the rider is all too often oblivious. It is only when the rider becomes more ambitious and begins to ask for more strenuous levels of performance that the problem begins to affect the results and the rider finally realises that something is wrong. By that time permanent damage is likely to have occurred, which will prevent the horse ever fully realising its original potential, although it may be possible to alleviate the problem to a considerable degree and enable the horse to continue a useful career.

When sizing up your prospective endurance horse, therefore, look first at its feet. Different breeds have slightly differing types of feet. An Arab, for example, will tend to have smaller, more upright feet, with denser horn than a Thoroughbred. After allowing for these differences, however, basic good conformation should be as follows.

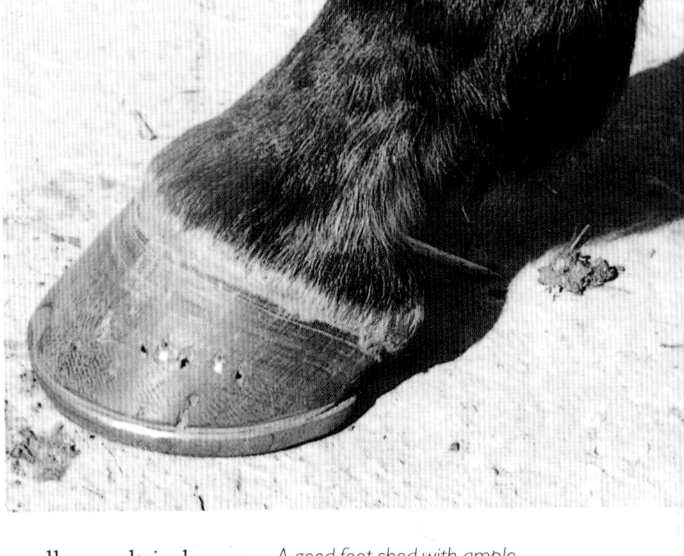

A good foot shod with ample width at the heel.

Each fore and hind foot should be a mirror image of its partner. Any deviation gives immediate warning of a problem, whether congenital or as the result of an injury or poor care and farriery. The angle which the front of the hoof wall makes with the ground and the angle of the pastern relative to the ground should be identical and this is more important than the angle itself, which is said to be ideal at between 45 and 50 degrees. If the hoof/pastern axis does not form a continuous line, it will appear either broken forward, which means that the toe has been artificially shortened or the heel has become overgrown, or broken back, in which case the toe has been allowed to grow too long and the heel has collapsed towards the ground. Both are serious defects, creating the potential for permanent damage and chronic lameness. Where the axis is broken forward, the stride is shortened and concussion is increased, which may eventually result in bony changes such as sidebone or ringbone. Where the axis is broken back – a more commonly found situation – there is serious strain, causing bruising and damage to the internal structures of the foot, which, in extreme cases, could result in traumatic laminitis. A further and more common effect is that the increased pressure on the heels, causing them gradually to collapse, restricts the blood supply to the area, which is thought to be a contributory factor to navicular disease.

The joints and tendons of the fetlock, pastern and hoof provide the means to absorb the jarring and concussive effects of the force of the horse's weight and action being transferred to the ground in movement. They are strong but complex and any significant strain may leave a weakness, with consequent doubt over the horse's future athletic success. The longer and more sloping the pastern, the greater the absorption of concussion and the smoother the ride. However, there is also greater strain on the tendons. The slightly more upright pastern is more prone to concussion but less to tendon strain.

There is some evidence that successful endurance horses tend more towards the slightly more upright hoof/pastern axis (up to 55 degrees in the front feet). However, this may also be linked to other aspects of foot conformation. It is worth remembering that tendon strain is immediately evident, whereas the effects of concussion may only gradually become apparent over several years.

The front feet should be round and open in shape, the hind feet will be more oval and the hoof/pastern axis more upright than in the front feet. The hoof wall should be smooth, without flaking or cracking, made of strong, dense but not brittle horn and the front of the hoof wall should form an even slope. The hoof wall is subject to considerable stress, both carrying weight and resisting wear and concussion. Defects which appear may be due to uneven growth,

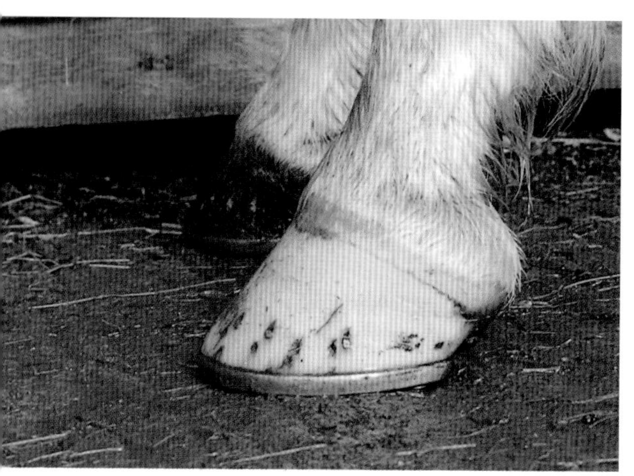

Horn strength does not depend upon its colour. Here is a white hoof with good heel growth and strong horn in good condition.

poor farriery, dietary deficiencies or bad management but, whatever their cause, something is wrong that must be investigated and corrected if the horse is to be asked to do strenuous work. The familiar rings which are often seen denote a change in the horse's diet or lifestyle. Sometimes the effect is quite drastic. For example, if a horse has changed from poor care and an inadequate diet to good care and a better diet, the appearance of the whole hoof will improve and this improvement can be seen growing progressively down the hoof wall over the course of the nine months or more required to grow a completely new hoof.

At the heels, the hoof wall returns sharply on either side to form the bars. As these extend the weight-bearing capacity of the foot, they should never be trimmed away.

'Open' feet have good breadth and support at the heels, with large, well-defined frogs. The frog plays a part in expanding the foot and cushioning against concussion. The conformation of the underside of the foot is particularly important for the endurance horse. Some horses have naturally flat feet, others have feet which have become flat through neglect, by allowing the toes to grow overlong and the heels to collapse, as already mentioned. If the sole is flat and close to the ground, the risk of injury through bruising is greatly increased. Thin soles, often found in Thoroughbreds, compound the problem. The sole needs to be sufficiently thick to protect the internal structures of the foot and sufficiently concave to bear weight without damage from ground contact over most types of terrain.

Strong Skeletal Framework

The horse's skeleton is the framework which supports the rest of its body. Inherent athletic ability, i.e. scope for powerful movement of various kinds, depends upon its shape and strength, as does the ability to carry weight. Developed athletic ability is the result of training but that will be partially limited by the raw material available in the individual undeveloped horse. Energy created in the muscles causes them to contract. The muscles are attached to the joints of the bones by a complex system of tendons and ligaments. When the muscles contract, the energy is transmitted to the joints via the tendons and ligaments, causing them to move.

The shape, size and angulation of the bones which make up the skeleton influence the ways in which the horse is able to move, the space available for strong attachment of tendons and ligaments and the stability of the overall structure as a moving, weight-carrying mechanism.

Bones develop from cartilage, which calcifies to become the solid structure

A seven-year-old Standardbred mare. This is a powerful, tough and solidly built breed. The long head is typical but is well balanced by the relatively short and well-muscled neck which rises from a powerful shoulder. The shoulder is well sloped with plenty of scope for forward movement. The withers are well shaped, flowing into a level back which makes for comfortable riding. The back is relatively long, the quarters well sloped and strong, the limbs well muscled with substantial bone and short cannons, all typical of the breed.

we think of as bone. A young horse's bones continue to grow until it is at least five years old, the growth taking place at the ends of the long bones, where cartilage is continuously produced and then calcified. If overfeeding, dietary deficiency or too strenuous activity should interfere with this process, abnormal growth can result and any deviation from symmetrical development will be a limiting factor of the horse's athletic potential. Bone takes longer to develop and mature than any other part of the horse's anatomy. Although growth ceases eventually, bone is not a finished, dead substance but a living, changing one and, once serious work commences, the bones continue to strengthen and become more dense in structure. Overstress of bones and joints, or injury, can result in various bone diseases such as splints (especially in young horses), spavin, sidebone and ringbone and, in older horses, in arthritic conditions.

The length and shape of the various bones, when put together to form the skeleton, give the basis of the horse's conformation.

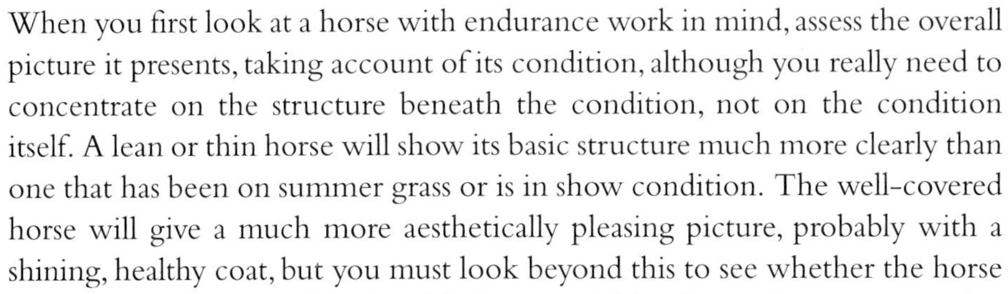

Athletic Conformation, Appropriate to Endurance Work

When you first look at a horse with endurance work in mind, assess the overall picture it presents, taking account of its condition, although you really need to concentrate on the structure beneath the condition, not on the condition itself. A lean or thin horse will show its basic structure much more clearly than one that has been on summer grass or is in show condition. The well-covered horse will give a much more aesthetically pleasing picture, probably with a shining, healthy coat, but you must look beyond this to see whether the horse has the athletic potential for the work you want to do.

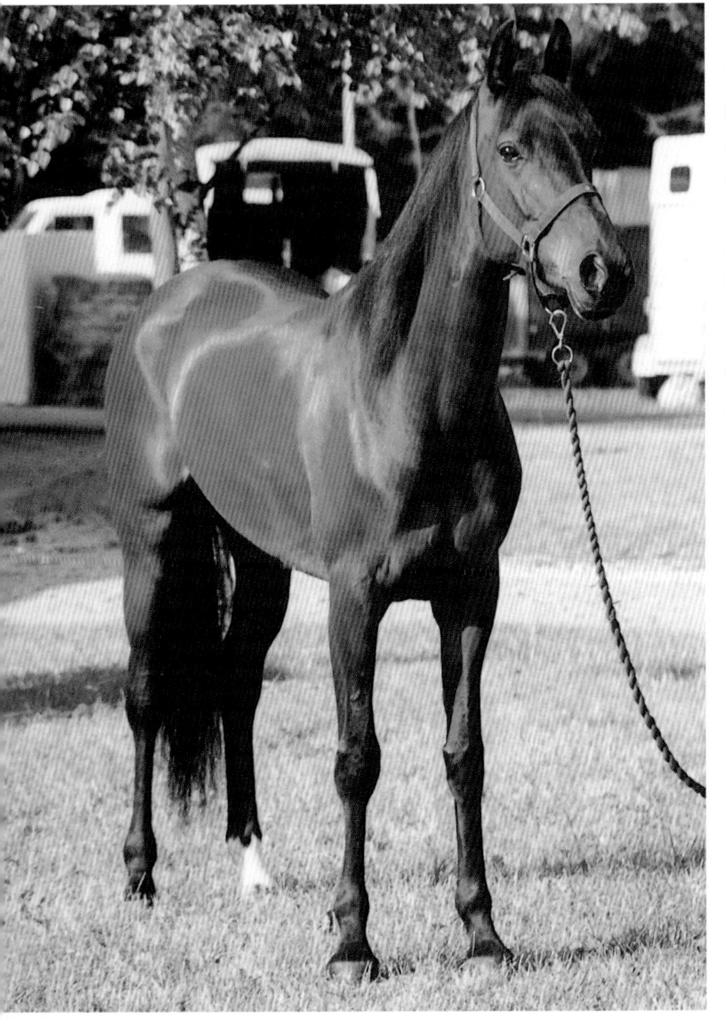

This Arab mare is a successful endurance horse who is tough and wiry, though slight bodied. The main difficulty with this type of horse is to retain enough bodily reserves to keep going to the end of a major ride.

There are many books which deal in detail with what constitutes 'good' conformation and we are not going to repeat this advice here. Instead, we shall look at how the basic points might vary in relation to endurance work. Of course, some aspects of good conformation are intrinsic to any type of successful performance – a horse with straight legs will always have better potential than one with knock knees and splay feet, for example – but we should be looking for attributes that will be positively helpful for endurance, as well as discounting obvious defects.

The first requirement is that the various parts of the framework should be in proportion to each other, so that the total shape is symmetrical and well balanced. As a general rule in life, things which work efficiently also look good. You can train your eye to appreciate good conformation but if you have not had any practice at this, begin by picking out a part of a horse which does not look good to you and then try to work out the reason why. Let us go back to that horse with the knock knees and splay feet for a moment. As a starting point, its legs are not straight, possibly due to some problem while it was growing up, or possibly it is a congenital defect. The tilt of its legs sends uneven pressure through its feet to the ground, so the hooves grow unevenly and its feet are asymmetrical and unbalanced. The higher forelimb bones will compensate for the knee problem, limiting the scope for movement. It will find it more difficult to support weight and abnormal tensions will be set up throughout its body. Its muscles will not develop efficiently and its overall appearance will be unathletic.

So, we want to begin with a picture in our minds of a basic framework which is in proportion. The various related proportions of the horse's physique have been studied and the so-called 'ideal' conforms to the comparative measurements shown in Fig. 1.

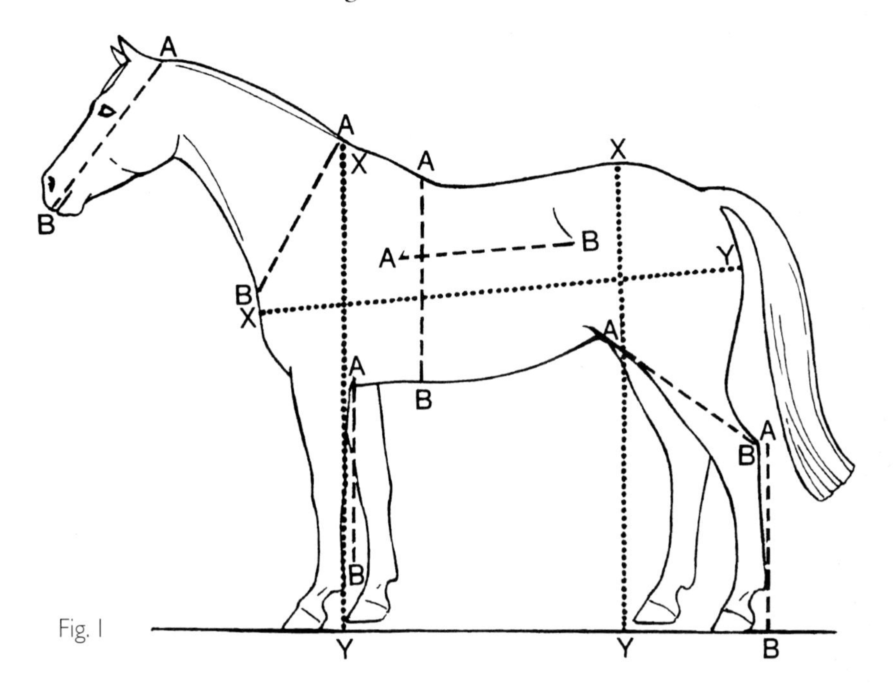

Fig. I

In conformation terms, the key to choosing a potentially good endurance horse is to choose one which is naturally well balanced. If you watch it free in the field, it will appear light on its feet, always in control of its body and always knowing exactly where its feet are. In endurance work, the horse, once trained, must share the responsibility for taking care of itself and carrying itself correctly with the rider on top. The rider in endurance competitions, while staying balanced and giving the horse guidance, cannot possibly maintain the intensity of physical effort used by the dressage or show jumping rider over the long period of the competition. His or her horse must stay balanced and perform in a relaxed way. A horse which needs extra training to overcome conformational problems in order to balance itself is inevitably going to find this more difficult than one which can do it naturally. A horse with all its parts in the correct proportions to one another will be more naturally balanced than one with some parts out of proportion. As few horses have perfect proportions, however, we should look for the closest we can find, bearing in mind what allowances can be made for the sport in question.

HEAD

Even a well-balanced horse still has to carry most of its weight through its front legs and the head is a comparatively heavy part of the horse, being made up of a considerable number of bones and the teeth. An out-of-proportion head, on a neck which lacks enough strength to carry it well, is a serious disadvantage which will make riding both tiring and uncomfortable as you attempt to keep the horse off its forehand. A few breeds – the American Standardbred, for example – have comparatively large heads. However, in good examples of this breed, a lean, muscular neck, which is perfectly set on to very strong shoulders, compensates for this. When assessing the various points of conformation, therefore, look for aspects which counteract one another.

Size of ears and eyes, the set of the eyes and shape of the face vary from breed to breed and are also believed to show characteristics of temperament. Look for alertness and an open, interested expression. The endurance horse needs to be calmly bold in its approach to life and curious to know what lies around the next corner. The timid, nervous individual will need much patience and reassurance for its confidence to be developed to cope with the pressure of

Cracker, the Standardbred, shows that her long head and short neck are no bar to flexion. There is ample width between her cheekbones for her windpipe and the curve of her neck to wither and shoulder is graceful.

competition, while the lazy horse, with a 'sleepy' eye, will not possess the eagerness and determination necessary for the work.

A broad forehead, often found in Arab and part-Arab horses, invariably denotes high intelligence and this may be a good or a bad thing, depending upon your personal ability to understand and communicate with horses. If a horse throws its head up and rolls its eyes, with its ears back, when you approach, this is a sign of nervousness or fear of human contact and also a warning to be careful how you handle it. A young, unbroken horse may do this simply because it does not know what to expect yet from humans but is prepared to challenge any treatment it doesn't like. Once its confidence is gained, the problem will be over. An older horse, who is supposedly trained to be ridden, should not do this, however, and if it does, this is a sign that it has not been handled with care and understanding. In such cases, the horse's natural willingness to co-operate has been blunted and its trust and confidence must be regained over many months before it is asked for serious performance.

The mouth and condition of the teeth are as important for the endurance

ABOVE LEFT *Much can be deduced about a horse's attitude from the facial expression. This top endurance mare has a kind eye, but a strong-willed, determined face – an exact reflection of her character.*

ABOVE RIGHT *Kelly has a typical Arabian expression, incurving ears, broad forehead, wide, open nostrils. Her eye reflects slight wariness about the proximity of the camera.*

horse as any other. Any problems in the mouth cause the horse pain which it tries to avoid by resisting or evading the rider's aids through the bit in various ways. As with problems in the feet, the results are transferred through the whole body as the muscles work to minimise the pain in the mouth rather than maximise athletic performance.

Conformation of the mouth varies as much as any other part. The roof of the mouth may be high or low, the bars may be thick or thin-skinned and narrow, the mouth short or long, the tongue thick or thin. Your choice of bit should reflect the conformation of the mouth and the ubiquitous single-jointed, thick snaffle is not the answer to every problem. Apart from basic conformation, there may be dental problems which need attention or abnormalities of jaw formation which might mean that the horse is not a suitable purchase, and your vet should take these points into account when assessing the horse's suitability for purchase for endurance work.

NECK

There are are three points to consider – the basic shape, how it joins the head and how it joins the body. The cervical vertebrae are not, as many people suppose, at the top of the neck, but buried deep beneath layers of muscle. The top line should therefore flow in a graceful, muscular curve, with the poll, where the bones are nearest the surface, the highest point. The bottom line, which comprises various muscles covering the trachea as it emerges from the throat at the top end and passes through to the chest at the lower end, should form a steeper but still concave slope, with no outward bulges.

The connection of the neck to the head must be sufficiently narrow to allow the horse to flex its head at the poll. If it cannot do this, it will find it difficult, in later stages of basic schooling, to work towards collection and better balance. The endurance horse does not need to work in a collected outline, but it does need the ability to achieve collection to cope in a balanced way with the natural obstacles of testing terrain, such as steep slopes and banks or very rough and uneven ground.

The set of the neck to the body may be relatively vertical, as in the warmblood, or relatively horizontal, as in the Quarter Horse. For endurance work at speed, a tendency towards the horizontal is preferable to a tendency to the vertical, but the main considerations are that the length of the neck should be in proportion to the rest of the body (see Fig. 1) and the back and hindquarters should be strong enough to keep the horse balanced and off its forehand.

WITHERS, BACK AND LOINS

The shape of the withers is related to the length of the spinal processes of the thoracic vertebrae, the design of which allows for muscle and ligament attach-

Passive exercises can improve suppleness in the neck and shoulders. As shown here, Kelly's neck is very supple, but some horses can bend only a short way before moving their quarters outwards. The bend must be asked for gently and only as far as the horse can manage easily; flexion will increase with practice.

ment. There are 18 thoracic vertebrae, extending from between the shoulder blades along the back, to which are attached 18 pairs of ribs, the first eight being 'true' ribs, attached to the sternum or breastbone. The spinal processes of the vertebrae at the front slope backwards and those at the back slope forwards. In a well-made horse, the fourteenth vertebra, which is upright, will be the point where the centre of the seat of the saddle should lie and where the rider can maintain perfect balance.

Continuing behind the thoracic vertebrae are six lumbar vertebrae, linking the thorax to the hindquarters. The strength of this section of the horse's anatomy is critical to its weight-carrying ability, bearing in mind that, at top-level endurance, horses must carry a minimum weight of 11 st 11 lb (75 kg). Arabian horses often have only five lumbar vertebrae and this contributes to their renowned ability to carry comparatively greater weight in relation to their size than other horses. A longer-backed horse often has a longer, smoother stride, whereas a short-backed horse may have an uncomfortably choppy action. The longer-backed horse requires more skilled training and riding, however, to keep it well balanced and to avoid strain. For endurance riding, therefore, look for a medium length of back with strong, well-muscled loins.

ABOVE *An 11-year-old Arab mare. This mare's conformation lends itself to speed. Her short back and comparatively long legs, coupled with a slightly upright shoulder make it difficult for her to stretch her back, lift her forehand and get her hocks underneath her body when working. Her quarters are a little shallow. The mare is approaching Intermediate level endurance and hillwork is improving her musculature. The head and neck are well balanced, she flexes easily and is a comfortable ride.*

RIGHT *This pair are having a lot of fun, but this pony's broad back would not make him the ideal choice as an endurance horse.*

SHOULDER

A sloping shoulder is a prerequisite for any horse which is expected to perform well over varying terrain at speed. In the horse, unlike other species, the thorax is connected to the forelimbs only by muscle and tendon, not by bone. This sling arrangement allows the shoulder great freedom of movement and it is essential that this remains unimpaired if the horse is to achieve optimum performance. The humerus forms the link between the scapula, at the point of the shoulder, and the forearm at the elbow. Its angulation and length affect the horse's scope for athletic movement and, with the scapula, it provides the basis for the attachment of the large muscles of the forehand.

The scapula is a long, flat bone which moves backwards and forwards over the ribs and a problem often occurs when the saddle impinges on the backward motion of the scapula as the horse stretches its leg forwards. This may occur either because the saddle has been placed too far forward or because conformation has not been taken into account in fitting the saddle, while, in extreme cases, the conformation is just not good enough to carry a saddle well.

A seven-year-old Anglo-Arab mare. This mare, at the same work level as the previous horse, has much more powerful conformation. The shoulder is strong and almost excessively sloping and the withers are very prominent, both points which made saddle fitting difficult. The overall picture appears long rather than tall, but the length is in the shoulder and quarters, which are also deep and strong, rather than in the back. She has adequate bone, natural balance and symmetrical action, but her ability to flex and raise her forehand will improve as her back muscles strengthen.

It can be a particular problem with Arab horses whose anatomy differs in several ways from other riding breeds, often including comparatively low withers combined with a rounded rib cage. The saddle needs to be carefully chosen, with a straight-cut flap and a seat which positions the rider centrally, not forwards, and attention needs to be paid to the girthing arrangements to keep the saddle in position and to avoid the girth slipping forwards and chafing the elbow. A crupper may well be the answer, at least in earlier stages of training, until muscular development provides some compensation.

An upright shoulder reduces the stride length and brings the saddle position and rider's weight further forward, increasing the weight on the forehand and making it more difficult for both rider and horse to achieve balance.

HINDQUARTERS

Same mare, back view. She stands foursquare, hocks turned slightly in and toes slightly out, which is natural to a well-made equine. Note the muscling of the thigh and second thigh (gaskin).

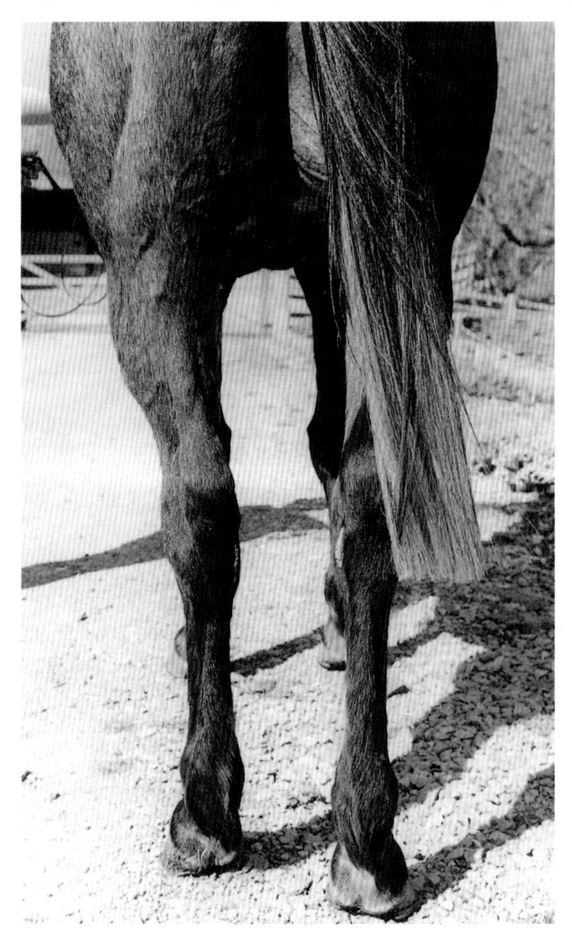

The hind limbs are attached to the pelvic girdle by a ball and socket joint at the hip and the pelvic girdle itself is attached to the spine at the sacro-iliac joint, where the lumbar vertebrae are met by five others fused together to form the sacrum. The pelvic girdle is formed in two halves, each of three connected bones. Adjoining the sacrum is the ilium, above which is the highest point of the croup, viewed externally. The ilium slopes down and forwards to the point of the hip (tuber coxae) and backwards to connect with the ischium which extends towards the point of the buttock. It then curves down and inwards to form the pubic bone, meeting with its mirror image on the opposite side. Where the ilium, ischium and pubic bone meet is the socket for the hip joint, into which the head of the femur is received. The femur (equivalent to the human thigh bone) and the ilium, being large bones, allow for large areas of major muscle attachment, while the hip joint provides the connection for forward propulsion between the hind legs and the rest of the body. It is clear that tremendous forces are at work in these areas and they need to be proportionately and strongly conformed to achieve balance when carrying a rider and to enable training to produce optimum muscle development.

LIMBS

Length, of the forearm in the foreleg and gaskin (or second thigh) in the hind leg, is obviously associated with length of stride and potential for ground-covering speed. Strong muscles, as well as tendons, support the long bones above the knee and hock. Below these joints, however, the bones are connected and moved only by a system of complementary tendons and ligaments. As explained in the earlier section on the feet, the stresses imposed by weight and movement are considerable and the cannon bones are stronger if comparatively short. The knee and hock are concerned with flexion, forward movement and shock absorption and each consists of a number of small bones. Strength and flexibility are denoted by comparatively large, clearly defined joints, free from puffiness, heat or any abnormal bony lumps or swellings. The sesamoid bones at the back of the fetlock and the navicular bone, linking the pedal bone and the short pastern bone, act as fulcrums for the flexor tendons, increasing locomotory power.

RIBCAGE, CHEST AND ABDOMEN

The endurance horse is often depicted as a lean creature of 'greyhound' shape and it is true that a fully fit, conditioned endurance horse will not carry any excess fat. However, if the ribs are clearly evident, that horse is not fit but in poor condition, which may equally well occur through overtraining as through an inadequate diet. It should be remembered that the ribcage and abdomen have a supporting system of muscles and tendons which carry the internal organs and are also involved in achieving the 'rounded' outline, necessary for balance when carrying a rider, which occurs when the horse raises its back and brings its hind legs further forward under the body. The depth of the chest and ribcage indicates the space available to accommodate the heart, lungs and gut, while the shape of the ribcage affects the horse's ability to carry a saddle and rider comfortably.

A thin, undernourished horse. Note the prominent ribs, but more particularly the lack of back muscle, prominent backbone and sunken loins and quarters.

A High Percentage of Aerobic Energy-producing Muscle Fibres

We shall look more closely at muscle fibre types and their capacity for energy production in the chapters covering fitness training. Muscles are made up of bundles of fibres, of which there are three different energy-producing types. Type 1 fibres are used for the production of energy aerobically, i.e. using oxygen. Type 2 fibres are divided into type 2a, which use oxygen and can also be trained to improve their energy-producing capacity using oxygen, and type 2b, which produce energy anaerobically, i.e. without using oxygen. Endurance horses must produce energy over a sustained period and this requires the most efficient aerobic energy-producing metabolism possible as energy can only be produced anaerobically in short bursts before fatigue sets in. The proportions of muscle fibre types in individual horses and horse breeds appear to be determined genetically. It is therefore helpful to select a breed or type which has a higher proportion of the right type of fibres.

A Strong and Healthy Heart

The health and efficient functioning of the heart are vital to the endurance horse. In competitions, recovery to an acceptable level (usually not more than 64 beats per minute) within a reasonable time (not more than 30 minutes) for each phase of the competition provides a parameter for elimination. In training, working heart rates and heart-rate recovery times are used to assess the horse's fitness.

The heart controls the circulation of the blood which carries oxygen and nutrients to the muscles and other organs. It is a strong muscle which acts as a pump, with four chambers. It first pumps blood from its lower right chamber (or right ventricle) through the lungs, where it takes up oxygen, and back to its upper left side (left atrium). The blood passes into the lower left chamber (left ventricle) and is then pumped out via the arteries and an ever-narrowing network of blood vessels down to the tiny capillaries. Nutrients are collected on the way and released with oxygen to the muscles and other organs. The capillaries then rejoin and progressively form the network of veins which return the depleted blood to the upper right chamber (right atrium), whence it flows down to the right ventricle for the heart to begin the process all over again. The flow of blood into and out of the heart is controlled by valves which operate rhythmically in sequence, speeding up during exercise and maintaining a steady, lower rate at rest. In some horses, the rhythm at the resting rate is occasionally interrupted, resulting in the 'missed beats' which a vet notices when taking the pre-ride pulse rate. This appears to be of no significance to the horse's performance, the regular rhythm being restored as soon as the horse begins to exert itself.

Heart disease or congenital defects causing faulty valve operation, arrhythmia, lesions or other changes have much more serious consequences. Unless the horse is obviously ill, the competitive prognosis is almost impossible to determine. Some horses continue working for years with apparently serious heart problems, but the possibility of collapse is, nevertheless, always imminent and it would be unwise to subject such a horse to the stress of endurance work or training.

Performance is limited by the availability of oxygen for energy production and a large, strong heart muscle is able to cope with a greater volume of oxygen-carrying blood than a smaller one. A larger heart can also work at a slower, and therefore less stressful, rhythm than a smaller one to circulate an equal volume of blood. Oxygen must be made available to the blood in the lungs, which brings us to our next essential quality of the endurance horse.

Healthy Lungs and Respiratory System

The swift supply of large volumes of air containing oxygen is essential for the continuous aerobic production of energy required for endurance work. Not only must the conformation of the respiratory system allow the free passage of as much air as possible, but the system itself must be able to perform its functions without the limiting effects of respiratory disease.

Air is taken in through the nostrils and filtered, to remove dust and foreign matter, by the mucous membrane and its secretions of mucus. At this point the air is also warmed. It then passes through the pharynx, larynx and trachea into the chest, where the trachea divides and subdivides to form the bronchi, bronchioles and alveoli, which make up the lungs. The alveoli are surrounded by tiny capillaries and oxygen passes into them across the alveoli wall, while the waste gas, carbon dioxide, crosses in the opposite direction, to be breathed out.

When the horse breathes in, the contraction of the intercostal muscles, which lie between the ribs and the diaphragm, creates space for the lungs to expand and fill with air. When the horse is working hard, the abdominal muscles also come into play. Breathing out requires less exertion as the muscles relax and the lungs retract to their original size when the air rushes out.

Respiratory function is adversely affected by congenital defects and, more frequently, by diseases related to people's insistence on the horse living in an artificial environment, often in unnaturally close confinement with many other horses. Respiratory problems which have long-term or performance-limiting implications will be detected by a vet, when carrying out a purchase examination, by listening to the horse's breathing at rest and during and after strong exertion. The precise nature and significance of a problem is best diagnosed by an endoscopic examination. The greatest enemy of optimum respiratory performance, however, is the system's reaction to overexposure to the dusty moulds found in hay and straw, compounded by poorly ventilated stabling.

A Tough and Assertive Mind

The more you have to do with horses, the more you will understand that their mental attitude and well-being are of paramount importance to good performance. We have already touched on the endurance horse's mental attitude in the Introduction – the will to go on is essential. A fit, healthy horse enjoys making use of its fitness. The desire to dominate is instinctive in all animals which live in social groups – it is the means by which the natural 'pecking order' is established. The better the horse is feeling, the more likely it is to want to test its place in the order. In competition, at race riding level, this manifests itself as going faster and further than the rest. This is why naturally bold and dominant horses make good endurance prospects.

For the same reason, mares often have a natual edge over geldings and even stallions. In the wild, it is the lead mare who decides where the herd will go and leads the way. The stallion's job is to bring up the rear, keeping the herd together and preventing stragglers from being left behind.

These are the attributes to look for when choosing a horse to train for endurance riding. In later chapters we shall see how these attributes are developed to turn a potential endurance horse into a successful performer.

This horse is coming towards the end of a big competition. He is a little tired, but calm and relaxed. One ear is cocked back, to listen to what his rider is doing, the other forward to take in what is happening in front of him.

CHAPTER 2

BREEDS FOR ENDURANCE

AT ANY endurance competition where there is a variety of classes, ranging from non-competitive pleasure rides up to endurance classes against the clock, horses of every description will be present. Hairy-heeled cobs from the local riding school frequently prove the point that the basic 20-mile (32 km) distance at a pleasure-ride minimum speed of 5 mph (8 kmph) is well within the practical scope of almost any sound riding horse. At the other end of the scale, horses competing for placings in rides of 50 miles (80 km) or more may be of a variety of breeds but will have an overall homogeneous appearance which is the result of being specifically conditioned for the sport. Lean-bodied, hard-muscled and eager, their task cannot be compared with that of the lower-distance horse.

Some unlikely horses do, over a period of years, make the highest grade – who could forget Margaret Montgomerie's wonderful cob Tarquin, with over 6,000 competitive miles (9,650 km) to his credit and still competing in his late twenties. However, as a general rule they take much longer to condition and are less likely to succeed than breeds more inherently suited to the demands of the sport.

The Arab

In many people's minds, endurance riding is synonymous with the Arab horse which has enjoyed more success in the sport than any other pure breed. However, it would be unfortunate if people prejudiced against the Arab were to be put off the sport as a consequence as, although the Arab is outstandingly successful, it is by no means exclusively so. Furthermore, the endurance sport

Pendavey Matra, known as Cassius, was one Haflinger who did make international level, carrying his young rider, Alex Nix, to second place for the British team at the Exloo Ride, Holland, in 1992.

The Arabian has proved itself the endurance breed par excellence. This good example, Impresario, started endurance competition only late in his life, but is the sire of 1992 ELDRIC Champion and European bronze medallist, King Minos.

has performed a service in increasing many people's understanding and appreciation of this oft-maligned breed. What makes the Arabian so successful in the sport?

Firstly, its physical qualities are ideally suited to working for long periods and, secondly, it is temperamentally suited to developing a close relationship with its rider. Its stamina and soundness will often outweigh any lack of finishing speed, although, on flatter courses with good going, Thoroughbreds and other longer-striding crosses may have the advantage, especially if the outcome is a racing finish.

The Arabian horse is a product of both the harsh environment of its desert origins and the needs and selective breeding policies of its Bedouin owners. The nomadic way of life predisposed selection for stamina and soundness, while tribal pride demanded horses of spirit and courage. At the same time, the fact that the Bedouin lived with their horses required docility and easy adaptation to a flexible domestic routine. The desert climate, while dry, varies between extremes of heat and cold and the Arabian horse can cope with both. What it cannot tolerate is the combination of cold and wet.

Probably the oldest breed in the world, its influence has pervaded a huge number of the more modern breeds, in particular the English Thoroughbred which, today, is the principal developmental breed used in competition horse production throughout the world. It is rather ironic that the Arabian itself is not considered up to the task of top-level show jumping, horse trials or dressage. Recent efforts by the Arab Horse Society to increase opportunities for pure-bred Arabians to compete have shown the breed to be extremely capable in all fields. Its only real disadvantage, compared to other so-called 'competition horses', is its smaller size, making the jumping obstacles found at top level somewhat beyond its scope. That smaller size, however, is an advantage in endurance riding where the larger the bodyweight the horse has to carry in relation to its strength and stamina, the more prone it is to injury. The combination of lighter bodyweight, coupled with proportionately greater weight-carrying ability, makes the Arabian ideal for the demands of endurance work.

For many years, concentration almost exclusively on production for the show ring did the breed a disservice and many inferior quality animals were produced in the attempt to breed evermore refinement of appearance. Fortunately, the revival of Arab racing and other competitive opportunities is now seeing a reversal of this trend and many more good quality Arabians, nearer to the old desert type, often incorporating Polish and Russian bloodlines, are available.

The quality performance Arab horse possesses stamina, soundness, courage and intelligence. The bone is fine but dense and strong, the conformation compact, with the anatomical variations peculiar to the breed affording great weight-carrying ability in relation to size. The conformation requires careful training to ensure the correct muscular development to carry a rider but,

Another Arabian, showing the enthusiasm and stamina for which the breed is renowned.

provided this is achieved, the springing, floating paces give a wonderfully comfortable ride, with the minimum of concussion to the joints. In a properly trained and conditioned horse, the musculature is lean and athletic, without excess weight. The nostrils are wide, with a considerable degree of flare, to allow the free passage of air into the lungs. For this reason, exaggeration of the normal slight dish in the face, seen in animals which have been overrefined for showing purposes, should be discouraged. The feet are notably hard, although often quite small. The sole tends to be usefully concave. Any tendency for the heels to contract should be averted by good farriery and, if well cared for, the feet should give less trouble than those of most other breeds. The coat and skin are fine and care must be taken when fitting tack to avoid any possibility of rubbing or chafing.

The Arab horse's natural courage helps it to tackle tough and demanding endurance courses, while the ability to settle and 'switch off', on arriving at vetgates or compulsory checks, helps it to recover well for the veterinary inspection. Natural stamina, enhanced by training, plus a streamlined body with the ability to dissipate heat from the muscles easily, means that the Arab horse generally exhibits rapid recovery of the heart rate to normal after exertion.

Thoroughbred

A few Thoroughbreds have done well in the sport, although the breed is generally of more value in adding speed, stamina and riding quality as a cross with hardier breeds. Advantages of the Thoroughbred are its speed and ground-covering ability, athleticism and stamina. Disadvantages include a more volatile temperament which makes it difficult for the horse to calm down and relax during veterinary inspections, an inclination to have flat, shallow feet which are susceptible to bruising and associated foot problems, and susceptibility to injury as a result of being selectively bred for fast growth and early maturity.

The English Thoroughbred, fast and powerful with plenty of stamina, but sometimes lacking strong feet and a calm outlook.

American Standardbred/Trotter

Closely related to the Thoroughbred but tougher and generally with better feet, is the American Standardbred, the breed used for the highly popular sport of harness racing. The Standardbred is a very muscular breed, with particularly strong shoulders and hindquarters, comparatively short, strong legs and a comparatively long back. For racing, the lateral gait, or 'pace' tends to be preferred to the diagonal trot, although races are held for both. The records for pacing are slightly faster than for trotting. Allied to the Standardbred are the breeds developed and utilised for trotting elsewhere, such as the French Trotter. Both the Standardbred and the French Trotter have enjoyed success in endurance riding, combining hardiness with economical, ground-covering action and a relaxed temperament. There have also been some very useful Trotter/Arab crosses, a trend which is likely to see further development in the future as the Trotter lends extra size and scope to all the qualities of the Arab horse, without detracting from its toughness and resilience.

Selle Français and Cheval de Selle

In France, one of the recognised top endurance-riding countries, many breeds will be found competing, including the major French competition breed, the Selle Français. This is a composite breed, developed specifically as a sporting horse, with a range of weight divisions, which has proved spectacularly successful in show jumping. Thoroughbred, Anglo-Arab and Trotter stallions are all used in the controlled breeding programme and the smaller, lighter-weight representatives of the breed, such as former French champion and world silver medallist Melfenik, certainly possess the qualities required for endurance. The Cheval de Selle is also often found. This is a horse of similar type but of less well-documented pedigree.

Shagya Arab

This breed from Hungary is an excellent example of the nineteenth-century development of a tough, utility saddle horse using Arabian stallions on indigenous mares. The aim was to produce a light cavalry horse and the qualities required then remain the essential ones needed for the endurance sport today. The type was fixed by careful line breeding but many vicissitudes of history all but destroyed the breed, so that the number of good Shagyas is small. Nevertheless, the Shagya has been well represented in competitive endurance history and the second European Championship, in Austria in 1985, was won by the Shagya Arab Samum, ridden by Hilde Jarc.

The Selle Français has never been better represented than by Denis Pesce's Melfenik, a world silver medallist at the age of 16 and a horse with many major wins to his credit.

Tersk

This is another Arab derivative, created in the Caucasus from the old Strelets Arab which was founded on crosses between the Arab and the Orlov breeds (the Orlov was Russia's principal trotting breed until superceded by the modern Russian trotter, a cross between the Orlov and the American Standardbred). Like the Shagya, it is principally grey in colour, although it tends to a bigger size. Like the Shagya, it should possess all the attributes necessary for endurance, although few have yet been exported from the former Soviet Union.

Andalusian

The Andalusian, its close relative the Lusitano and the Hungarian-bred Lipizzaner, which derives from the Andalusian, all possess the attributes of spirit, elegance and ideal riding conformation which led to the Andalusian being prized as the 'horse of kings' during the Renaissance period. Strongly built and quite heavily muscled, the pure Andalusian has no Arab blood but has been almost as pervasive as the Arabian in influencing other breeds. Its extravagant action may detract from the pure-bred's usefulness as an endurance horse, but its comfortable ride and gentle, easy-to-handle temperament offer other essential qualities and it makes a superb horse when crossed with the Arab to modify the action and lighten the musculature.

Barb

An ancient breed whose origins may pre-date the last ice age, the Barb lent influence to the development of the Andalusian but is itself less well developed as a saddle horse, retaining various primitive characteristics. However, it has depth, strength, courage and inherent soundness which provide an excellent basis for crossing with the Arab to produce endurance horses for today.

Australian Stock Horse

Australia is a strong endurance riding nation and, apart from the pure-bred Arab, of which Australia has a good supply, the mainstay of the sport (and all other equestrian sport in the country) is the Australian Stock Horse. Developed for livestock tending in the outback from a number of breeds, including the Arab, Thoroughbred and probably heavy horse and pony breeds, the Australian Stock Horse provided all the qualities needed for coping with stock management on the huge cattle and sheep stations. It is strong, comfortable, tough, agile and has a sensible disposition.

Criollo

The Argentinian Criollo is of interest because it is the tough breed on which the world's most successful polo ponies are based. Crossed with the Thoroughbred, it produces an agile, small riding horse of great soundness and stamina. In 1925, Tschiffely used two Criollos for his famous ride from Buenos Aires to New York. Polo ponies of Criollo stock, retired sound and appropriately retrained, can make excellent endurance horses.

Appaloosa

The success of the Appaloosa as an endurance horse depends much upon its basic type, the heavier examples being less suitable. However, the breed is very versatile, generally with sound limbs and feet, and should not be discounted.

The Appaloosa is popular, but care is necessary when making a choice as the breed varies from Arabian to heavyweight in type.

British Native Pony Breeds

The larger native breeds, in particular the Welsh Cob and Connemara, but also the Dales, Fell and New Forest, can be successfully crossed with Thoroughbred or Arab to produce versatile riding horses. The native element provides the horse with a strong sense of self-preservation and an ability to cope well with rough or varied terrain. Conformation, soundness, basic recovery rates and temperament all vary considerably, however, and should be carefully considered when selecting horses of this type of breeding for endurance work.

British native crosses are often strong, sound performers, with the ability to look after themselves on difficult terrain. This one, Burton Nimbus, is a Dales/Arab cross.

A smaller version is this Dartmoor cross. Dartmoor ponies make willing, equable, forward-going mounts.

BELOW *The Exmoor pony is certainly strong, but often too strong for young riders and though he is capable of carrying an adult for long distances, his comparatively heavy muscling and short legs make him an unsuitable choice for working at speed, especially in hotter weather.*

ABOVE *Cawdor Honey is undoubtedly the best known Welsh Riding Pony in British endurance. Still competing at the age of 22, she has carried her diminutive owner, Jan Lloyd Rogers for many thousands of miles both in competition and at home in the Welsh mountains.*

LEFT *The Welsh Cob gives a strong, energetic ride and is very hardy. The pure-bred, shown here, lacks the speed and has too much knee action to win at top level, but crossed with the Arab or Thoroughbred can produce an excellent prospect.*

Quarter Horse

Quarter Horses have performed successfully in endurance competition, although, theoretically, the breed is too heavily muscled, with a high proportion of muscle fibres predisposed to sprinting rather than the slower, steady work of endurance, to be ideally suited for the sport. They are compact, strong and tough, however, and if trained to go in Western style, could easily prove comfortable mounts for the less competitive spheres of the sport, such as set-speed or pleasure rides.

Irish Draught, Cleveland Bay and Warmbloods

These larger, heavier breeds are not really suitable for endurance work, although, at the lighter end of the scale, there have been some very successful Trakehners and Trakehner crosses, this being one warmblood breed with a history so steeped in hardship and trials of endurance that it must retain some of the inherited toughness of the survivors of the flight across Prussia from the

This Thoroughbred/Irish Draught mare is tough and has an excellent recovery heartrate. She has enjoyed a long and successful career at medium level.

Russian invasion during the Second World War. In general, however, these breeds have large, bulky muscles from which heat is slow to dissipate, thus also slowing down the rate of recovery from strenuous exertion. The bigger size and greater bodyweight make them less agile and therefore less adept at coping with varied terrain and they are more prone to suffer injuries such as joint and tendon strains.

ABOVE *The Pottock is a native pony breed from France. This one, Neron, has successfully completed several major rides.*

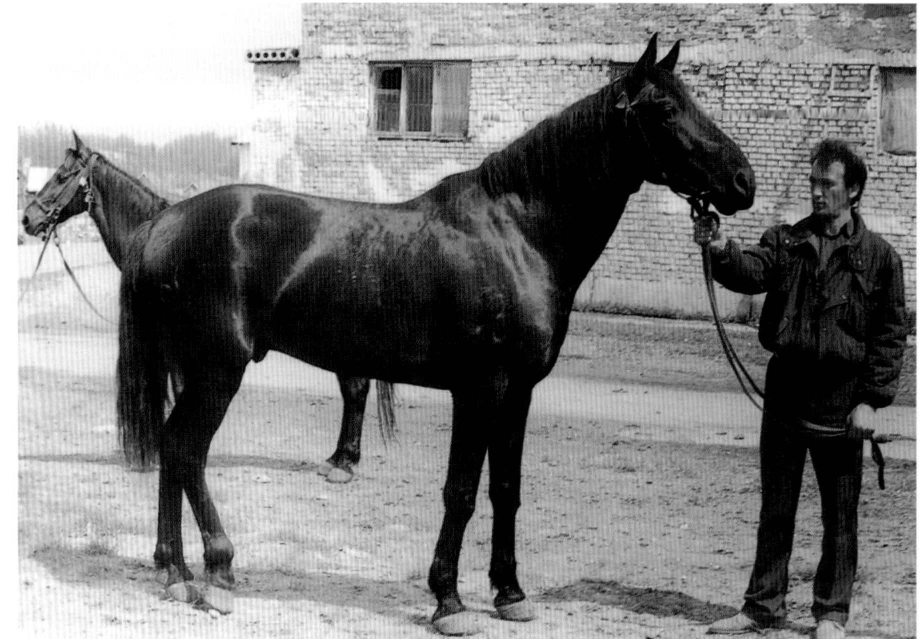

RIGHT *This Kabardin stallion, Karo, from the Caucasus was the first of his breed to participate in international endurance competition, at the 1990 World Equestrian Games.*

The Akhal-Teke, admired for the metallic sheen which often occurs in the coat, has extraordinary conformation, the neck rising almost vertically from the shoulders, the chest and quarters narrow, the back long and the body shallow – all faults to be avoided. The breed is renowned for its hardiness and stamina in desert conditions, but does not adapt well to a damper climate.

In summary, the ideal type and breed for endurance work is a horse which is light and agile on its feet, extremely hardy and sound, of compact, strong conformation, with lean, streamlined but powerful muscles, well proportioned for the purpose of carrying a rider, not too large (ideally 15.0–15.3 hh), with a healthy constitution and body systems and having a courageous, determined, but calm and easily managed disposition.

CHAPTER 3

WORKING OUT A ROUTINE

IT IS A GOOD idea to work out a planned routine and training programme for your horse. At the beginning, it is immaterial whether your goal is limited to basic-level, set-speed competitive riding or whether your ultimate aim is to compete in proper endurance riding. The horse must still master the first before it can be trained on to tackle the second.

Rides fall into various categories, further complicated by which organising body is running them (see Appendix 1), but the main types are as follows.

Pleasure Rides

These are rides up to a maximum of 25 miles (40 km), with a minimum speed of 5 mph (8 kmph), and their purpose is to give people an enjoyable day out, introducing them to the sport without the pressure of actual competition. The vetting procedure is usually limited to a trot up at the start and finish to check for soundness, although the vets are on hand to deal with any problems. Rides at this speed, which approximates to the normal speed of hacking out for exercise, rarely cause any difficulties other than occasional lameness. Rosettes are awarded for successfully completing the distance.

Competitive Trail and Qualifying Rides

These vary in distance from 20 to 60 miles (32–96.5 km) at set speeds, depending upon the class, from 6 mph (9.66 kmph) upwards. The set speed usually has a lower and upper limit, for example a novice CTR would be a 25-mile

Two young riders enjoying good going on a competitive ride.

(40 km) ride, to be completed at between 6 mph (9.66 kmph) and 7 mph (11.26 kmph). Sometimes there is a minimum speed to be attained, for example a 40-mile (64.37 km) qualifier for the Golden Horseshoe Ride must be completed at not less than 7.5 mph (12.06 kmph). Endurance riding is an evolving sport and the exact classifications vary from time to time as the rules are amended. However, the general principle is that, as the horse progresses, both speed and distance are increased, therefore the longer-distance qualifiers have higher speeds than the shorter ones, with around 7–9 mph (11.27–14.48 kmph) being the norm for rides of 40–60 miles (64.37–96.56 km). Similarly, in CTRs, the speed range for senior Open classes is higher than that for Novices and Juniors.

Awards and points in these classes are based on a combination of successfully completing the distance within the required speed limit, the horse passing all veterinary inspections and, in some cases, the degree of fitness of the horse based on its heart rate at the finish and the imposition of penalty points for minor injuries. There are usually no actual placings for first, second, third, etc. with regard to other competitors. The aim is to achieve a personal goal. The majority of rides are of this type and this element of non-competition against the other participants is one reason why the sport has such a friendly atmosphere, with everyone willing to help everyone else.

Endurance Rides

(These are often referred to as 'race' rides.) They are the ultimate form of competition and the basis of the sport internationally. The distances vary from 40 to 100 miles (64.37–160 km) in one day and many more miles in multi-day rides. The international championship class, however, is the classic 100-mile (160 km), one-day ride. Horses which have progressed successfully through the various levels of qualifying rides and CTRs are ready to begin tackling endurance rides.

There is a difficulty of nomenclature and definition of this level of ride. The sport, over all, is referred to as endurance riding, although the rides previously referred to are not 'endurance' rides in the strictest sense but competitive rides. Endurance rides, according to international definition, have a minimum distance of 50 miles (80 km) and usually involve horses being placed on a first past the finishing post basis (although they may be run on a set-time basis), in conjunction with meeting strict veterinary criteria before, during and after the ride. A 'winning' horse can be eliminated from the entire competition at its final veterinary inspection, which takes place within 30 minutes of finishing.

The basis of placings leads to endurance rides often being referred to as 'race' rides, although, clearly, it is impossible for horses to be involved in a flat-out race against each other over such distances with any hope of meeting the fitness criteria at either the vetgates (compulsory veterinary inspections *en route*) or at the final vetting. The only stage when the horses might truly

Four abreast on the Spirit of Sherwood 150-mile, four-day endurance ride.

become involved in a 'race' is if two or more enter the final stage together and actually do race for the finish line, which should always be roped off and organised on private ground. This distinction is important because most rides take place through open countryside, sharing the route with other users such as walkers and cyclists. Actually to race in these conditions would be both dangerous and, in some areas or countries, might well be against the local land laws. At this level of competition, the advantage is gained not by neck and neck racing but by a combination of other factors: the horse's fitness and experience; the rider's ability to pace their horse and use tactical riding, taking into account variations in terrain and ground conditions; actual riding ability; and the skill of rider and crew in getting the horse quickly through the vetgates.

Throughout this book, this type of competition will be referred to as an 'endurance ride', while qualifying competitions and CTRs will be referred to as 'competitive rides'.

In the northern hemisphere, endurance riding is mainly considered a summer sport, although in many countries it now stretches almost right round the calendar, with just one or two months off in the depths of winter. In Britain, the earliest rides are towards the end of February and the latest in early October. Most serious riders, however, tailor their competition season to a slightly shorter length, so that the horses have a four- or five-month break from the sport, with probably two months' complete holiday included.

When your horse is working during the off-season, it is an excellent idea to introduce some variety into its life through other activities, such as hunter trials, dressage or show jumping, and, most importantly, to have some lessons together to get you both in shape for the new season. Endurance work tends to encourage horses to run on, get on their forehand and become unbalanced. Lessons and flatwork will rebalance the horse and show you how to overcome this tendency, while also improving your own riding. Lessons should be taken seriously; the other extra-curricular activities are for fun and relaxation.

To compete successfully in a top-level endurance ride, a horse needs to have developed supreme physical fitness, with all its body systems functioning at peak efficiency. The pursuit of this goal has caused a minor revolution in traditional methods of stable management, turning some ideas upside down and rediscovering others that had been almost forgotten. Even if your sights are set much lower initially, it is still obviously logical to pursue the same aim of maximising your horse's health and fitness as far as possible.

The guiding principle is simple – that maximum health and the most efficient functioning of the body systems are achieved when the horse is kept in conditions as close as possible to those in which nature intended it to live. Equine evolution took around 60 million years, finally producing a creature that closely resembled some of today's principal breeds, at a time well before the human race itself had developed to the point where it suddenly realised how useful the horse could be. In the process, the horse acquired a number of

There is effort in every fibre of this galloping horse. The head is stretched forward and down, nostrils distended to draw in as much air as possible. The eyes are wide open and the teeth bared in determination. Also note the strain on the fetlock, pastern, knee and hock joints which occurs when the horse is travelling at speed.

characteristics which enabled it to survive in its wide-ranging prehistoric environment. In this context, it can only be considered rather presumptuous of humans to think that, in the space of a few thousand years, they could expect the horse to adapt completely and successfully to a totally changed way of life in an artificially imposed environment. We have already touched on the unique co-operation between the two species, which developed over the centuries and settled the direction human history would take. No less remarkable is the extent to which the horse has managed to cope with human interpretation of its physical needs in terms of food, exercise and environment. However, problems of management regularly arise – colic, laminitis, small airway disease, influenza epidemics, dietary deficiencies, to name but a few – and all of them affect the horse's ability to carry out its owners' wishes, while some may result in serious illness or even death.

What physiological characteristics did the horse develop in its natural environment, which are affected by the way it is kept today?

1 A respiratory system that is designed to deliver large amounts of oxygen quickly to the blood to fuel the production of the great energy needed to move a large body mass at speed.

2 A digestive system that is capable of converting substantial quantities of low-energy food into energy-producing nutrients.

3 A requirement for a balanced range of nutrients that are all obtainable from a wide range of plants – grasses, herbs and, to a lesser extent, bushes and trees.

4 A skeletal structure and musculature that are capable of great speed of flight from predators, but also needing considerable space for continuous roaming in search of food, which also provided sufficient exercise for the body.

5 A body shape that is designed to carry suspended weight, slung between the four supports of the limbs, not compressed weight bearing down from above.

How has human interference affected these needs?

1 Its design as an efficient oxygen collector also makes the horse's respiratory system susceptible to invasion by infectious viruses and dust and mould spores which trigger an allergic response. Keeping numbers of horses closely confined in stables which may not have a continual free exchange of air exacerbates these risks, resulting in the rapid spread of infectious disease and in allergic respiratory conditions, such as small airway disease, which seriously limit performance.

2 Feeding of high-energy 'concentrates', coupled with the restriction of bulky forage intake, as in the 'traditional' method of feeding working performance horses, upsets the horse's natural digestive processes (see Chapter 4), causing colic and other digestion-related disorders.

3 Feeding of a much more limited range of foodstuffs than the horse would find when foraging in the wild results in dietary deficiencies and imbalances which, at best, limit performance and, at worst, cause serious illness.

4 The horse's natural inclination is to wander 20 miles (32 km) or more a day in the search for food. Confining it in a stable for many hours slows down the circulatory systems, thus slowing the supply of tissue-repairing and energy-producing nutrients and the removal of waste products. In a fit horse, this restriction of freedom of movement and the lack of opportunity for the horse to exercise itself results in muscle and joint stiffness and filled legs. It also results in boredom, often accompanied by so-called 'stable vices', such as weaving or crib biting.

Taking good care of horses when travelling can make the difference between success and failure. This horse is being given a leg-stretch at the docks after a Channel ferry crossing, while droppings are removed from the lorry. Water and food are offered and haynets replenished.

5 The imposition of the weight of a rider on a structure which was not designed for this purpose requires careful control by training to develop those muscles which make it possible for the horse to carry this weight comfortably. If this training is not correctly carried out, the result is constant strain and accumulated stress on the muscles, ligaments and joints, causing pain and a shortened working life for the horse and, probably, a short temper too. (It also causes discomfort for the rider.) This subject is considered further in Chapter 5.

Here is a well-balanced combination, both horse and rider looking towards an approaching turn.

All of these potential problems should act as danger signals to the aspiring endurance rider. You are going to commit a considerable amount of time and energy, not to say money, to managing, training and competing your endurance horse and it will pay great dividends to be aware of these common problems of mismanagement and to take obvious preventive measures.

We have already established that no special extra training is needed for a normally fit and healthy horse to take part in pleasure rides. Before you begin to think about training for anything else, however, you should look at your horse's daily environment, your management routine, the horse's general health and condition and the time you have available for looking after and training it.

Environment

For years, people have used a method of keeping the working horse, which was very convenient to themselves (especially if paid help was available to do the work, whereas most private owners today are obliged to do their own mucking out!) but not necessarily beneficial to the horse. When this system first evolved, horse keepers did not have the benefit of the extent of scientific knowledge which is available today. The empirical methods of observation and trial and error enabled them to learn to cope with, or avoid, most serious problems, but they also gave rise to many of the dogmatic misconceptions which many people – especially traditionalists or those coming new to horse keeping – pick up and adhere to, even though a more reasoned approach, with an appreciation of up-to-date scientific knowledge, would produce better results. A further effect of this attitude was that when a problem occurred, the emphasis was placed on finding a cure, rather than trying to establish the cause and seek a means of prevention. Thus, for a health problem, there was always a recommended 'physic', and for a training problem, a 'gadget'.

The working horse may often be stabled all night, or even on a permanent basis, so that the only time it is out of its stable is for work. For the physiological reasons already outlined, even the industrialised world of flat racing is beginning to recognise the limitations this puts on the horse's performance potential. The first aim, therefore, when considering your horse's daily environment, should be to turn it out of its stable for as many hours as possible. Really, the only good reason for putting a healthy horse indoors is as a compromise for the sake of good pasture management, for example when excessive poaching of the ground during bad winter weather would destroy the potential for grass production the following spring. Bad weather in itself is not a good reason – the horse is better off outside in a good quality, well-fitting waterproof rug, provided there is also a hedge or wall which will provide shelter from strong wind or driving rain.

A fit horse in summer condition, turned out on well-kept pasture with the minimum of weeds.

What are the advantages and disadvantages of the average field? Firstly, the single horse owner may have only one paddock available – trying to keep a competition horse outdoors on anything under 2 acres (8,000 sq m) is labouring under a serious disadvantage. Ideally, the horse will have the company of another horse, so, for year-round outdoor living, we want at least 4 acres (1.6 hectares) of grazing for our two horses. Not everyone has access to this much land, so when we have defined the ideal method of outdoor management, we shall look at good ways of compromising to make the best use of less space.

Even at the rate of 2 acres (8,000 sq m) per horse, the animals are still confined in a much smaller area than in the wild. They are, in fact, restricted to roaming the same area over and over again. This is significant with regard to parasite infestation as grazing over the same ground means that the horse cannot avoid taking in worm eggs, whereas in an undomesticated condition the horse would move on and leave its droppings and the worm eggs behind. The most efficient method of dealing with this problem is to remove droppings from the pasture regularly, at least twice a week. If this is too time-consuming, harrowing in hot weather will spread the droppings, allowing the eggs to be dried out by the sun. The eggs will live in the pasture right through cold winter weather, however, and worm activity is greatest when the atmosphere warms up, but is still damp, in the spring. Rotational grazing with sheep or cattle is another way of helping to clear the pasture of eggs as the different species are affected by different types of parasite.

The available land should be divided into at least two enclosures, so that part can be rested while another part is being grazed. This also enables management activities to be carried out on the vacant areas in turn. The principles of good pasture management should, of course, be followed, with harrowing, fertilisation, rolling and reseeding, if necessary, carried out in turn at the appropriate times of year. Weed control is essential, both to allow the growth of a good sward and to remove poisonous plants. Thistles, docks and nettles can be sprayed, although spot spraying is preferable as clover will also be killed by the spray. An excess of clover produces pasture that is too rich in nitrogen for horses but some clover is still valuable as bacteria in the roots have the ability to 'fix' atmospheric nitrogen which is later released into the soil to improve grass growth.

A continuous, fresh, clean water supply is necessary, either from a natural stream which is deep enough to allow the horse to drink without picking up sand from the bottom and which is also free of pollutants – an increasing problem in the modern industrial world – or a supply piped to troughs set into the hedge or fence line.

Two acres (8,000 sq m) give a horse just about sufficient space for its psychological well-being. You will find that, apart from the obvious dunging areas, where the horse will also not eat the grass, the horse will choose different spots for different activities, such as for rolling, lying down to rest in the sun or for surveying the view (psychologically, a horse likes to be able to see all round itself for a good distance in order to feel safe from predators). You may also notice that your horses follow a routine, using different areas at different times of day. The ideal field, therefore, provides not only a specified amount of grazing, but a varied environment of vantage points, shelter, shade, sun traps, etc.

What has all of this to do with training for endurance? Quite simply, the horse that is able to follow at least a semblance of its natural inclinations during its non-working hours will be much more relaxed and settled in its mind than one that is unnaturally confined. When it comes to training, it will be less worried, less tense, more interested in what is happening and better able to cope with the significant physical and mental demands of the sport.

What adjustments can you make if you do not have this much land available? Firstly, it is still advisable to divide what you do have into two equal parts. That way, in winter at least part of your grazing is being saved from poaching and will provide better grazing in the spring. It may be more convenient or practical, when managing a smaller area, to use electric fencing which can be moved around, rather than putting up a permanent dividing fence. Horses adapt very well to electric fencing, whether of the purpose-designed type for horse-paddock fencing, or the lightweight, portable type which is also convenient to take to rides where you have an overnight stay.

On a small area, picking up droppings is absolutely essential, ideally twice a week. Not only will this minimise parasite infestation, it will also limit the dunging areas and therefore increase the available grazing. Despite the fact that your grazing is limited, occasionally arranging for a few sheep to spend a week or so there will also help to keep the ground clean. Weed control is even more important than on larger fields.

With limited grazing, your horse is likely to have to spend at least some time in the stable, so pay particular attention to ventilation. Install high-level hoppers if necessary, or have door openings back and front, with upper halves which can be left open during dry weather. The bigger the stable, the better for the horse. Good rugs and no gaps at ground level will prevent the horse from suffering from draughts. Think about fencing off an area of yard around the stables so that the horses can at least wander outside, even if they cannot go out in the field (make sure they can't get into the feed store!). Use dust-free bedding and be particular about the quality of your hay or feed ensiled grass, or haylage, instead. Hayracks, if fitted, should not be so high that the horse has to pull the hay down from above its head. Where grazing is limited, the variety of herbage is also limited, so improve the nutritional value of your forage by feeding alfalfa and a herbal supplement.

Company is good for the horse but a mixed blessing for the manager. A horse is definitely happier when it has a friend to pass the time with, who will whisk flies off its face, indulge in mutual back scratching, help to keep a lookout and generally lend a sense of security. At feeding time, however, these benefits are forgotten and kicking matches can ensue if the subservient horse does not show sufficient respect. The dominant horse is also likely to want to try its companion's breakfast as well as its own, which may not suit the owner feeding according to individual needs. The dominant one also usually eats faster and will then take what its companion has left, thus getting more feed than it needs and depriving the other. An extra bucket does not solve this problem! It is generally sensible, therefore, to separate the horses for feeding. Endurance horses can be particularly difficult in this respect as the nature of the sport encourages the development of dominant personalities and pecking orders may be constantly challenged.

Management Routine

This has to be tailored to the time available and will also vary according to the time of year and level of training. It must also take account of the fact that changes must be introduced gradually, whether of exercise level or diet.

Many endurance riders also work full time during the day and this limits their training time during the early part of the year. Riding in the dark is not much fun and, especially if you have to ride on public roads, should be avoided whenever possible, for safety's sake. In some parts of the world this may not be a problem but in Britain the end of January sees many riders in the saddle at first light, doing what they can before going to work. This may be a sign of the dedication which has brought British riders so much success in the sport, however, unless you are aiming at the early qualifiers at the end of February or beginning of March, it is not absolutely necessary. It might be a better plan to start your competitive season a little later, ride your horse at weekends, maybe take it for a lesson to an indoor school on a weekday evening and wait until there are more hours of daylight before you begin serious training (see Chapter 6).

Annual Routine

Whether your horse has had a complete holiday for a couple of months or has been doing other things, such as riding club activities during the winter, early January is a good time to start planning your endurance competition year. We shall assume that your horse has been living mainly outside, coming into the stable when necessary, has been doing only light or no work and has been on a basic, low-energy, 'maintenance' diet.

From around the third week of January, you will be thinking about more regular exercise. Now is the time to clip, if your horse has not previously been clipped for winter activities. Clipping the winter coat from your horse's neck, chest and belly will reduce sweating and the risk of a chill. A chaser clip is practical, although some people prefer a trace clip. If the horse is living out, as recommended, it can cope with either of these with the benefit of a good New Zealand rug. A blanket clip, where all the neck hair is removed, is less satisfactory as the horse will feel the cold more unless a neck cover is used.

In winter, even when snow covers the ground, turn your horses out for as long as possible, in well-fitting New Zealand rugs.

The ideal time for the annual influenza and tetanus vaccinations is during the horse's winter break but now is the time to check that they are up to date if you have not already done so. An influenza certificate, complying with Jockey Club rules, is compulsory for most major rides today and you may not be allowed to compete if it is not in order.

Before serious training starts, the horse's teeth should be checked, both to be sure that it is gaining the maximum nourishment from its feed and to check that no problems are likely to interfere with its acceptance of the bit when being ridden. Now is also the time to give a wormer which is effective against bots as well as the other forms of parasite.

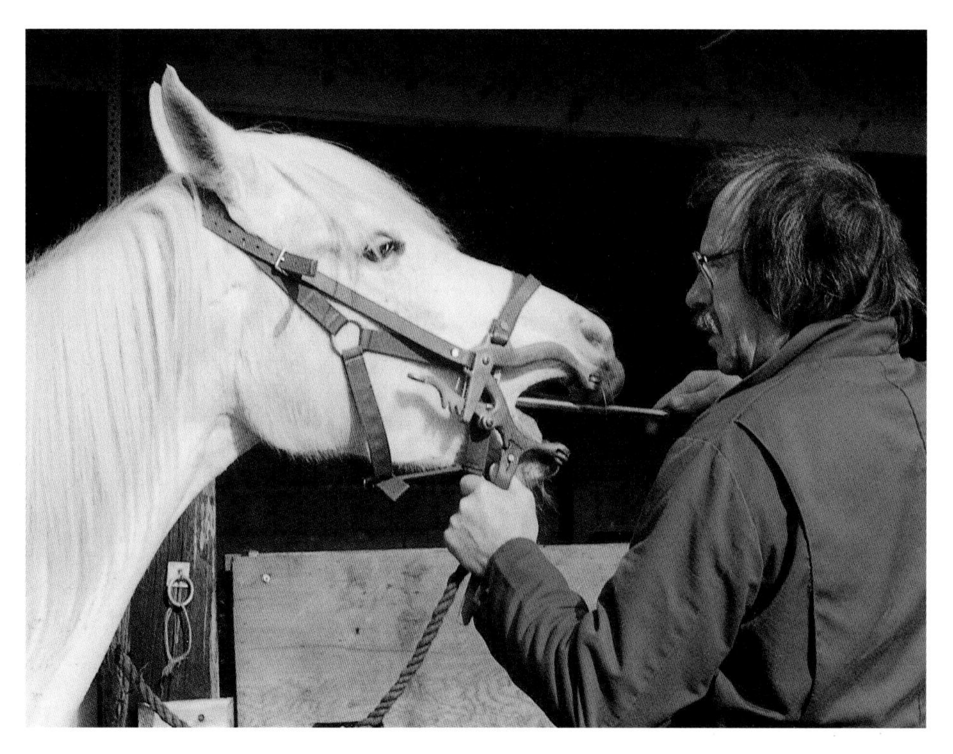

Annual tooth rasping is part of essential routine management

The feet should have been kept in good condition over the winter, whether or not the horse has had its shoes removed. Discuss the horse's action with your farrier and decide what its shoeing requirements for the season will be and whether any special shoes, such as wide-web shoes, would be helpful. The horse in endurance training will wear out shoes faster than horses in other forms of work, especially if a considerable proportion of the work has to be done on metalled roads. Therefore, make your farriery bookings regularly in advance, say, every four to six weeks, depending upon how fast your horse wears its shoes.

Changes in diet and exercise programmes through the year will be considered in the following chapters.

Weekly Routine

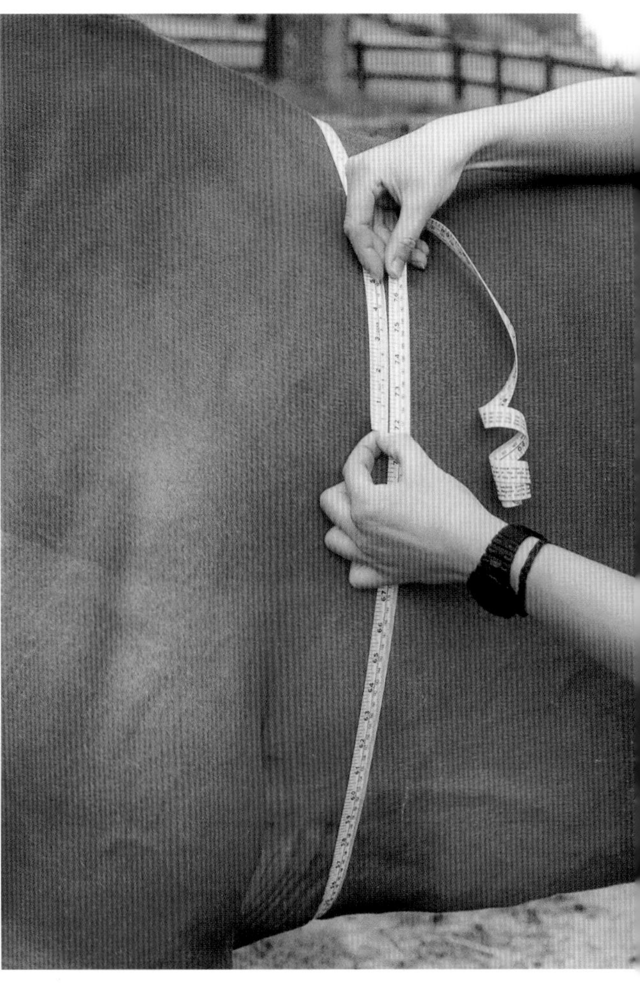

Checking the horse's bodyweight with a tape on a regular basis can provide a guide to changing condition. The tape must always be placed in the same position, behind the withers and around the girth area.

Exercise is best planned on a weekly basis and recorded in a diary so that you can keep track of whether your actual work is in line with your planned programme. For the first few weeks, fittening exercise will follow that suitable for any horse recommencing work, beginning with walking out for an increasing length of time and gradually introducing trotting. The aim is to get the various body systems functioning more energetically, stretch the muscles, improving their 'tone' and ability to produce energy, and start conditioning ligaments and bones, i.e. accustoming them to increasing amounts of controlled stress and inducing changes which increase strength and resilience.

Your horse's weight and shape will change as the season progresses and it is useful, both for training purposes and to help you judge condition, to keep a regular note of the horse's weight. A weigh tape, available from saddlers and some feed merchants, will help you to do this easily. The tape will show actual body weights, or a table corresponding to different girth measurements. It is not very accurate as to any individual horse's exact weight, but will serve well enough to show any changes in its condition. Check the weight once a week, at the same time of day and following the instructions on the tape precisely, so that you measure at exactly the same points around the horse's girth each time.

At the end of each week, take a good look at your horse, in conjunction with the reading on your weigh tape and decide if and how its condition has changed. On this basis, introduce any change of diet or increase or decrease in the quantity of feed.

Daily Routine

This can be divided into essential tasks and non-essential tasks. Essential tasks are feeding and watering (or checking water supply), checking for injuries or ailments, checking feet and shoes and exercise/training. Non-essential tasks include almost everything else, varied by how you have organised your day. Mucking out, for example, is reduced to skipping out if your horse is only in the stable for feeding, grooming and tacking up.

The horse is best adapted to a more or less continuous intake of low-energy food. For performance work, the diet has to be supplemented with higher-energy foods and it is preferable if these can be given as several smaller meals rather than one or two large ones as this is less likely to cause digestive upsets. Of course, the change to eating high-energy food is less marked if the horse is kept outdoors where the digestive system is at least kept functioning by a fairly continuous intake of grass, whereas, once it has finished its haynet, the stabled horse has to wait for the next meal to arrive. Many horses have a limited capacity as to how much they will eat at one time, so extra meals may have to be included to make sure the hard-working horse gets its full ration.

Checking for illness involves noting your horse's general attitude and condition. Is it eager and waiting for breakfast or moping in a corner? Are its eyes bright and clear and its nostrils clean? Is the skin loose and elastic and is the coat flat and shining? If stabled, is everything as normal, or is the bedding churned up? Are the droppings normal? A quick response to any such indication that all is not well can often save money and time off later. Always check the legs for injuries – mud and long hair can hide a lot – and check under rugs for chafing.

Grooming definitely takes second place to exercise if your time is limited. There are a number of basic points to bear in mind.

1 Feet must never be neglected. Pick them out before and after exercise, at the same time checking for loose, displaced or worn shoes and raised clenches. A horse with feet that have overgrown the shoes at the heels can easily develop painful corns which often take a long time to clear up. Raised clenches can cause self-inflicted injury, while a loose shoe can be caught by another foot or a tree root and be ripped off, causing damage to the hoof which may take a long time to grow out or, even worse, serious strain to the small ligaments of the fetlock and pastern joints, which might leave a permanent weakness. None of these risks is worth taking.

2 A horse living outdoors benefits from the natural oils in its coat, which help to keep it warm, even when rugged. In winter, therefore, keep grooming to the minimum, just removing dried mud and sweat with a dandy brush (use a body brush on the tummy if the horse is clipped). The mane, tail and feather at the fetlocks also afford protection from the weather. Leave them longer and do not trim in winter.

3 Never clip an endurance horse's legs – they need all the protection they can get.

4 Bathing is seldom necessary for a working horse. Provided dust and sweat are brushed out, a healthy coat takes care of itself. The mane and tail may occasionally benefit from shampooing if they have become dirty and tangled to the extent that brushing breaks the hairs. A mare's hind legs may sometimes need bathing if she has been in season. Endurance horses soon become accustomed to having copious amounts of cooling water poured over them during competition and often finish a ride cleaner than they started. After a competition in conditions of sticky mud, a sponge down with a soothing wash will make the horse more comfortable and get rid of stubborn mud that won't brush off the tummy and legs (clay particles often get into the pores and irritate the skin). Otherwise, leave bathing to the showing people.

5 Although thorough daily grooming is unnecessary, old-fashioned strapping, correctly carried out on the large muscle masses, stimulates the circulation and improves muscle tone. However, wait until the summer coat is through before trying this on a horse living outdoors.

6 Of rather more use are the methods of muscle massage which help a horse to relax both mentally and physically. For this, some knowledge of anatomy is required. If you want to try these methods, get a qualified person, such as an equine physiotherapist, to show you the correct movements, since incorrect massage will hurt. The aim is to improve circulation whilst reducing stiffness and pain and it is necessary to understand how the various muscles lie so that the massage strokes follow the direction of the fibres and circulatory vessels, moving towards the heart. The principal stroke used to help a horse relax is called effleurage and consists of a firm movement of the flat of the hand over the muscles of the affected area, repeated rhythmically for several minutes. Effective massage takes time, patience and energy and good technique develops through becoming aware of the normal texture and elasticity of the muscles and the ability to feel any abnormal tightness, swelling or spasms.

A somewhat different technique, developed for the owner/rider to practise on his or her own horse, is the Tellington Touch, as advocated by Linda Tellington-Jones, which is based on the methods of Dr Moshe Feldenkrais, an Israeli physicist known for his work in the field of human physical dysfunction. The Tellington Touch offers a method of identifying and resolving problems in the horse's body, using the hands, based on the theory of using non-habitual movements to open new neural pathways to the brain. The system has found wide acceptance, not only in the endurance world but in other equestrian disciplines throughout the world and especially in America where it was developed. Combined with ground exercises, it forms the method known as TEAM, or the Tellington-Jones Equine Awareness Method.

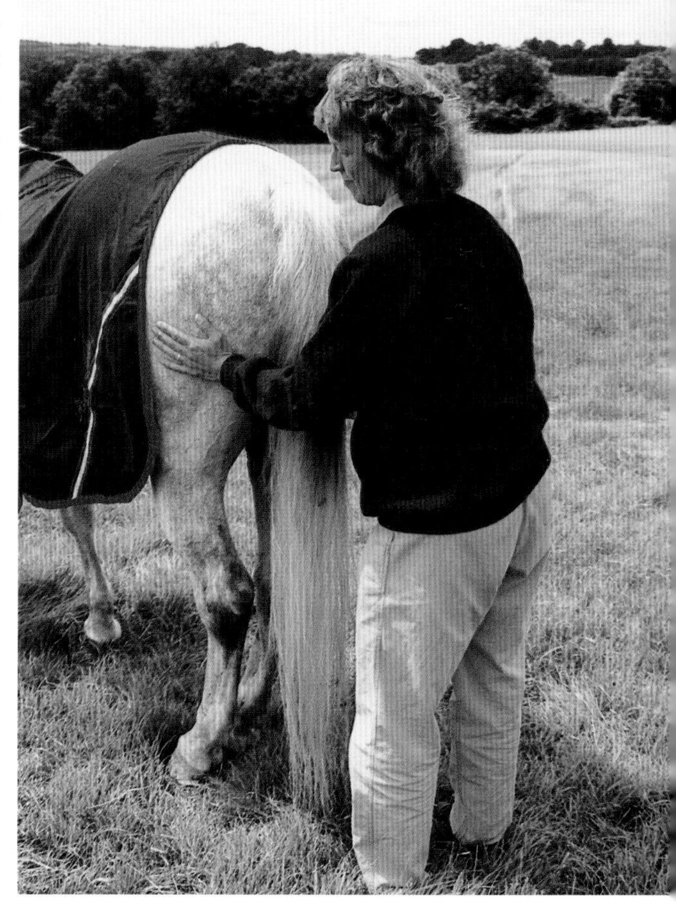

Carrying out massage and relaxation techniques to prepare for vetting.

Whatever your views about such systems, there is a great deal to be said for the fact that it involves the rider in spending a lot of time observing and getting to know their horse better. It also has a place during the endurance ride itself, where the relaxation methods are valuable in preparing a horse for presentation at the vetgates. This is recognised to the extent that a rule has been introduced to preclude the handler from actually touching the horse while the veterinary inspection is in progress, on the basis that using the Tellington Touch could result in a falsely lowered heart-rate reading.

The final item to consider before getting down to serious work is your horse's physical condition prior to the start of your training programme. What we hope to have at the end of the winter break is a horse in good health, with routine veterinary care and farriery attended to and in stable, good condition which has been maintained by good management and an appropriate diet. If the horse is too fat or too thin, problems lie ahead.

In fact, the overweight horse may pose less of a problem than the thin horse. Obviously, it is important to train the horse in such a way that it loses its excess weight and this is going to mean steady, regular work of increasing duration, coupled with a carefully monitored feeding regime. This horse probably eats everything it sees so it will be necessary to restrict its intake of low-energy, bulk food, while ensuring that it receives just sufficient higher-energy food to cope with its work. It must be fed rather more below appetite than is the norm, while still endeavouring to keep its digestive system functioning properly with regular feeding. From the rider's point of view, this horse can be frustrating because it takes months, or even years, rather than weeks, to achieve an appreciable difference, converting fat to muscle and training the horse's body to use up its surplus reserves as energy. In the meantime, the horse's performance will be limited.

A thin horse, conversely, should not even be started on a fitness training programme until it has built up enough condition to produce energy, first, for body maintenance without further weight loss, second, for the repair and strengthening of body tissues and, third, to cope with the demands of the imposed workload. A thin horse put into training will not become fit; it will merely become overstressed, unwell and at risk of exhaustion if put into competition. At endurance ride level, at distances of 50 miles (80 km) or more, the energy demands are considerable. The horse needs sufficient resources to cope with the inevitable loss of weight associated with these demands, which can quickly be regained, but without incurring actual muscle wastage and damage.

CHAPTER 4

DIET AND FEEDING

THIS ASPECT of competition horse training seems to worry owners more than any other, perhaps because it provides a lucrative commercial market for the feed and supplement producers and so generates an excessive amount of publicity and, frequently conflicting, advice. Also, feed industry research has produced a bewildering variety of feeding methods and systems, each claiming superiority in terms of performance results. The accompanying glossy literature, however, tends to make powerful claims of success in more generalised terms, without necessarily giving detailed facts concerning either the ingredients of the products or how they work. Experienced endurance riders are not prepared to accept such inadequate information, while less experienced riders need basic, common-sense guidance on their horses' needs. How is the owner or rider without a scientific background to choose?

Crudely defined, digestion is the process of breaking down and converting food into substances capable of use by the body to sustain life. To a certain extent, this process will happen whatever herbivorous food the horse eats. However, as we shall see later in this chapter, different foods are digested in different ways and the competition horse owner's aim is to feed his or her horse in such a way that: (a) all the food given will be used to optimum advantage; (b) none of the food will cause digestive upsets; (c) all the horse's nutritional requirements will be met in a balanced way. What the endurance rider needs to know is how to assess and feed for the difference between the horse eating to stay alive and eating to produce optimum endurance performance.

Research into equine nutrition has not yet produced the definitive answer to this problem, which is why feed manufacturers are able to package and market such a variety of systems, each incorporating their particular interpretation of the knowledge available.

What the serious competitor must do, however, is to devise his or her horse's diet on the basis of the most up-to-date facts known, in accordance with tested principles. This will give the best chance of achieving the desired result and is not as difficult as it might sound.

The Purposes of Nutrition

Horses need food for two natural purposes and one imposed by people. The natural purposes are, first, to sustain life and maintain basic condition and, second, for growth and physical development. The purpose imposed by people is work.

The Nutrients Required

Six groups of basic nutrients must be included in the diet to fulfil these purposes.

Proteins are required for tissue maintenance, growth and development.

Carbohydrates are required to produce fuel for energy production, including that needed for the functioning of the basic body systems as well as muscle contraction. Soluble carbohydrates consist of sugars and starch which comprise a high proportion of the traditional cereal concentrate ration. Insoluble carbohydrates consist mainly of cellulose, the principal fibrous constituent of the forage ration.

Fats are also utilised for energy production. The horse has proved capable of digesting fats efficiently, although the natural diet does not include fats in significant quantities. Fats may have a significant role in the diet of the endurance horse and we shall consider them in more detail later.

Minerals are necessary for essential body functions and defined as major or trace elements according to the levels required in the diet.

Vitamins are necessary for essential body functions. At least 15 vitamins have been identified as playing a role in equine nutrition. There are two types: water-soluble vitamins which are mainly manufactured in the horse's gut, and fat-soluble vitamins which are mainly found in fresh forage and can be stored in the body, primarily in the liver.

Water is essential to sustain life and for various body functions. Up to 75 per cent of the adult horse's bodyweight may be comprised of water.

The 'pecking order' is never more strongly enforced than at feeding time. This yearling filly has to wait while her mother and older brother clean up the remains of her breakfast.

Measurement of Nutrients

Various foods containing these nutrients are combined to form a ration which provides the horse with its daily nutritional needs. Equine nutritionists and researchers have produced tables which show these nutritional requirements, measured in various appropriate ways.

Protein requirement is usually expressed as a percentage of the total ration. For the adult horse this is about 8 per cent for maintenance purposes. As the horse becomes fitter through training, the energy proportion of the diet is increased to meet the demands of the extra workload and it is generally found that this also includes the slight increase in the protein level required for the extra workload. Higher protein levels are required only for breeding stock and immature horses which are being worked, such as young racehorses, or for horses recovering from seriously debilitating illness with associated muscle wastage.

Carbohydrate levels are best expressed in energy terms, i.e. as megajoules of digestible or metabolisable energy (MJ DE or MJ ME) per kilogram of food. Digestible energy is the energy produced from food minus that lost in the faeces. Metabolisable energy is digestible energy minus that lost through urination and gases produced during digestion. Metabolisable energy is used by the competition horse for warmth, maintenance and work. Fat levels are also expressed in terms of energy produced. For example, 0.5 litre (1 pt) of corn oil provides approximately 18 MJ DE.

Minerals and vitamins, required in much smaller amounts, are usually expressed by weight as grams, milligrams or micrograms per kilogram of food, or per recommended dose of proprietary supplement. Some vitamin requirements are expressed by the statutory measurement 'international units' (iu).

Relationship of Feeding to Breed/Type, Bodyweight and Workload

So far, we have been concerned with principles which apply to all horses. However, the next problem which leads to confusion and uncertainty for the horse owner, is the emphasis that must be given to treating each horse as an individual and formulating a ration accordingly. The variables to be considered are breed or type, bodyweight and workload.

Some breeds are able to obtain energy more efficiently from food of lower nutritional value than others. For example, native pony breeds need very little supplemental winter feed, whereas the Thoroughbred needs considerably more, as well as a more protected environment. Some breeds, types and individuals also burn the fuel which produces energy at a faster rate than others, for reasons which may vary from keeping warm to nervous excitement.

An approximate guide to the weight of food (in dry matter) which the horse will eat per day is 2.5 per cent of bodyweight. This is an average assessment of the capacity of appetite, not a minimum quantity. The actual weight consumed will be much higher if the food has a high moisture content, for example when the horse is getting more of its energy from grass in the growing periods of the year, than if it has a lower moisture content, for example when the horse is eating cereals and hay. The actual nutritional value of this quantity of food will depend upon its composition and the respective nutrient and energy values of the different ingredients. If it comprises nothing but hay, for example, the energy value will be much lower than if it comprises a combination of hay and concentrates. Nutrient values are expressed either as a proportion of the dry matter content of the food, or on an 'as fed' basis, in which cases the figures will be proportionately lower. The dry matter content of most common concentrate foods is approximately 88–90 per cent.

The assessment of how much energy is required for various types of work is subjective and extremely variable, depending upon many factors such as speed, duration and intensity of the work, level of fitness, weather conditions, ground conditions, the horse's athletic scope and economy of movement, and rider skill. Clearly, it may vary considerably from day to day, depending upon the horse's routine (for example, rest day, light work, two days' heavier work, day off, competition day), yet no one would suggest adjusting the ration so drastically on a daily basis as to do so would inevitably upset the delicate balance of the horse's digestive system. In actual fact, light work requires comparatively little extra energy; the introduction of fast work, at a relatively advanced stage of training, produces an additional energy requirement approaching that required for maintenance alone; and strenuous competition work (i.e. endurance ride level) increases the energy requirement over that for advanced training by about 75 per cent

Nutritionists have devised a system of 'scoring' to calculate how much extra energy a horse needs for various forms of work, which we shall apply to the endurance horse when we come to work out a ration (see page 90).

Training increases the body's energy production capability, necessitating the rapid replacement of fuel metabolised from food. If sufficient, easily digestible, good quality food is not provided, the reserves of readily available fuel, stored as glycogen in the muscles and liver, will be progressively depleted. Experiments have shown that exhaustion occurs before these reserves are completely used up and part of the aim of training is to increase their accessibility.

In endurance competition, the available fuel will be used up faster than it can be replaced via the digestive system. This is one reason why a recovery period of at least several days, during which fuel stores are replenished, is needed following a major ride. The faster the average speed, the greater the risk of exhaustion. This is why official endurance rides are no shorter than 40 miles (64.3 km) – the temptation to go faster over a shorter distance poses a greater risk to the horse than to go at a slower average speed over a longer distance. Methods of feeding for endurance seek to widen this margin of risk, firstly, by providing a continuous, steady release of fuel for energy into the system, and, secondly, by providing alternative energy sources which help to conserve the stores of muscle glycogen, thus delaying the onset of fatigue.

To work out a ration that will do this, we need to have a basic understanding of how the different stages of the digestive system deal with the various nutrients.

The Digestive System

Food may take up to three days or more to pass right through the digestive system, although some types of food will be digested much more quickly. The digestive system is basically a tube, beginning at the mouth and ending at the anus, and can be thought of rather like an underground railway system, with passengers getting on and off at various stations along the way. The horse is a very selective feeder – a source of frustration to the owner who has carefully worked out a diet only to find that a particular ingredient is carefully sorted and left at the bottom of the manger. The various food components are sorted by the lips before they arrive at the first station in the mouth, where saliva joins the train (at a rate of about 17–21 pt or 10–12 litres a day) to help to lubricate, moisten and bind together the food which has been ground to a pulp by the molar teeth. This passes down the line along the oesophagus (gullet), with a one-way ticket through the cardiac sphincter muscle – one-way because this powerful muscle does not allow regurgitation and so the horse cannot vomit.

The horse uses its lips and sense of smell to sort through potential food. Grass and herbage are bitten off with the incisors, then passed back with the tongue for mastication by the molars.

The pulped food, mixed with alkaline saliva, is now in the acidic station of the stomach, where gastric juices join the party and begin to attack the food constituents. However, the stomach has a relatively small capacity and its shape means that it is no more than two-thirds full – containing about half of a normal feed bucket in volume – at any time. If the horse continues to eat, the food in the stomach must move on, so the stomach is responsible for only the beginning of the digestive process, a period lasting from 30 minutes to about three hours.

From the stomach, the food enters the small intestine, where new passengers board the train. Pancreatic juices and bile arrive from ducts on the first stretch of track, which is the duodenum. The following sections are the jejunum and the ileum. The small intestine, which is about 65–89 ft (20–27 m) long, has an enormous internal surface area, augmented by finger-like projections along the internal walls which are lined by enzyme-producing cells.

Now the serious part of digestion begins as the small intestine is responsible for dealing with most of the non-fibrous, soluble constituents of the feed, including the sugars, some of the starch, the protein from grain and other concentrates, plus the fats.

The horse has no gall bladder and bile is continuously trickled in from the liver via the bile duct, while pancreatic juice is also continuously produced. Both are alkaline and counteract the acidity of the digestive material which arrives from the stomach. The pancreas controls levels of blood sugar and the juice also contains digestive enzymes. Bile gets to work on emulsifying fats, so that enzymes can break them down to fatty acids and glycerol.

Several different enzymes work on each category of nutrients. The fatty acids and glycerol produced by the fat-digesting enzymes are absorbed into the lymphatic system and carried into the bloodstream where they are available to produce energy. The amino acids produced by the protein-digesting enzymes are absorbed through the gut wall into the blood. The majority of soluble carbohydrate, comprising sugars and starch, is also broken down, principally to glucose and galactose which pass to the liver – making a sort of rail-link connection – whence they are available for energy production, or to be converted to glycogen or fat and stored for future use.

Up to this point, the journey of the food nutrients has been rather turbulent – the passage of some nutrients through the small intestine can take as little as one hour. Many changes have occurred and all but the toughest passengers have left the train. It should now be clear that most of the nutrients provided in a concentrate feed are available for energy production within about four hours of eating. As we shall see, this presents both advantages and problems for the endurance horse.

The digestive material still remaining on our train now consists mainly of insoluble fibre, plus any soluble carbohydrate – particularly starch – which was not in the small intestine long enough to be fully digested and absorbed. This part of the journey through the large intestine takes much longer than the earlier stages (up to two days) and its progress is unique to the equine species. The large intestine comprises two parts – the caecum is a large fermentation chamber, equivalent to the station buffet, while the large colon continues the onward journey. This is the part of the system which allows the horse to obtain significant amounts of energy from insoluble fibre, by providing an alternative method of breaking the material down into usable fuel. The method is one of bacterial fermentation, made possible by the large capacity of the hind gut and the presence of millions of micro-organisms which work on the fibre (cellulose, hemi-cellulose and pectin) which makes up plant walls to produce volatile fatty acids which are absorbed into the bloodstream to become available for energy production.

This system is particularly advantageous for an animal which obtains a high proportion of its natural food as insoluble fibre. It is designed to work continuously, so the output of energy is also continuous. The better the nutritional value of the fibre being digested, the greater the steady output of energy. The population of micro-organisms in the gut is self-adjusting, to take account of the type of diet being received by the horse, and it varies according to the proportions of forage and concentrates being fed. These micro-organisms do take time to adjust to any changes, however, whether of proportions, quality or type of food, and this is why it is vital that new or different foods are introduced gradually.

The small intestine cannot always cope with digesting all the soluble carbohydrate it receives – particularly starch as the natural high-fibre diet is low in starch – and the bacteria in the hind gut must therefore deal with the remainder as well as with the insoluble fibre.

The fermentation of starch in the large intestine happens very rapidly, accompanied by a rapid rise in the level of available 'fuel' in the bloodstream. This is the basis of the so-called 'heating' effect of grain-based diets, which is also compounded by overfeeding high-energy food during the fitness training programme. Overfeeding is frequently the reason for excitable behaviour, accompanied by high heart rates, at Novice level.

The bacteria which digest the soluble carbohydrate produce lactic acid which must then be converted to volatile fatty acids. If the two processes are not synchronised, a lactic acid build-up can occur, which upsets the balance of micro-organisms, leading to the production of endotoxins. These are absorbed into the blood and can cause laminitis, acidosis or endotoxic shock, resulting in serious illness or even death.

Too rapid fermentation of soluble carbohydrate can also cause a build up of gas, resulting in flatulent or tympanitic colic.

During the fermentation process, water is also absorbed through the gut wall, so what remains to continue the journey via the rectum to the outside world as faeces is a drier mixture of the indigestible material from food, plus waste products, including a high proportion of dead bacteria from the constantly self-renewing population in the gut. The propulsion of food through the digestive system – the progress of the train – is aided by regular muscular contractions of the intestinal walls, called peristalsis, which is stimulated by the presence of bulky, fibrous food.

Before we leave the subject of the digestive system, what happens to any fuel that is not immediately required for energy? Some is stored in a readily available form – glycogen – in the muscles and liver. Any excess, however, undergoes a further conversion process and is stored as body fat. The laying down and taking up of body fat reserves is an ongoing process which we can see happening in the horse's changing condition according to the time of year, grass growth, feeding regime, etc. However, it is a slow process relative to the take up of muscle glycogen.

Training helps the endurance horse to speed up its metabolic rate and make more effective use of body fat reserves than less fit horses. Increasing the proportion of fat in the diet by including vegetable oil in the ration may also stimulate the metabolisation of body fat reserves, although the extent to which this may happen, or how much oil is needed in the diet to bring this effect about, is not yet known. Neither is it known whether substantially increasing the fat content of the diet would produce any detrimental side effects. However, a controlled amount of oil, fed as part of the ration, does provide an alternative source of readily available energy, which helps to conserve the limited stores of glycogen, thus delaying the onset of fatigue.

Oil also provides a high concentration of energy in relation to the quantity consumed. As the workload and concentrate ration increase, the addition of oil to the diet, rather than a greater volume of grain similar in energy value, reduces the risk of too much undigested starch reaching the large intestine and causing the metabolic problems previously mentioned. Oil is also a useful means of providing a higher energy diet for a horse whose appetite for a grain ration sufficient for its workload has waned.

This three-year-old filly is growing fast and in almost too good condition, living off summer grass. However, the reserves she is building up now will help maintain condition when the grass becomes less nourishing. It is essential to be aware of the effect the changing quality of pasture through the year has on growing youngstock.

Summary

Let us summarise the points we have established so far:

1 The horse needs food to maintain life, to grow, to repair body tissues and to work.

2 It requires a balanced diet, including all six groups of vital nutrients.

3 It requires a diet tailored to avoid digestive and metabolic problems.

4 It requires food of high digestibility and good nutritional value, to minimise wastage and maximise a continuous, steady output of energy.

5 A horse's daily appetite in weight of food will be in the region of 2.5 per cent (dry matter) of its bodyweight.

6 The total energy value required in an individual horse's diet is assessed by reference to breed or type, condition and workload.

7 Nutrients digested in the small intestine (principally the concentrate ration) begin to provide energy after about four hours. Nutrients digested in the large intestine (principally the bulk ration) provide a slower but steadier source of energy.

8 The size of the stomach dictates that the maximum volume of any one concentrate feed should be not more than about half a standard feed bucket.

Specific Requirements of the Endurance Horse

The endurance horse is asked to work for long periods of time, mainly at a 'sub-maximal' level, i.e. a rate where it is not asked for maximum output of power and speed, unlike the sprinter. Only rarely, for example, in a racing finish, would the endurance horse be asked to extend itself to this degree and, even then, the rider's knowledge of the need to pass the final vetting would act as an inhibiting factor.

The traditional feeding method for hard-working horses dictates that the forage ration is decreased in proportion to the increase in the concentrate ration, to a point where 75 per cent of the diet is given as concentrates and only 25 per cent as forage. This results in more emphasis being placed on digestion in the small intestine and less in the large intestine, thus reducing the activity of fibre-digesting micro-organisms, with the hind gut ultimately shrinking in size. It was thought that this reduction of size and weight helped the horse to gallop faster and reduced the strain on its body when working hard.

In reality, this change of emphasis from the high-fibre diet intended by nature makes the system vulnerable to the various digestive problems and

Steady work builds fitness, and shorter distance competitions can be used as part of the process, to prepare for longer ones.

metabolic illnesses already mentioned. Peristalsis and gut motility are reduced; the balance of bacteria changes, increasing the risk of an imbalance, with lactic acid build up and consequent problems; the risk of colic is increased; and problems of appetite loss and 'overheating' occur.

Even in racing and eventing, the extreme traditional view is beginning to change as our understanding of the horse's digestive system becomes more enlightened. For the endurance horse, however, which is rarely asked to gallop anyway, there are no disadvantages and many advantages in a diet based primarily on good quality, digestible fibre. Concentrates should be regarded as necessary supplementation to meet energy demands but not as the foundation of the ration.

What to Feed

From all of the many foodstuffs available, how do we initially decide what to feed a horse coming fresh into the sport? It may be a horse coming back from its winter break or into endurance from another discipline; it may be one which has just been purchased, whose previous diet is unknown, or which you want to change to suit its new way of life and your management routine. In all cases, the basic principles will be the same.

The first consideration is to avoid putting any sudden new pressures on the animal's digestive system. Therefore, the initial diet should be as simple and natural as possible. (If it is a new horse and you do know what it was fed previously and want to change it, begin by continuing to feed the foods you want to phase out of the diet, reducing them gradually and then introducing the new ones.)

The most natural food of all is grass and if your new horse arrives during the summer, after the first flush of growth and the danger of too much sudden richness are past, there is no problem. Simply turn it out and allow several days for adjustment, feeding the minimum of concentrates to which it is accustomed, commensurate with its workload. In any case, a new horse should be allowed time to settle into its new environment before being asked to go for more than a short ride.

A nicely balanced horse, working well. He is in ideal condition for his type, for a horse in medium level training. His muscles are developing and he is well covered with flesh, but not too fat.

In winter, or when pasture is limited, feeding requires more thought. The basic essential is the best quality hay you can get and it really is worth paying more per bale for a top quality product. Bales of barn-dried and seed hay are invariably heavier and more densely packed than meadow hay, so each bale lasts longer. There is nothing wrong with well-made meadow hay and horses do like it, but the nutritional value is more variable and generally less per kilogram than for seed hay. Do not accept poor quality hay, whether made too late and of poor nutritional value, dusty, rain-washed, mouldy or mow burnt. (Mow burnt hay has overheated in the stack, due to being baled too damp. Moulds develop during the drying process, especially in hay which was baled with too high a moisture content, and they cause chronic respiratory problems which seriously inhibit performance.) Good quality hay should fulfil two criteria: (a) high nutritional value; (b) a minimum of dust and mould spores. Good quality hay will have the following approximate feed values: dry matter 86 per cent; crude protein 9–10 per cent; crude fibre 30 per cent; digestible energy 9 MJ/kg.

A sample of good hay.

The practice of soaking hay to remove dust and moulds also removes a considerable proportion of nutrients and if your horse really cannot take even good hay without suffering the effects of small airway disease, it will be better to feed one of the proprietary forms of haylage instead.

Silage is sometimes fed to horses but however vigilant the control when it is made, there still remains the risk of contamination from the soil or other foreign matter, resulting in abnormal fermentation and the growth of dangerous bacteria. Unless feeding large numbers of horses, the impracticality of handling big-bale silage hardly makes it worth the risk, however slight, of losing your horse through botulism poisoning.

Haylage, however, is grass which has been cut a little earlier than it would be for hay, partially wilted, then baled, compressed to about half its original size and packed in heat-sealed plastic bags, with most of the oxygen removed. The little that remains is used up by bacteria naturally found in the grass, resulting in a slight fermentation which prevents mould growth. The product is therefore dust-free and is usually very palatable, with slightly higher nutritional values per kilogram than good hay, although individual analysis is required to obtain exact figures.

In the United States and other parts of the world, alfalfa hay is commonly fed. The climate is not conducive to the production of much alfalfa hay in Britain, but alfalfa is available in both a chaffed and a pelleted form and provides a valuable additional form of highly digestible, highly palatable, good quality forage. It is higher in protein, calcium and some B vitamins than grass

TOP PICTURE *Chopped, molassed alfalfa is a very useful mixer and is highly palatable.*

SECOND PICTURE *A chaff made of 50 per cent chopped alfalfa and 50 per cent oat straw. It can be used as a mixer or as a total hay replacer.*

hay. It can be fed to complement the nutritional value of the forage ration, thus helping to minimise the requirement for concentrates. It can be fed as a mixer or separately and is often acceptable to tired horses when hay is left untouched.

Chaffed straw adds bulk but little nutritional value and has little place in feeding the competition horse. However, a 50:50 mix of molassed, chaffed alfalfa and oat straw provides a dust-free total hay replacer as an alternative to haylage. It has lower energy values than pure alfalfa but provides good quality bulk, helping to keep the digestive system working well. It can also be used as a mixer and is a useful feed when minor adjustments to the nutritional value of the diet are required.

Another basic essential, which can be considered partly a forage and partly a concentrate foodstuff, is sugar beet pulp which is available dried as either pellets or shreds. It must be well soaked before feeding, for up to 24 hours (follow the instructions on the bag), to prevent it continuing to swell when actually in the gut. Soaked beet pulp provides a little sugar for immediate energy, a high level of digestible fibre for steadily released energy, a protein level of 7 per cent and is high in calcium. Digestible energy is 10.5 MJ/kg (dry weight). Horses can be fed up to 1 kg ($2\frac{1}{4}$lb) (dry weight) per day, which equates to about three scoops of soaked beet pulp. Always soak in a minimum of double the weight of water for the weight of dry beet pulp. Make it fresh each day as it goes off quickly.

Concentrates come in many forms and may be fed either as 'straights', i.e. mixing the ingredients yourself, or as compounds, which are ready-prepared feeds, designed to be fed without extra additives. Most endurance riders are incapable of keeping to this rule! Provided you do understand the implications of adding different ingredients and the risks of unbalancing the ration, this need not be a disaster. The newcomer to the sport, however, is advised to follow the basic rules to avoid problems. The critical aspects of feeding various extras do not really come into play until you reach full endurance ride level and by then you should know exactly what your horse needs for a given workload, during competition, etc. It may take a little time to resolve any problems, such as loss of appetite, condition or performance, but it is necessary to understand the cause before you can put the situation right. Grasping at straws, or at the latest additive or remedy to be advertised, is never the solution.

Oats are traditionally considered the most suitable grain for horses, basically because they are fairly easily digested, with a higher fibre content and lower energy value than many other cereals. Their light weight for volume (due to the fibrous husk) means that a relatively high volume must be fed in comparison with other grains to give the same energy value. This may necessitate increasing the number of meals if the horse won't eat enough otherwise. Adult horses should be able to cope with whole oats, although most feed merchants today sell the bagged product rolled. The nutritional value starts to deteriorate as soon as the oats are rolled, however, and it is often difficult for the one- or two-horse owner to obtain good quality oats in sufficiently small quantities on a regular basis, causing a problem in keeping track of the energy value of the horse's feed. For the endurance rider, other forms of concentrate are probably more practical.

A new strain of oats, known as 'naked oats', has been developed, which loses its husk during harvesting, leaving the whole kernel. These do not lose nutritional value during storage and because they are much more energy-dense by weight than ordinary oats, the weight fed should be reduced by 20 per cent, i.e. 800 g (1¾ lb) of naked oats is equivalent in feed value to 1 kg (2¼ lb) of ordinary oats. They are higher in protein and oil than other oat types and much lower in fibre and they are dust-free. They can, therefore, form a very useful high-energy feed for the performance horse but it is essential that they are not mistakenly overfed and that the horse also receives sufficient good quality fibre.

Barley must be crushed, boiled or subjected to one of the modern processing methods before being fed to horses, as the small grain is tightly encased in the indigestible husk which prevents the digestive enzymes from working on the nutrients inside. Barley is heavier than oats on a weight for volume basis, contains more starch and less fibre and has a higher energy value. These factors are responsible for barley being known as a fattening food. The various cooking processes – micronisation and extrusion – help to make the barley more digestible by breaking down the starch, so that more is digested in the small intestine. Micronised or extruded barley is, therefore, a very useful food for helping to keep, or put, condition on the competition horse and generally seems to be very palatable.

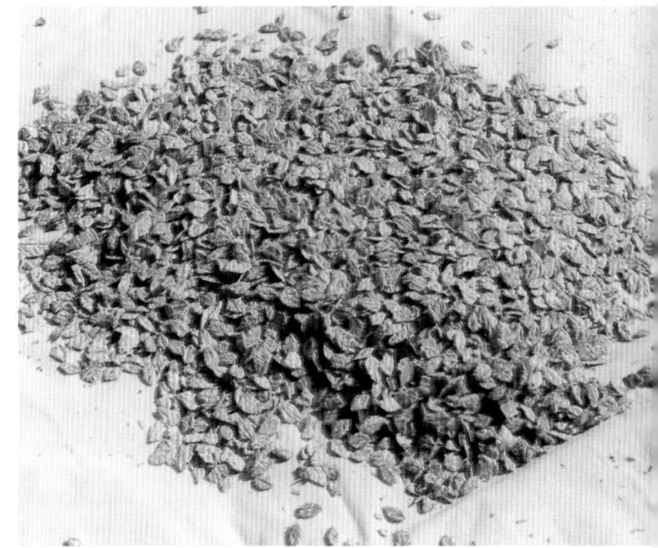

Micronised barley, useful for putting weight on.

Maize is more rarely used and will also help to put weight on, being high in energy value. It can be fed whole or steamed and flaked, but is probably not economical outside major growing areas.

All the commonly fed straight cereals are comparatively low in good quality protein, which is why it is generally recommended that horses on cereal-based diets are given a broad spectrum vitamin and mineral supplement which also contains the essential amino acids lysine and methionine. Alternatively, one of the modern 'oat balancers', designed to remedy the deficiencies in cereals, can be used. Essential amino acids are those which the horse cannot manufacture either at all in the body, or in sufficient quantity to meet the protein requirements for tissue maintenance. Proteins are made up of chains of amino acids in different combinations for different body structures. There are over 20 amino acids, all working in conjunction with one another. An imbalance or deficiency of one amino acid can seriously affect condition. If protein is overfed, however, it is broken down and stored as fat – an expensive and wasteful method of energy production.

Compound feeds come in many guises, the simplest two options being either cubes or coarse mixes. The ingredients are stated on the bag, together with a nutrient analysis. The feeds vary from low-energy compounds to very high-energy compounds, such as racehorse cubes. The protein level is also increased as you move up the scale, some of the racehorse compounds having a crude protein content as high as 16 per cent or more, which is a good reason to think twice before feeding them. The idea of compound feeds is that they are balanced in terms of energy, protein, fibre, fats, vitamins and minerals, to be used in conjunction with average quality forage, to form a diet based on the horse's workload. This theory makes them a simple and manageable option for the less experienced owner. All you have to do is to choose a compound which suits your horse's current workload, such as a low-energy coarse mix during the winter, or a competition mix in the competition season, and feed the recommended quantity along with your hay. Compound feed products designed for competition horses are also sold guaranteed free from any prohibited substances under FEI and Jockey Club rules, which removes another worry from the competitor's mind.

A typical coarse mix, containing a variety of grains, a proprietary pelleted feed, plus vitamins and minerals.

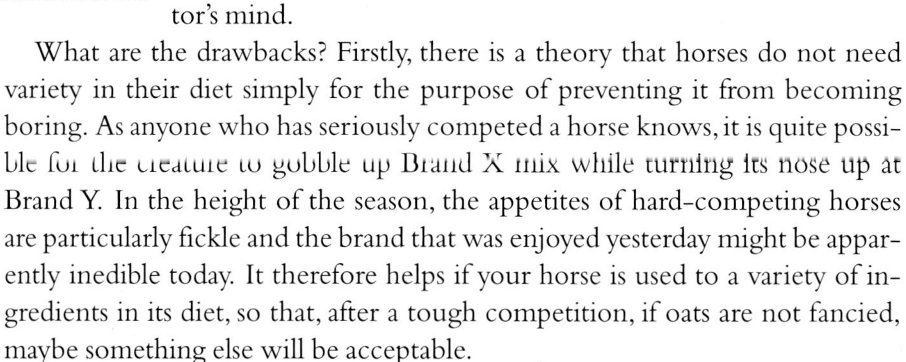

What are the drawbacks? Firstly, there is a theory that horses do not need variety in their diet simply for the purpose of preventing it from becoming boring. As anyone who has seriously competed a horse knows, it is quite possible for the creature to gobble up Brand X mix while turning its nose up at Brand Y. In the height of the season, the appetites of hard-competing horses are particularly fickle and the brand that was enjoyed yesterday might be apparently inedible today. It therefore helps if your horse is used to a variety of ingredients in its diet, so that, after a tough competition, if oats are not fancied, maybe something else will be acceptable.

Secondly, compounds reduce the flexibility of the ration, in that the horse's requirement for particular levels of protein or energy will change through the year according to condition, workload, grass availability, etc. This is one of the endurance rider's excuses for fiddling with the feed and it is a valid one for a rider who understands enough to know when an increase or reduction in a particular ingredient will make a difference to well-being and performance. Also, although compounds are designed to reduce the margin of error, the wrong compound, with the wrong proportion of inadequate-quality forage, can easily result in a horse under par or an unmanageable beast.

Thirdly, if you are relying on a particular compound and the manufacturers change the specification, or you have supplier problems in mid-season, you will be forced into an unanticipated change of diet. The answer in this case is to use well-established brands from major feed companies. If you then do experience any problems with their products, you need have no hesitation in telephoning their nutritionists for advice.

Despite advice that a horse on a well-balanced natural diet should require no extra vitamins and minerals, a good, general-purpose supplement is usually advisable for a hard-working competition horse, provided care is taken not to overdose. The beginner horse on a compound concentrate ration will not need a supplement, but by the time the horse is competing in endurance rides it will almost certainly not be on a pure compound concentrate ration any longer and a supplement should be given accordingly. For example, if half of the concentrate ration consists of a compound, with cereals and/or beet pulp forming the other half, give half the dose of supplement.

The most important mineral to be considered for the competition horse is calcium, which is inadequate in cereal-based diets and is required particularly for the health and development of the bones during training – remember that bone continues to change and develop throughout the horse's life, not just while it is growing up. Phosphorus is also involved here but the normal diet usually provides an adequate supply and the problem, if any, is to ensure that the diet maintains a high enough ratio of available calcium to phosphorus, usually recommended to be between 1.5:1 and 2:1. Calcium is also involved in various chemical changes relating to muscle and nerve function and in enzyme activity and is implicated in connection with a possible cause of azoturia. Calcium and phosphorus will both be included in broad-spectrum supplements, but extra calcium may be required, in a form such as limestone flour, to provide the correct balance.

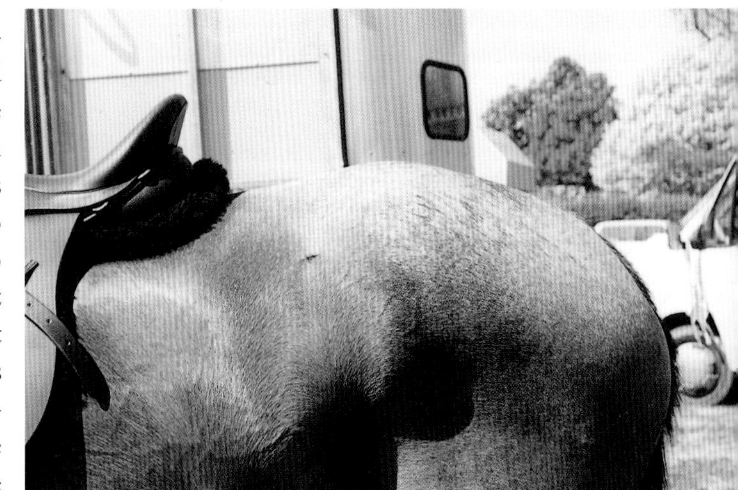

Salt deposits left on the coat following the evaporation of sweat are clear evidence of the loss of electrolytes when the horse is working hard. Both salts and fluids must be replaced to prevent dehydration.

Essential salts, mainly sodium, chloride and potassium, are lost through sweating during heavy work and the former two are often lacking in the diet of the stabled horse, although forage contains more than enough potassium. Vitamin and mineral supplements may not include sufficient sodium and chloride to replace that which is lost and it is good practice to include common salt in the diet (up to 40 g or $1\frac{1}{2}$ oz per day) and/or provide a salt lick. The horse cannot store these essential salts in the body and any excess is simply excreted. Giving electrolytes as a feed supplement, therefore, is a waste of time unless there is some good reason, for example if the horse has become dehydrated through illness or stress and needs the electrolyte balance to be restored. Some electrolyte preparations are designed to be diluted and the dilution ratio recommended by the manufacturer should be followed. Electrolytes designed to be administered in concentrated form should never be given to a dehydrated horse until it has started to drink well, as the salts will draw water into the gut and away from other parts of the body where it is vitally needed, thus worsening the horse's condition. We shall consider the role of electrolytes further in Chapter 10 (see also Appendix 3).

All other minerals and vitamins should be provided in sufficient quantities in a normal diet. There may be a deficiency of something specific, such as selenium or copper, in the soil in certain areas, but if this is suspected it needs to be verified by your vet before you start feeding individual mineral supplements.

Selenium is required, together with vitamin E, at higher levels than normal if the diet is high in oil and this should be taken into account when choosing your broad-spectrum supplement.

Specific extra vitamin supplementation is rarely required, although rapidly growing youngstock and horses showing loss of appetite, anaemia and poor condition may benefit from supplementation with vitamin B12 which is linked with folic acid in the production of red blood cells. Folic acid itself occurs at adequate levels in good quality forage.

How Much to Feed

For centuries, knowledgeable horsemen have fed horses with no better guide than their own eye for the horse's condition. This 'eye' varies, depending upon the job the horse is going to do. To the endurance rider, a show horse simply looks fat. To practically everyone else, an endurance horse looks scrawny, if not thin. The practised eye of someone who also knows the horse well – how it responds to training; how it behaves when going well – can be sufficient to control the levels of feed in a balanced diet. If you haven't yet developed this feel for the task, however, it helps if you can at least check that you are working on the right lines.

It should be clear by now that, in feeding horses, there is considerable scope for error but there is also considerable leeway for getting it about right. Scientific measurement will never give all the answers but it will help you to develop your own judgement as to what your horse needs.

We shall explain the basic calculations that can be used to formulate a ration, then look at one or two alternatives, taking into account some of the variables that concern the average horse and rider. For the purposes of calculation, we shall assume that we have a typical endurance horse, 15 hh, in good condition, but not overweight, fit enough to compete in 20- or 30-mile (32 or 48 km) rides.

Estimating Bodyweight and Appetite

First, we need a guide to the maximum weight of food, in dry matter terms, that this horse is likely to eat, which is 2.5 per cent of its bodyweight. The best way to check bodyweight is by using a weighbridge but most people don't have access to one so we have to use another method. The simplest is a weigh tape, available from good feed merchants; alternatively, you can find formulae for calculating bodyweight in books on nutrition. None of these methods is particularly accurate – as an experiment, the author tried two different tapes and a formula and arrived at three wildly differing answers, from 390–579 kg! Weigh tapes give a guide to weight by reference to girth measurement, although it appears that a heavier type of horse does not always necessarily have a much greater girth than a lighter one as depth also comes into the equation. The following table gives an approximate guide, applicable to endurance horses:

Height (hh)	Girth (in/cm)	Weight (lb/kg)
14.0	65–67/165–170	860–926/390–420
14.2	67–69/170–175	926–992/420–450
15.0	$68\frac{1}{2}$–71/174–180	992–1080/450–490
15.2	70–73/178–185	1058–1146/480–520
16.0	73–75/185–190	1146–1214/520–550

For an average-height endurance horse of 15 hh, with a girth of 69 in (175 cm), the bodyweight will be approximately 1014 lb (460 kg). The daily appetite, on a dry matter basis, will be 1014 × 2.5% = 25 lb 5 oz (460 × 2.5% = 11.5 kg). The actual weight eaten could be much more, for example if the horse is on grass, because of the high moisture content. The stabled horse, on a high-energy diet, may well eat less in total weight, but if the dry matter content of the food is somewhere near this figure, the horse is getting enough to eat in terms of quantity.

Energy Calculations

The energy required for maintenance, i.e. staying alive, is worked out by a formula to give the megajoules per kilogram required per day:

$$18 + \frac{\text{bodyweight (1b/kg)}}{10}$$

Our 1014 lb (460 kg) horse therefore requires 64 MJ of digestible energy (DE) per day for maintenance.

As previously mentioned, reducing the amount of energy required for work to a mathematical calculation is difficult because of all the variables involved. However, a table for guidance for the endurance horse would be as follows.

For each 110 lb 4 oz (50 kg) of bodyweight, add:

Type of Work	Work score (MJ DE)
Walking (1 hour)	+1
Walking and trotting (1 hour)	+2
Walking and trotting ($1\frac{1}{2}$ hours)	+3
Introducing cantering, or up to 2 hours	+4
Introducing 20–30 mile (32–48 km) rides	+5
40–50 mile (64–80 km) set-speed rides	+6
50–80 mile (80–129 km) endurance rides	+7
100-mile (160 km) rides and major multi-day rides	+8

Our 1014 lb (460 kg) horse, competing in 25-mile (40 km) CTRs on a regular basis, will therefore need +5 MJ DE for each 110 lb 4 oz (50 kg) bodyweight, i.e. 46 MJ DE for work per day.

Maintenance level	64 MJ DE
Work level	46 MJ DE
Total energy required per day	110 MJ DE

Choosing the ration

It would be possible to provide the total requirement as forage. For example, good hay provides about 9 MJ/kg on an as-fed basis. To provide 110 MJ we would need the horse to eat 27 lb (12.2 kg), the dry matter content of which would be about 86 per cent, i.e. 23 lb (10.5 kg) and within the appetite/bodyweight amount of 25 lb 4 oz (11.5 kg). However, there are two reasons against this course of action. Firstly, as work increases, the energy level will also have to increase and concentrates will have to be included. It is therefore sensible if the horse's digestive system is attuned to coping with a minimum level of concentrates, so that the balance of micro-organisms in the gut is not suddenly upset. Secondly, the quality of hay is extremely variable and unless you are prepared to have each batch analysed, there is no sure way of knowing the true energy value.

Ideally, we want to maximise the amount of good quality fibre fed while enabling the horse to carry out its work programme and keep its appetite keen by aiming to feed slightly below the full weight to satisfy that appetite.

Let us assume that we shall provide at least half of the quantity required to satisfy the horse's appetite in good hay, so we shall feed 15½lb (7 kg), which will provide about 9 MJ/kg of energy = 63 MJ DE.

We also want to include other good quality and digestible forms of fibre, so we shall add another 10–15 per cent of the total made up of chopped alfalfa and sugar beet pulp: 2¼lb (1 kg) chopped alfalfa provides 9.3 MJ DE; 1½lb (0.67 kg) dry sugar beet (about two scoops soaked) provides approximately 7 MJ DE. We now have:

15½ lb (7 kg) hay	63.00 MJ DE
2¼ lb (1 kg) alfalfa	9.30 MJ DE
1½ lb (0.67 kg) sugar beet	7.00 MJ DE
Total	**79.30 MJ DE**

To meet a total requirement of 110 MJ DE we still need 30.70 MJ DE to be provided by concentrates. We have reached 19 lb (8.67 kg) in weight, leaving us up to 6¼lb (2.83 kg) to make up in concentrates. We can choose a single type of concentrate or a combination. For example:

Food type	Approx. MJ/kg	Weight to make up 30.70 MJ
Barley	13	5.2 lb (2.36 kg)
Oats	11	6.15 lb (2.79 kg)
Low energy mix	10	6.76 lb (3.07 kg)
Competition mix	11.5	5.88 lb (2.67 kg)

We see that using barley will achieve the aim of feeding slightly below appetite, while still fulfilling the energy requirement. In fact, all the alternatives are within the limit, including the low-energy mix, if we allow for the difference between the weight as fed and the dry matter content. For practical purposes, the dry matter value can be taken as roughly 90 per cent of the weight of a hay and concentrate ration.

At the point where the dry matter weight exceeds the appetite limit, we have the options of: (a) increasing the percentage of concentrate to forage;

(b) gradually changing to a higher-energy concentrate or combination of concentrates. Assuming we decided to feed competition mix, our final ration is:

Hay	15.4 lb (7.00 kg)
Alfalfa	2.2 lb (1.00 kg)
Sugar beet (dry weight)	1.47 lb (0.67 kg)
Competition mix	5.88 lb (2.67 kg)
Total	**25 lb (11.34 kg)**

Percentage of fibre:concentrates = 76%:24%, which is quite acceptable for this level of endurance work.

Most competition horse diets worked out on an energy basis will contain sufficient protein, but we can check:

Food	Protein %	Protein in ration
Hay	9	22.22 oz (630 g)
Alfalfa	16.01	5.64 oz (160 g)
Sugar beet	7	1.65 oz (47 g)
Competition mix	12	11.28 oz (320 g)
Total		**40.8 oz or (2.55 lb)**
		(1,157 g or 1.157 kg)

The percentage protein in the diet is therefore 2.55/25 (1,157/11,340) × 100 = 10.2%. This is somewhat higher than strictly necessary, mainly due to the high protein content of alfalfa. However, we have assumed good quality hay with a relatively high protein content, while even good hay can be variable and average quality hay might well have a protein level of about 6–7 per cent. A hay protein content of 6.5 per cent would reduce the protein in the hay ration to 15.8 oz (448 g) and the total protein percentage in the ration to 8.6 per cent. Also bear in mind that not all of the crude protein is available to the horse and estimated levels of digestible protein given by feed manufacturers are often based on research done with other species, not horses. An estimated crude protein content of around 10 per cent in the diet of an increasingly hard-working horse is therefore acceptable.

Approximate nutrient values of some basic foods are shown in the following table, but be aware that they can vary and, if in doubt, obtain an analysis. For compound feeds, always follow the analysis printed on the bag – one competition mix is not the same as another!

Food	Crude protein (%)	DE (MJ/2.2 lb/kg)
Oats	9–11	11–12
Barley	9–10	13
Maize	8.5	14
Chopped alfalfa	16.01	9.3
Alfalfa/oat straw chaff	10.5	8
Sugar beet pulp	7	10.5
Good hay	9–10	9
Average hay	5–8	7–8
Oil	0	35

We have now worked out one example of a basic diet for a horse competing at Novice level in the sport. Should you add anything else to this diet?

If using a compound feed, the answer is no. The feed will be balanced with vitamins and minerals and the food ingredients of the diet will provide sufficient levels of all the important nutrients. If using straights, the recommended dose of a broad-spectrum vitamin and mineral supplement is advisable.

As the horse progresses in fitness and workload, adjustments will need to be made to cope with the demand for more energy. Adding vegetable oil, for example, is one way of providing more energy without greatly increasing the volume of the concentrates. Begin with a small quantity, say, a tablespoon per feed, and gradually increase, up to 1 pt (0.5 litre) per day for a really fit horse competing in major rides. As with all high-energy feeds, don't increase the amount beyond what the horse shows it really needs, judging by its attitude to work and its condition.

From Novice level upwards, you can add salt to the feed, although some horses won't take it, so making sure that a salt lick is available is a good alternative. A reduced salt intake leads to dehydration and reduced sweating, limiting the horse's ability to dissipate heat when working hard.

There are many other foodstuffs – soyabean meal, peas and beans, linseed, bran, succulents such as carrots and apples, molasses – and the principles for adding any of them to the diet are the same as those outlined above for the usual basic foods. Be aware of their nutrient values and how they will affect the balance of the diet.

Beware of the tradition of 'bran with everything'. Bran offers little of value in the way of nutrients which cannot be better obtained elsewhere, is high in phosphorus and low in calcium and may be a cause of mineral imbalance. Unless prescribed, for example after colic, the notion of the 'comforting bran mash' is a panacea for the owner rather than the horse. Would you want a dollop of laxative if you were tired out and hungry?

Many people like to use herbal supplements and these are available for various specific problems as well as for general health. Horse pasture often lacks a wide range of herbs, especially if overgrazed, and there is nothing wrong with adding a supplement produced by a reputable company to the diet if you wish. The best known and most frequently fed herb is garlic, which is thought to 'cleanse' the blood, help cure coughing, relieve inflammation and to have a healing and antibiotic effect. However, do remember that some herbs can cause illness if fed to excess; comfrey is one commonly used herb which may possibly be toxic in large quantities.

There are also various other products on the market, such as probiotics and so-called 'performance enhancers', such as carbohydrate boosters and simple sugars. We shall consider the effect of these on the horse in high-level competition in Chapter 11 (also see Appendix 2).

Summary

Finally, let us summarise the basic rules of feeding the endurance horse.

1 Make any changes to the diet progressively over several days. This is the single most important rule for avoiding upsets and keeping the digestive system working efficiently.

2 Base the diet on good quality digestible fibre.

3 Add concentrates progressively, as demanded by the workload.

4 Feed all foods by weight, not volume.

5 Ensure that plenty of fresh, clean water is available at all times.

6 Feed concentrates in as many small meals as is practical, especially if the horse's grazing time is restricted.

7 Monitor changes in condition. Changing bodyweight can be checked using a weigh tape.

8 Don't use any 'additives' unless with good reason. Apart from a general vitamin and mineral supplement, the additives most likely to be required for an endurance horse are: salt, limestone flour (calcium) and, if feeding oil, extra vitamin E and selenium.

CHAPTER 5

ENDURANCE EQUITATION

FOR ANY other equestrian discipline there is an accepted style of riding. Endurance, however, is such a young sport that a definitive style has not yet been fully established. In fact, as the sport involves riding in varying situations – on the flat, on steep hills, over natural country, in a racing finish – it is likely that one style will not suit all situations and the rider may need to shorten or lengthen their stirrups as appropriate. The 'pioneer' spirit of the sport has encouraged some riders to think that they do not need to learn riding technique at all but simply leap on a horse and go. Perhaps this chapter will show why this attitude is not a good idea.

Why Do We Need Endurance Equitation?

The absolute aim of endurance riding is to finish the distance of the competition with the horse fit, sound and in the best possible condition. To achieve this, the rider needs to help the horse as much as possible. The best ground management and crewing in the world will not compensate for incompetent riding. Bad riding over a long distance will result in an exhausted horse, if not an injured one. Any aspiring endurance rider owes it to his or her equine partner to learn to ride as well as possible.

As we saw earlier in the book, the horse is not designed to carry a rider, therefore we have to adapt its physique, through training, to enable it to do so without distress. Luckily for us, most horses respond well to such training and even seem to enjoy their partnership with people. Over the centuries an idea has evolved of the most appropriate equine conformation for our purpose. Some horses, however, are less well conformed than others and this makes training more difficult and lessens the chances of success in a sport as demanding as endurance.

We have covered the points of conformation in Chapter 1 and it might well be worth checking back to see how they apply to the requirements of riding. The skeletal structure and muscle development of any individual horse will be taken into account by a good and committed rider.

This Thoroughbred/Irish Draught mare, Phaedra, ridden by Eileen Baxter, won the Scottish Championships in her first attempt at a 100-mile ride, the only finisher over a tough course at a slow average speed. Her innate toughness and determination, plus careful riding, kept her going.

Let us assume for the moment that you have a well-schooled, well-balanced horse, with symmetrical action and good basic paces. What is the most appropriate basic position to adopt for endurance work?

A look at the various endurance saddle designs on the market will show a variety of ideas on the subject – some more thoughtfully conceived than others. The Western cowboy and the cavalryman knew about riding for long hours at a time. From their experience saddles were developed which provided for the rider to sit with a long, almost straight leg and a very upright seat. This was fine, of course, provided you weren't going anywhere very fast, although the Western 'lope', a slow canter, is ridden in an upright position. Such a style also suited the wide-open level plains. When going up and down hills, these saddles needed high pommels and cantles to help to keep the rider in place.

Conversely, the sports of jumping and cross country riding resulted in the invention of the 'forward seat', with saddles having forward-cut flaps and knee rolls and the rider adopting a relatively short stirrup. This enabled the rider to unfold the angles at hip, knee and ankle to rise forwards out of the saddle to take a fence. The forward position of the rider, when out of the saddle, also encourages the horse to move forward faster. This effect is further exaggerated in racing. However, when the show jumping rider sits down in the saddle, the angles of the body are compressed to achieve a correct riding position, with the shoulder, hip and heel in alignment. Such a position would be extremely uncomfortable for an endurance rider who is in the saddle for hours, rather than minutes, at a time. Also, the forward position can encourage the horse to go too fast and, if not carefully controlled, to fall on its forehand and become unbalanced. The rider must expend more energy to maintain a forward position in balance than in a more upright position.

The endurance rider needs to find a comfortable, balanced position which can be maintained for long periods without muscle cramps or strain, but also needs some adaptability of seat to cope with variations in terrain and speed. The sport does not involve jumping, except for small logs or ditches which

A big, strong, fit and well-muscled Arab with a lot of scope.

might be found *en route*, therefore the short stirrup used for cross country event riding is not required. A dressage- or Western-length stirrup, however, would be too long for most rides as it would not allow the rider sufficient angulation and anchorage to cope with minor natural hazards and to stay balanced going up and down steep hills or banks, nor to get out of the saddle if a racing finish was necessary. The optimum would be a stirrup just short enough to cope with these needs, but no shorter than necessary in order to minimise cramps and strain. A further point is that the saddle will, ideally, provide some support fore and aft, but will not be so heavily encumbered that the rider has no freedom to get his or her weight forward when necessary.

As the most appropriate stirrup length is longer than that required for jumping, the knee rolls of a forward-cut general purpose saddle are usually too far forward to support the endurance rider's leg. A straighter-cut flap, with a knee roll that extends upwards to support the front of the thigh – very useful when trotting or cantering long downhill stretches – is what is required. The stirrup bars are also often set too far forward on general purpose saddles, making it difficult for the rider to balance over the centre of movement. The bars should be set in a similar position to those on a dressage saddle.

We have already discussed the central positioning of the saddle on the horse's back, with the seat level. If the rider then adopts a classically correct riding position, with a vertical line through shoulder, hip and heel, but with moderate angulation at hip, knee and ankle, we are beginning to get the static picture of the ideal endurance riding position. It could best be described as a modified military or dressage position, being somewhat closer to this than to the opposite position used for jumping.

Some riders, especially older riders, with a hunting and jumping background find this position difficult to achieve and therefore have no option but to use a more forward-cut saddle. Pushing the lower leg forward, as in the old English hunting seat, can relieve some of the tension of cramped leg muscles but this will have the effect of unbalancing the rider, making him or her more dependent upon the reins and harder on the horse's mouth and will be more tiring for both horse and rider.

Conversely, some riders, usually with a Western background, ride with a totally long leg and never post to the trot (English trot). Maintaining a correct sitting trot is strenuous for the rider at the best of times and, over a long ride, is impossible, so the rider will inevitably end up bumping up and down on the horse's back. Even if the horse is trained to the smooth Western jog, it is more tiring for a rider to maintain this over a long period than to shorten the stirrups slightly, even in a Western saddle, and post to the trot.

Some endurance saddles are built on a lighter-weight Western theme and generally encourage a good position. Others follow the military patterns of earlier centuries, sometimes with extended panels, said to provide better weight distribution, but which, in fact, are often too long for the horse's back, especially on Arabian horses. Others still are built like armchairs, with deep, quilted seats intended to provide comfort for the rider on a long ride. In fact, with the majority of the distance covered at a posting trot, the extra padding is unnecessary and usually just serves to sit the rider further away from the horse's back, detracting from the desirable close contact which enables the rider to follow the horse's movement well.

Some excellent saddles are purpose-designed for Arabian and Arabian-cross horses, following the traditional English pattern of wool-stuffed broad panels, with straighter-cut flap and knee/thigh rolls as previously mentioned. These saddles are designed with the particular comfort of the female rider in mind.

Other excellent designs are based on a 'suspension' system, where the panels can move independently of each other and with the horse's movement, thus affording great freedom of the shoulder. An individual rider's choice of purchase requires considerable thought and the comfort of both horse and rider should be taken into account.

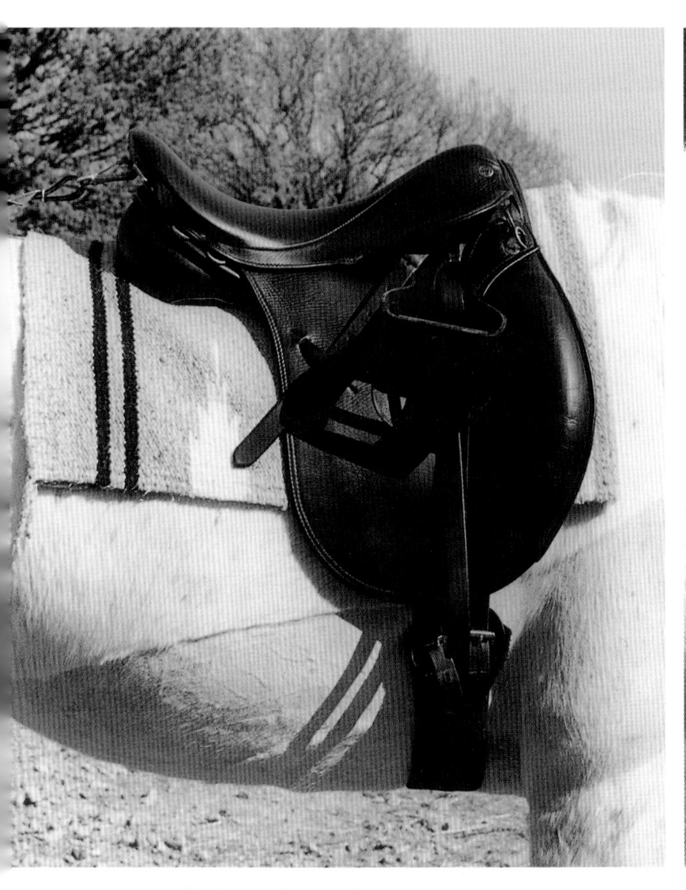

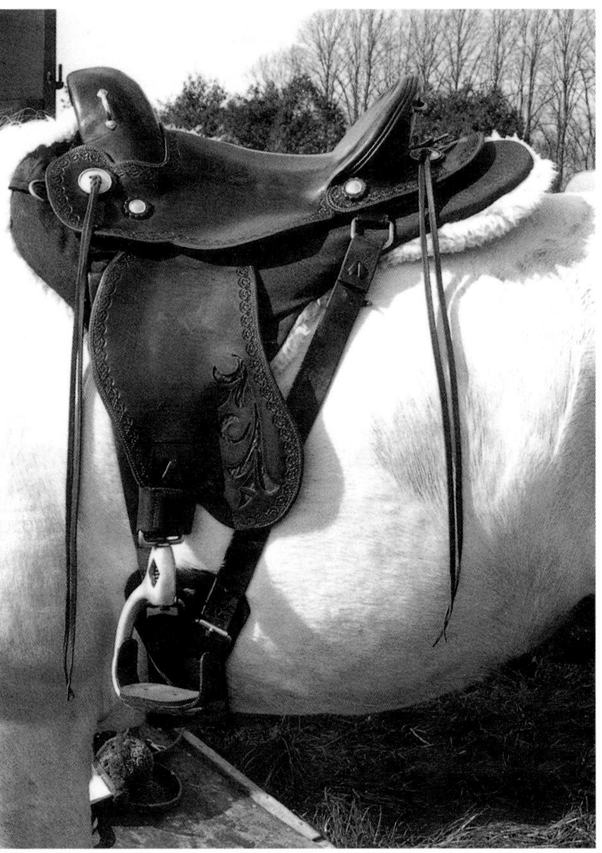

ABOVE LEFT *An Arabian Saddle Company endurance saddle, specifically designed for the Arabian horse, but soon adopted for other breeds because of its good fit, broad panels and rider comfort.* ABOVE RIGHT *An Orthoflex traditional pattern endurance saddle. The Orthoflex, with its 'suspension system' and independent panels, represented the beginning of a revolution in endurance saddle design. It allowed the horse much greater freedom of movement, spread the weight more effectively over the horse's back and thereby reduced stress and back injuries and improved performance. The spring-loaded stirrup was another innovation. It reduced pressure on the rider's foot, but tended to be bouncy.*

We have the horse saddled and the rider mounted, sitting correctly. What happens when the horse begins to move?

As soon as the horse begins to walk forward, the rider's body must go with, and absorb, the movement, otherwise the rider will be unbalanced and the horse will be unable to maintain a rhythmic, symmetrical progression, due to the shifting, uneven weight on its back. Imagine giving a piggy-back ride to a child who keeps twisting, wriggling or leaning to one side then the other or leaning back. It would be very difficult to keep an even, forward-going pace with such a load on your back!

How does the rider sense and absorb the movement? Firstly, the seat must be in the saddle, balanced on the seat bones and buttocks, with the pelvis vertical, the spine straight but relaxed and the head erect and balanced on top. In this balanced position, it is possible to relax all unnecessary tensions in the body, maintaining just sufficient muscular effort to keep the body in equilibrium, i.e.

The author and Rani Tarina (right) on their way to third place in the gruelling Red Dragon Ride in the Black Mountains of Wales. To tackle rides like this successfully the horse must be trained to move in balance, minimising energy expenditure and the risk of accidents.

The author and Rani Tarina at the Golden Horseshoe Ride. The culmination of Tarina's career was winning the Arab Horse Society's endurance trophy for the most successful British pure-bred Arabian in 1993.

to stop it from falling over! In the same way that the balanced horse can move in self-carriage, so the balanced rider has the freedom of movement to allow the horse's back to move underneath him or her and to use the various parts of their body independently and effectively. This ability to *allow* the horse the full scope of its movement is extremely important. A stiff, tense rider will block the horse's freedom and thus contribute to tiredness and wastage of energy. The position should be such that if the horse were suddenly removed from underneath you, you would land on your feet. In this position the hip joints will be free and open and the legs should hang without any gripping and free from tension, with hips, knees and ankles flexible and ready to give light, precise aids.

If, however, you are in a position of rigid tension, with a hollowed back, you cannot absorb the horse's movement and will have a jarring ride with your seat bones digging into its back. The horse will show a shortened stride, raised head carriage and hollowed back, resulting in strain and earlier fatigue than would otherwise occur. Similarly, if you slouch, with a rounded back and head thrust forward, your seat will be unbalanced and you will be unable to use hands and legs independently. This type of rider is likely to be behind the movement, again jarring the horse's back, often hanging on the reins and causing the horse to fight the bit, hollow its back and go on its forehand. Both of these undesirable types of riding are, unfortunately, commonly seen, yet, given the number of hours the endurance rider spends in the saddle, part of the goal should surely be to ride as well, as sympathetically and with as much understanding as possible.

As the horse walks, the rider should be aware of what its legs are doing at any given time. It should be possible to feel, through each buttock alternately, the sink of the back as the horse brings the hind leg forwards and the rise as it brings the foot to the ground and pushes back. The rider absorbs this movement by keeping the hip joints open and mobile, allowing the seat bones to slide forward alternately in rhythm with the movement, keeping the lower back soft and the thigh muscles relaxed. If you cannot obtain this feeling and its regular rhythm, check your position. Tuck your buttocks underneath you on the saddle, stretch your back upwards and then relax it, keeping erect, with your head balanced on your spine, and allowing your shoulders and arms to hang freely, without tension. Let your legs hang free without tension, relaxing all the muscles and joints and letting your weight drop naturally down through your heels. Walk the horse on again and try to be aware of the rhythm of the horse moving under you, first one side then the other, without allowing any part of your body to stiffen.

As the horse moves into trot, it changes from a four-time, (left hind, left fore, right hind, right fore) movement to a two-time diagonal movement. If you sit to the trot, however, you can still feel the alternate sink and lift of the back as the hind legs swing forward or take weight. In rising trot, you sit as the inside hind leg (and outside foreleg) come to the ground and rise as the inside hind leg pushes your buttock back up. This is the most important gait for the endurance rider and the cause of many aches and pains due to tension. Your weight should be carried evenly on both sides, with your seat still following the rhythm of the movement and your stirrups a rest for your feet, not a barrier to push against. Hips, knees and ankles should all act as shock absorbers, flexing as you sit and releasing as you rise.

The above is just a brief description of the most basic essential riding technique, the minimum you must learn if you want your horse to have the best chance of competitive success. Obviously, there is much more to it and we have not even begun to look at the application of the independent aids of hand and leg, nor at more detailed aspects of balanced schooling. Balance is the key to everything. If the rider is in balance, the horse can perform with the minimum of effort and the rider can ride with the least expenditure of energy. In

It is essential that the rider can feel the movement of the horse as its balance moves from one limb to another. In walk the sequence of footfalls progresses from left hind to left fore…

…left fore to right hind and…

…right hind to right fore.

both cases the onset of fatigue is considerably delayed and the risk of strain vastly reduced. Many books have been written on equitation and it is well worth pursuing the subject in more detail, both by reading and by taking lessons from an instructor who understands the needs of the sport. Sally Swift's book *Centred Riding* offers a great deal of valuable advice for endurance riders. Finally, if you cannot ride in balance, you cannot train your endurance horse to move well, nor develop its physique correctly.

Hillwork is an essential part of the training of any horse intended for serious endurance competition and if you don't live near any hills suitable for riding up, it is worth the effort of boxing the horse to the nearest range for training. Teaching your horse to stay balanced on hills at speed, whether going up or down, can gain valuable time over the opposition. Hill training also vastly increases the amount of effort a horse has to put into its work and it extends the scope for movement and use of the muscles and joints to a very significant degree. Just consider the difference in effort and the differences in pull on the various muscles which you use for walking up or down a steep hill, in comparison with the effort required for walking on the flat. The amount of extension

The rider is upright and well balanced, the slight curve in the rein shows that she has the lightest of contacts and the horse is moving freely and lightly in rhythm. He is not collected and his nose is in front of the vertical, but this is right for endurance where the horse needs to stretch out freely to cover the ground. Because his muscle development and outline are correct, it would be easy to school him for greater collection if desired.

and flexion required of the muscles and tendons to keep you on your feet and propel you up- or downhill, is clearly much greater than if you were walking on a level plain. Over a period of time, this stretching and contracting enhances strength, suppleness and resistance to injury through unaccustomed strain, by promoting full use, through training, of the horse's locomotory system. Also, because hillwork requires so much more effort from the horse, more fitness is achieved in fewer miles and at a slower speed, reducing concussion and the potential for strain.

When teaching a horse to deal with hills, it is essential that the rider keeps the horse straight and stays balanced. Young horses often try to attack uphill stretches at a canter, but may be reluctant or very uncertain about how to go down steep hills. Going up or down hills is often easier for the young horse at a faster pace and this tendency must be checked, to avoid the horse becoming unbalanced and to teach it to control its own body. However, provided balance is maintained, it does no harm to let the youngster take a slightly faster pace while it builds up strength and confidence. Going uphill, the horse should propel itself forward using the strength of its quarters, bringing the hind legs well forward at each stride. The rider's weight should be inclined slightly forward from the hips, not the waist, lightening the seat and giving the horse the freedom it needs to move energetically forward. Going downhill, the rider's weight should again be slightly forward, in a light seat which allows the horse to get its hocks underneath itself. The thigh should be flat against the saddle and thigh or high knee rolls help to keep the rider in position. The horse must learn to stretch its head and neck forward for balance while doing hillwork and must not raise them, which results in a hollow back with the hind legs failing to come through and the stride restricted.

Hillwork often shows up a very one-sided horse, or one with a back problem as the horse will tend to throw its quarters out sideways and move on three tracks to minimise the strain on the weaker side.

A horse well trained to hills can gain considerable advantage in competition, simply by being able to tackle them faster, whether up or down. Trotting downhill, particularly on tarmac, is generally considered damaging to the horse, due to the strain imposed on the joints. However, the endurance horse does need to learn how to trot downhill as this will be necessary in competition. Once the horse has mastered the technique, however, trotting downhill in training should be kept to an absolute minimum. It is a considerable advantage to the horse if the rider is fit and well balanced enough to dismount and run down steep hills alongside the horse and we shall look further at the pros and cons of dismounting during competition later in the book.

Balance is also required in order to guide the horse through difficult going at speed. A balanced rider can indicate a chosen path to the horse by a minimal adjustment of weight in the saddle, coupled with neck reining. A really skilful horse and rider partnership bounding down a mountainside in a

ABOVE *Hillwork strengthens the horse's physique, improves his balance and cardiovascular performance and reduces the time needed for fitness training.*

RIGHT *Moving at speed downhill must also be practised.*

well-contained canter or fast trot, with the horse responsive and balanced yet on a free rein, is beautiful to watch. When you are in balance, you have the feeling of being able to control every stride and, at the most advanced level, when your body has learned to make the correct response automatically, just the thought of what you want to do is enough to effect a tiny aid which communicates itself to the horse.

A well-trained horse which has settled into its work can often be ridden on a free rein. However, most of the time most horses require a light, supportive contact to avoid too much extension or falling on the forehand.

The majority of the distance of most rides will be ridden in trot. The pace you should aim for is an active, balanced, working trot, with the power coming from the horse's hindquarters. It used to be considered that a long-striding, extended trot was the ultimate endurance pace. However, the extended paces

The endurance horse must be capable of coping with all types of terrain at varying speeds.

require tremendous energy from the horse and cannot be kept up for many miles. It is better that the horse works within its maximum capacity than at the limit of it, thus conserving energy and making optimal use of stamina.

Where the ground conditions are good enough, the trot can be varied by cantering and, again, the optimum pace is a balanced, in-hand canter. Once a horse learns to move in balance, you can work on increasing speed while maintaining that balance. If balance is compromised, both energy consumption and the risk of injury through strain or accident are increased.

On the question of whether trot or canter is the most energy-efficient pace, it would appear that, at the average speeds achieved in most endurance rides, there is little difference. However, the horse does not keep going continuously. There are stops to cope with gates, road crossings and checkpoints, and also crewing stops, which all have the effect of decreasing the average speed. Steep hills will also slow the pace to a walk. When the horse is able to move on at a trot or canter, therefore, it is likely to be going faster than the final average speed suggests.

A recent (1994) study of endurance horses using a treadmill at the Bristol Equine Sports Medicine Centre showed that horses would maintain trot on

Although this rider is leaning slightly forward to go with the faster pace of the canter, she is not interfering with the horse, who is working in a strong but steady rhythm, bringing his hocks well underneath his body. He is using his whole body well, minimising stress and energy expenditure.

the flat at speeds up to 15.66 or 17.9 mph (7 or 8 m) per second, before breaking into canter. When they did break into canter, however, their heart rates tended to fall from around 150 bpm (beats per minute) to around 120 bpm, thus the canter at these speeds was more energy-saving than the very fast trot.

Another interesting point of note was the ability of horses to synchronise their breathing not only with the canter rhythm, which is well documented, but also with the fast trot, and individuals differed as to whether they did this at all and, if so, as regards the number of strides per breath.

Another factor to be considered under the heading of equitation is the weight of the rider as the placing of additional weight on the horse and how it is carried can make a considerable difference to the horse's potential for success. It is fairly well established that a lightweight rider, riding well and in balance, poses less of a question for the horse than a heavier rider also riding in balance. The lightweight rider will tend to achieve better results purely because the horse has an easier task. However, if the lightweight rider is made to carry lead as deadweight in order to bring his or her weight up to the level of the heavier rider, does the deadweight merely equalise the situation or does it actually disadvantage the horse compared to the one carrying a heavier rider? It would appear from research carried out in France that if the deadweight carried by the horse is carried as close to the horse's centre of balance as possible, the disadvantage is minimal, if any. If, however, the rider carries the lead on his or her body, in order to try to lighten the load for the horse, then it does become a disadvantage because the rider becomes tired more quickly and, when tired, no longer rides in a balanced way.

This does not resolve the question of disadvantage to the horse carrying lead if both light- and heavyweight riders dismount to save the horses' energy when they are becoming tired. Clearly, the horse carrying the lead will now be at a disadvantage because a proportion of weight is still on its back, whereas the heavier rider has removed all the weight from his or her horse's back.

The organisers of international endurance rides have tried to achieve a relatively level handicap by introducing a minimum weight requirement for top-level competition of 165 lb (75 kg), including tack. For the majority of riders this does not, in fact, involve carrying very much, if any, lead, although a significant number of particularly slim or small women are at a disadvantage.

The same could be said for particularly small horses. Is it really fair to expect a 98 lb (45 kg) rider, on a horse under 15 hh, to carry 66 lb (30 kg) of lead? Should there, perhaps, be a sliding scale of weights, dependent upon the size of the horse? No one has yet suggested such a scheme and if you consider that three-times World Champion Becky Hart carried around 55 lb (25 kg) of dead weight on the 14.3 hh R.O. Grand Sultan, perhaps lightweight riders should not complain too much about the minimum weight requirement. Becky and Rio, of course, were outstandingly brilliant performers. In any sport there are going to be riders (and horses) at the periphery who, however enthusiastic, simply do not possess the physical capacity to make it to the ultimate level. (The show jumping arena would be poorer today if Nick Skelton had not grown too big to be a jockey!) It is impossible to cater for absolutely everyone and many north European men are precluded from top-level endurance simply because they are too heavy compared with their south European counterparts. Endurance does, however, do an excellent job of catering for allcomers at everything but top race-riding level.

Riding, like any other sport, is a physical activity which requires physical and mental fitness from the participant. This means taking care of your body by keeping it healthy and ready for competition. Riding alone is not sufficient exercise. In fact, the body needs other forms of exercise to negate the detrimental effects of hours of riding – exercises which stretch contracted muscles, liberate tensions and keep joints and ligaments free and mobile. Other forms of sport, such as swimming, running and skipping, help with cardiac and respiratory fitness, building up stamina, and also exercise muscles in different ways from riding, again relieving tension. These are not, of course, alternatives to regular riding. An expert in exercise physiology, both equine and human, when asked about the benefits of regular swimming as fitness training for horses, said: 'You will end up with a horse that is good at swimming.'

When you begin endurance riding, it is certainly noticeable that your first 20-miler (32 km), then your first 30-miler (48 km), then your first 50-miler (80 km) all result in agonisingly stiff muscles, usually two or three days after the event. However, after a couple of seasons it is only the first qualifier that hurts. Once you are into the swing of competitions, you can ride 50 miles without really thinking about it. The 100-miler (160 km), of course, is another matter and requires specialised preparation (see Chapter 11), but it is the shorter rides that you have done which give you the basis of fitness upon which you can even contemplate tackling a major event.

Another aspect which needs to be developed is the rider's mental ability to cope simultaneously with riding the horse and concentrating on the demands of the competition. All too often riding technique is forgotten in the midst of route-finding, crew stops, veterinary checks and timing and the horse is treated as a machine-like object, rather than a living, breathing participant. Ultimately, your body should become so attuned to riding well that you scarcely have to give it conscious thought – a totally different matter from not giving it due consideration in the first place. There are various techniques which can help your brain to help your body ride well, such as centring, mental rehearsal, etc.

Finally, if you make the effort to understand and learn equitation as it applies to endurance riding, you will reap the benefits in energy conservation, minimising risk of injury or strain as well as simple aches and pains, and will be able to achieve a true partnership with your horse.

CHAPTER 6

THE BASIS OF CONDITIONING

IN THE previous chapters, we have considered the demands of the sport, decided what sort of horse we want, worked out how to keep it in good health and manage and care for it on a daily basis and what to feed as a nutritious basic diet. We have discussed how to ride it and now we are ready to begin training.

The ultimate aim is supreme physical fitness. However, the initial aim of training is very different. If you simply pile on the work in an effort to have a super-fit horse in double quick time, you will end up with a horse which is mentally soured and physically overstressed. True conditioning for endurance work requires the complete training of all aspects of the mind and body. There are no short cuts and it cannot be hurried beyond the horse's capacity to accept the work and new experiences. A young horse which has been properly educated by being introduced to a variety of experiences before beginning serious ridden work will be far more mentally mature and able to cope with the demands of training than a young horse which has simply been left in the field until being broken in. A golden rule throughout all training is this: if your horse becomes upset, resistant, reluctant, off-colour or obviously unable to cope with what is being asked of it in any way, ease off on the workload, go several steps back to reinforce what was previously learned and rebuild your horse's confidence and strength until it is ready and willing to progress to the next stage.

At what age should a horse begin training for endurance riding? A study of the results of major endurance rides has suggested that six-year-old horses do not do well in 100-mile (160 km) rides, although for many years six was the minimum age at which horses were permitted to compete at this level. In Britain this has been raised to seven years, although in some countries five is still the minimum age. Obviously, a 100-mile ride is a major event, for which a

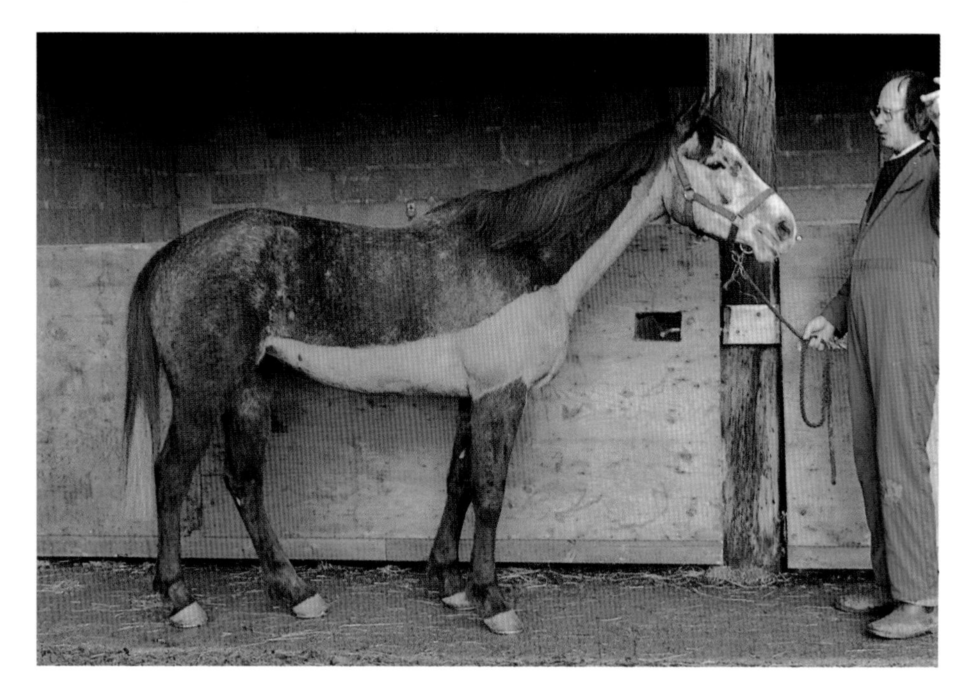

A six-year-old horse about to begin winter training. She has a good basic framework, but her muscles are undeveloped and soft. Compare this photo with the photo of the same horse photographed six months later (SEE OPPOSITE PAGE).

horse should not only be well trained but physically and mentally mature. If a horse is to have a long career, it should not be asked too much too soon and in practical terms this means it should be at least eight years old before being asked to compete for a win or a placing in a 100-miler, and at least seven before being ridden for a steady completion.

Between six and seven, the horse can progress through the intermediate levels of rides, gradually being asked to go longer distances at increasing speeds. At five years old, it can be introduced to its first competitive rides. As a four and five year old, after being backed, it will also go through its basic schooling and education. An older horse coming into the sport should progress more quickly, but time is still needed for the muscles to develop properly, the tendons and ligaments to become accustomed to the work and the bones to strengthen, as well as for mental adjustments to be made. It is generally considered that it takes three years of training and competing at progressively difficult levels for a horse to reach the stage of competing with consistent success in major national and international competitions. Endurance horses are considered to be at their best from ten to 13 years of age.

We have already mentioned the early education of the young horse. This can include anything that introduces new experiences, from handling and groundwork lessons at home, to going to shows. The aim is to have a well-handled, well-mannered young horse with a balanced outlook on life and a calm, confident attitude. If the youngster has spent all its life in the field before being broken in, with little human contact, every new thing introduced will be something to worry about and more confidence-building time will be needed than if the horse has already learned to trust you.

The same horse six months later enjoying an early competition, looking alert, enthusiastic and well balanced. The author on Tawmarsh Tara.

Time spent with your horse, other than for riding, is very valuable, whether handling, grooming, massaging, mending the fence in the field or just sharing the view. So many horses never reach anything like their full potential just because their owners don't spend time watching, listening, thinking and just getting to know them better.

Basic Schooling

For a horse, and indeed for the rider, schooling is rather like learning a foreign language. You never really forget but unless you practise you make mistakes and your knowledge becomes rusty. Therefore, never think of basic schooling as something that only happens to the young horse in the course of being broken in. The horse may never progress beyond that basic level to the heights of formal dressage, but it is vital that it does achieve a correct, balanced way of going and, having achieved it, continues to maintain it throughout its life, so that it can carry a rider without unnecessary strain. All horses and riders develop bad habits unless someone is there on a regular basis to correct the mistakes. Frequently, a rider is not even aware of a fault which may seriously limit his or her performance and which could be corrected with a few schooling sessions under the eye of a good teacher.

The idea that endurance horses do not need to be schooled is completely misplaced. The nature of the sport, with much high-speed trotting, encourages horses to run on and to go on the forehand, causing excessive strain and concussion to the front legs and placing the rider's weight forward of the centre of gravity where it cannot be carried in balance. The further forward the rider's weight, the faster the horse goes in an attempt to rebalance. In this forward position, the rider cannot use seat and weight aids to slow the horse down and so must have recourse to pulling back on the reins. The horse resents the pulling and pulls back in its turn and the final result is an exhausted rider with aching shoulders and arms and an overstressed horse, barely under control. In the short term, incorrect muscle development will make the horse uncomfortable and resistant to ride and will prevent it from working efficiently. Ultimately, the extra physical stress will shorten its career.

Flatwork for the endurance horse should follow the same classical principles as for any other horse. There is no space in this book to discuss it in detail, but a course of lessons with a good teacher, perhaps during the winter, is strongly recommended. There is no substitute for formal school work to concentrate the horse's mind, improve its balance and suppleness and encourage correct muscle development. Lungeing is also a useful way of improving suppleness and teaching the horse to rebalance itself without the encumbrance of a rider. Lungeing must be done correctly to be of benefit and if you are not sure of your ability, ask an experienced person to teach you.

Don't forget about schooling when you leave the *manège*. Much can also be done while out riding, by concentrating on how your horse is going, asking it to work correctly, straight and in hand, and using suitable, safe places on your rides to do various exercises, such as leg-yielding or turns on the haunches or forehand.

Trail Schooling

Apart from being well balanced, correctly muscled-up and supple, the endurance horse needs to be well mannered, handy and co-operative on the

Lungeing is useful not only when the horse cannot be ridden for some reason, but as a means of helping the horse to rebalance itself without the rider's weight on its back. Kelly is lunged in a chambon to encourage her to lower her head and stretch her back.

ride trail. A horse which shies at every bird in the hedge is a risk on public highways and byways, while one which naps or baulks at every new hazard is a frustrating nuisance. It will also slow down your progress and affect your ride time. Horses become half-fit remarkably quickly with regular work and the half-fit horse is often a difficult horse to ride. Not yet fully settled into its work, it nevertheless feels very well and keen. If you recognise the description of the horse which wants to go fast before it has learned to watch where it is putting its feet, takes hold of the bit and ignores your hands and legs, bucks or tosses its head when you try to attract its attention and is too busy looking at the distant horizon to notice what is under its nose, you have dealt with a typical half-fit horse. The situation usually occurs in the spring, when the grass begins to improve and the horse is probably receiving a little too much energy in its diet for the level of work reached. The diet must be adjusted and the situation worked through. Going out in company and working at a brisk pace, whether at walk or trot, usually helps.

The first thing the potential endurance horse must learn about trail schooling is to go forward when asked. Many hazards may be met *en route* – other traffic on wheels or legs, barking dogs and frightening objects of household or farmyard life, such as chickens, tractors, washing lines, holes in the road, fallen

trees, rivers and streams, bridges, rail crossings, construction or industrial sites, forestry operations, pig farms, double-decker buses and low-flying aircraft. Whatever it is, if you tell your horse it's all right to go past, it has to believe you. The travel-seasoned horse will not turn a hair at being unloaded in a motorway car park for a leg stretch; the unschooled youngster will panic at the sight of a bicycle. Between the two lies an education which must be conducted with patience, firmness, kindness and confidence.

When first ridden out, the young horse must be given time to look at strange things. This tends to be a stop-go progress because, at first, everything must be looked at, however briefly – a shadow on a wall, a leaf trembling in the breeze, sunshine reflecting from a puddle. Most horses are very responsive to the voice and if encouraged forward with your leg and a firm confident tone of voice, this stage will quickly be overcome. Use a firm, natural and rather deep tone; a high, cajoling or uncertain tone will usually just make a horse more nervous. Company can be helpful, provided the companion horse is well trained and forward going, communicating confidence, not nappiness, to the youngster.

Learning to cope with banks and ditches adds interest and variety to training rides.

Note the tension through the muscles and tendons of the quarters and hind legs as Tara powers herself up this bank.

BELOW *Teaching a horse to go through water must be tackled with tact, understanding and determination.*

The more worrying the hazard, the more time must be given. For example, the tenth shiny puddle you meet on a sunny, showery day should not require a second glance. However, crossing your first flowing stream will require more tact. A lead is desirable, if available, for a first attempt at this, but don't be surprised if the youngster still isn't convinced. Give it time to approach the stream, encouraging it forward confidently but calmly and be convinced in your own mind that the horse will cross the stream. Let it put its head down and have a good sniff around. Be prepared for a leap forward but don't allow turning away. Keep your leg on and nudge the horse forward, with your hands steady and your seat in the saddle. Bring the lead horse back into the stream for encouragement if necessary. If you are on your own, you will have to be prepared to wait until the horse concedes the point. Once you have embarked on a lesson of this nature, you must not give up. Kicking the horse's sides or flapping the reins and your elbows will not help. Just keep the horse straight and continue to encourage it with leg and voice aids. The whip may be used to reinforce the leg aid if the horse is not responding at a point where fear of the water has been replaced by a stubborn refusal to cross. It is essential that you can tell the difference between a frightened or nervous horse and a stubborn or naughty one. If you are not sure about this, don't risk starting a battle without experienced help.

Going through water can be one of the most difficult things to teach an unwilling horse, but a similar approach can be used to teach the horse to pass any other hazard.

The second early lesson for the young endurance prospect is to go first or last or in the middle of a group, as required. Some are natural front runners but there may well be times when you don't want to be in front and the horse must be taught to accept that it must go slower and keep its distance from the heels of the horse in front, if asked. Some young horses also dislike having another horse behind them and try to scamper out of the way, while others don't like another horse alongside and try to kick or bite. Patience and practice will overcome these problems and stand you in good stead when you start competing. If you ride in company, make sure you take turns to lead or follow.

Horses must be happy to go first, last or side by side.

Equally, don't always ride in company. There will be many times in later competitions when you and your horse will find yourselves alone on the trail, perhaps for hours at a time, and taking your young horse out on its own will teach it to have confidence both in itself and in you, its rider. It will also teach it to develop its own, natural paces, uninfluenced by its companions and to pay attention to your aids, thus developing the rapport between you.

As in the *manège*, the young horse out on the trail must be allowed and encouraged to find its own level, at which it can stay balanced, without being either restricted or allowed to run on. The rider should sit quietly in the saddle, with an upright position and the stirrups just short enough to cope with any high jinks and to adjust the weight when going up- and downhill – having the footrest level with your ankle bone when your legs are hanging straight down out of the stirrups is about right. Rein contact should be very light and elastic, indicating direction and helping to give the horse confidence in obeying the aids. It must never be used to hold the horse up, nor to restrict it from learning to carry itself and its rider in balance. It is vital that the endurance horse learns to use the full scope of its athletic potential in a controlled way. A horse which is constantly held in and never allowed the freedom of its natural paces will use more energy than necessary in covering the ground with shortened strides on an endurance ride. A horse which is allowed always to run on, however, will suffer the strains and incorrect development mentioned earlier. To achieve freedom of movement in balance requires tact and finesse from the rider.

Stride for stride with balance goes the development of rhythm. The development of good rhythm demonstrates even paces and symmetrical development. A balanced rider can create good rhythm and a horse moving in rhythm helps the rider to stay balanced. Interference with the horse and stress on its limbs is minimised. Rhythm ultimately also helps the rider to assess the horse's speed and pace. The speed at trot can vary from around 6 mph (9.6 kmph) to over 15 mph (24 kmph) and, with experience, the rider can tell his or her horse's approximate speed within this range at any given time.

The final aspect of trail schooling is teaching the horse to cope with natural obstacles and gates in a co-operative and handy manner. We have already discussed teaching the young horse to go through water. Once it ceases to be worried by this, the next step is to stop at water and encourage it to drink. Young, unfit horses frequently get thirsty on their early rides out and it is easier to instil the habit of drinking at clean streams and other available unpolluted water supplies at this age than later. Be patient about this training – after all, it does no harm to the horse's legs to stand in a stream for a few minutes. If, after a reasonable wait, the horse clearly shows no indication to drink, for example by persistently pulling towards the grass on the bank, move on. There will be other, thirstier times.

Endurance does not involve much jumping, but there is no point in wasting precious minutes going round a fallen tree if your horse can pop over, so teach

Opening and closing gates efficiently can save many minutes on some rides.

it to take such small obstacles as logs and ditches in its stride. Also ride over as varied terrain as possible. In competition you may have to tackle anything, including turf, roads, muddy bridlepaths, rock, chalk, sand, stones, peat moor and clay.

Lastly, in countries where boundary gates abound, such as Britain, teaching your horse to cope with them efficiently can save countless minutes of competition time. It takes practice, forethought and patience. Initially, the young horse will probably be frightened of a gate swinging against it and the noise it may make and will try to back off or jump away. Going through or around a gate, it will also probably not move very quickly and easily off the rider's leg. Start with easier gates, in other words, those that have a reachable catch and will swing clear of the ground when you try to open them. Encourage the horse gently alongside the gate and put both reins, at a fairly short, even length, in the hand you do not need to operate the catch. Keep your outside leg against the horse's side behind the girth while you bend down to unhitch the gate. Don't let your leg swing back. If the gate opens towards you, ask for a gentle, straight rein-back, raising the hand with the reins, lightening your seat and squeezing with the legs. If it opens away, push it, while keeping your seat in the saddle and encouraging the horse forward. Either way, try to keep hold of the gate. When the gate is open, ask for a turn on the forehand around the gate, then, still holding the gate, ask the horse to move either back or forwards, as appropriate, to close the gate. Then ask it to stand while you fasten the catch. A young horse that is wary of the gate might well jump away from it several times, forcing you to let go. Remain patient and quietly bring the horse back into position until it gets the idea.

Gradually progress to more difficult gates. If necessary, for example with a gate which swings open as soon as it is unfastened, stay mounted for part of the procedure and dismount for the awkward bits. Finally, the horse should learn to hold a gate closed with its chest while you fasten the catch. A really good horse will even open gates with its nose, but as the horse becomes more practised at this, watch out that it does not nip through the gate too quickly and get itself jammed or catch your knee on the gatepost!

Basic Fitness Training *(see also Chapters 9 and 11)*

Once your horse has gone through the basics of progressive walking and trotting to become riding fit, to the point where you can go out and enjoy an hour or two's riding with some canters and without overtiring the horse, it is time to think about fitness training for your first competition. Ideally, your horse will have done the basic roadwork alongside its schooling and trail training and will be starting to become more settled mentally as the work becomes easier for it physically and it becomes accustomed to the hazards and obstacles encountered on your rides together.

The purpose of fitness training is to increase the efficiency of the various body systems to produce improved stamina, strength and power. The formal schooling already referred to is another form of fitness training which improves power and suppleness.

The body systems most affected by training are the locomotory, circulatory and respiratory systems. We have seen how poor management can threaten the efficient working of these systems. Now we shall explain how training enhances their efficiency when they begin that training in a healthy state. We can.define fitness training by stating that it comprises the imposition of controlled, progressively increasing amounts of stress on the systems involved, so that, through acclimatisation, the body adapts to support an increased level of work or athletic activity, with commensurately increased resistance to injury or distress.

Many aspects are involved – developing the strength and bulk of muscles, increasing strength and density of bone, maintaining elasticity of tendons, oxygen uptake and utilisation, metabolisation of various nutrients, heart size and function, to name a few. In recent years a tremendous amount of research into equine exercise physiology has taken place, but it is such a relatively new field that far more work needs to be done and the conclusions of various studies may be conflicting as often as they are helpful. Also, much of the work has centred on horses used for sprint-type competition, such as Thoroughbred racehorses and trotters, with little work done on the needs of endurance. Nevertheless, valuable data are being accumulated, which are helping the veterinary profession to gain a better understanding of the physiology of the endurance competition horse, some of which is filtering down to the practical training level.

Effect of Training on the Locomotory System

Bone is not a finished poduct. The calcium content is continuously exchanged and bones increase or decrease in size and strength depending upon the pressures to which they are subjected. Nutrients and waste are carried through blood and lymph vessels which supply the bone cells and the nervous system also extends into bone. Changes to bone are slow in relation to other parts of the body as the shape and size of bone can only be altered by the resorption of old bone, followed by the laying down of new bone. The most common bone problems occur when intermittent pressures over a long period, i.e. concussion, have caused excessive growth of bone in unwanted places, resulting in problems such as ringbone or spavin. The opposite also occurs, when longer, repetitive periods of excessive pressure cause damage and loss of bone, resulting in the sudden stress fractures that sometimes occur and the damage that shows up as navicular disease.

All of the stresses of movement that are applied to the muscles and tendons – stretching, twisting, compression, bending – also affect the bones. The muscles and tendons support the bones and cushion them from some of these forces,

Even in a well-trained horse with excellent conformation, such as this compact Arab, the strains placed on the lower limbs are clearly considerable. Anne Newton on Dacoit.

which is very necessary as bone itself is rigid and very limited in its ability to stretch and contract. Training programmes are rarely planned with specific concern for bones – it is assumed that the bones will strengthen as training progresses – however, we need our endurance horse to develop strong, dense bone and an awareness of the way in which this happens, and the problems which occur, is useful knowledge.

Bone adapts to be no stronger than the body needs it to be. Lack of exercise therefore results in resorption and loss of bone strength. Regular, controlled levels of work over a long period will maintain the strength of the bone commensurate with the amount of regular stress. Too much concussive work of this type will lead to the bony growth type of problems mentioned above. Galloping stresses the elasticity of bone, requiring time for recovery, which then results in increased strength. If the horse is galloped too often without allowing time for adaptation, however, the reverse happens and the bone is weakened.

In practical terms, intensive work for short periods, on a regular but not too frequent basis, coupled with regular steady work, avoiding too much concussion and including a variety of terrain to vary the types of stress imposed, will help the development and maintenance of strong, healthy bones.

Tendon injury is comparatively rare in endurance horses as it appears that it is the stress of galloping for longer periods than nature intended, as in racing, which causes the damage. Tendon, like bone, loses its functional ability through inactivity, although scientific research has not so far demonstrated appreciable improvement in tendon function as a result of training. Several factors contribute to tendon injury. The heavier the horse's bodyweight, the greater the force transmitted to the tendon. Hard going also increases the risk, as does poor foot balance and inadequate farriery. The idea that roadwork 'hardens' tendons has not been supported by scientific evidence, but the general benefits of this work in reducing body fat (i.e. weight) and improving muscle tone and fitness probably do help to reduce the risk of tendon strain.

Muscles produce the energy which operates the locomotory system. To provide for both flexion and extension of the limbs, many muscles operate in opposing pairs and, to maintain equilibrium, there is always a slight tension between these opposing muscles, which is known as muscle tone. Without it, the muscles would become flaccid and wasted. Most endurance riders will be familiar with the concept of muscles as bundles of slender fibres, or cells, which, by moving over one another, contract the muscle, enabling movement. As mentioned earlier, these fibres are of three types. Type 1 fibres are called 'slow-twitch' fibres and are long, thin fibres which take a relatively long time to contract and which use oxygen to produce energy. These are the fibres most useful in endurance work as they can provide a continuous, steady supply of energy for submaximal work, provided they continue to be supplied with nutrients and oxygen. Type 2 fibres are shorter and bulkier, contract more quickly and are therefore called 'fast-twitch' fibres; they are further divided into type 2a and type 2b fibres. Type 2a fibres, like slow-twitch fibres, have a high capacity to use oxygen to produce energy and are therefore also useful for endurance work. The ability of these fibres (or possibly of a further subtype which has not yet been conclusively researched) to use oxygen can also be improved with training – a fact which is very significant in the attempt to increase the endurance horse's capacity for sustained energy production. Type 2b fibres produce rapid bursts of energy without using oxygen, but become fatigued (i.e. have their glycogen stores depleted) very quickly. The 'aerobic' method of energy production uses oxygen; the 'anaerobic' method produces energy without using oxygen.

In Chapter 4 we established that fuel for energy production is stored in the body as glycogen or free fatty acids. These are metabolised in several ways to produce a chemical called ATP (adenosine triphosphate) which is the essential final form of fuel needed to produce energy. In anaerobic energy production, ATP is produced in the cells from stores of muscle glycogen or from glucose transported in the blood, without using oxygen, by a process called glycolysis, producing lactic acid as a byproduct. This build up of acid impairs the muscle function and finally forces the horse to slow down. Lactic acid has been blamed for many performance problems but is of less consequence to the endurance horse than to the sprinter as the extreme situation, where the body cannot remove or resynthesise the lactic acid fast enough to prevent an excessive build up, rarely occurs. Possible exceptions might be a very fast finish to a long ride or a very fast, short endurance ride of less than 40 miles (64 km). Whenever the horse is suddenly asked to go faster or make a much stronger effort, the anaerobic metabolism comes into play, recruiting type 2b muscle fibres.

If we want to produce a steady supply of energy over a long period, we must therefore concentrate on the energy produced via the aerobic method. This occurs in a part of the cell which can be likened to a power generator, called the mitochondrion. Here, fuel, in the form of pyruvate (which is derived from glycogen) and, more significantly, free fatty acids are converted, with the help of oxygen, to produce the essential ATP plus carbon dioxide and water. A substance called carnitine is sometimes found in highly priced, competition-horse food supplements. This also occurs naturally and its function is to help to transport fatty acids to the mitochondria, encouraging their use for energy production. The oxidation of fatty acids is, in fact, the most efficient method of ATP production.

It should be clear that the aerobic metabolism requires both the presence of oxygen and the disposal of carbon dioxide. If insufficient oxygen is transported to the muscle cells, the production of ATP is limited. One of the aims of training, therefore, is to condition the respiratory system to carry more oxygen through the lungs to the blood and to dispose of carbon dioxide effectively.

What happens to ATP when the muscle cells have produced it? To obtain movement, the muscle cells must contract. To stimulate contraction, a nerve impulse alters the normal electrical charge of the muscle cell, causing a temporary release of calcium, which begins a series of chemical changes resulting in the release of the chemical energy from the ATP, which has the effect of contracting the cell.

How does training improve the ability of the muscle cells to produce the type of energy we want for endurance work?

Muscles respond to the stimulus of the demand for varying types of energy. Therefore, if we want our endurance horse to improve its capacity for aerobic-energy production, we must give it the type of work which stimulates the muscles to produce energy in this way, i.e. relatively long periods of steady work.

A resting horse obtains all the energy it needs to keep its body functioning via the aerobic method. When it begins to work slowly, more slow-twitch muscle cells go to work, concentrating mainly on fatty acid metabolisation and minimising the need for the cells to expend their limited stores of glycogen. As the work speeds up a bit, or goes on longer, the type 2a fast-twitch fibres are recruited, using their oxidative ability to continue aerobic-energy production. At some point along the graph curve of increasing intensity and duration of exercise, the demand for energy begins to outweigh the ability of the oxygen-using cells to produce it. This is the point, known as the 'anaerobic threshold', when the type 2b, non-oxidative fibres begin work. They cannot metabolise fatty acids and, once they are recruited, they rapidly use up the available stores of glycogen so that the level of lactic acid begins to build up and, as previously mentioned, after a short time the horse becomes fatigued. The extent of glycogen depletion in the muscle cells and the tolerance of different horses to different levels of lactic acid are the subjects of ongoing research but, for practical purposes, the important thing for the endurance rider to know is the horse's anaerobic threshold. The capacity for aerobic-energy production is improved by working the horse at a heart rate just below this level. Work above the anaerobic threshold, i.e. fast work, is required only to a limited degree by the endurance horse, as we shall see later.

The Effect of Training on the Respiratory System

In Chapter 1 we saw briefly how the respiratory and circulatory systems work. Now we shall see what changes occur through training.

The principal aim of training, as far as the respiratory system is concerned, is to increase the supply of oxygen which is available for energy production. This is done in two ways: firstly, by making sure that the route by which oxygen reaches the lungs is clear of mucus and the rubbish which it collects and, secondly, by encouraging the development of more capillaries around the alveoli, to increase the area across which the process of gaseous exchange can take place. (Gaseous exchange is the reciprocal movement of oxygen across the cell wall from the lungs into the blood and of carbon dioxide in the opposite direction.)

Both of these changes are encouraged by an increasing workload but, in the early stages, until they begin to take place, the horse cannot provide enough oxygen for a protracted demand for energy and the respiration rate rapidly increases to the point where the horse must slow down or stop. The elevated rate of respiration then continues until the horse has absorbed enough oxygen to recover its basic condition. Slow, steady work of gradually increasing duration and intensity is required to bring about the desired changes.

In former years, respiration recovery rate was used as a parameter for elimination of unfit endurance horses in competition. This was discontinued a few years ago when veterinary surgeons acknowledged the difficulty of obtaining a reliable reading of respiration rate due, among other variables, to the fact that hot horses may also pant in an effort to dissipate heat. However, veterinary judges at rides will still consider respiratory rate when assessing the overall clinical condition of a horse and whether it is fit to continue.

The Effect of Training on the Circulatory System

The blood is the medium of transport for carrying various vital substances to different parts of the body and is also used to carry waste substances away. From the endurance rider's point of view, training enhances the rate at which the blood can transport oxygen and nutrients to the muscles and remove carbon dioxide to the lungs and other unwanted byproducts of energy production to the kidneys. Excess heat is another product of energy creation and an efficient circulatory system also assists in its rapid dissipation.

The heart is controlled by special structures called pacemakers. These are influenced by nervous impulses and subtle changes in the concentration of certain hormones in the blood. When the horse is asked to work harder, the muscles demand more oxygen and nutrients from the blood and also produce waste products at a faster rate, which have to be carried away. To respond to these demands, the heart has to beat faster so that blood is circulated more quickly. As with the respiratory rate, this increase cannot be maintained for very long when the horse is untrained.

As with the capillaries around the alveoli, training also encourages the number of capillaries in the muscles to increase dramatically, thus vastly improving the available area through which oxygen can be supplied from the blood to the muscle cells. This is a long-term process which goes into reverse if the horse has a long lay off.

The final effect of training is actually to increase the size of the heart muscle itself, thus making it stronger and capable of pumping a greater quantity of blood with each beat.

The horse's heart rate is of considerable significance for the endurance rider, both in training and in competition, as it is the single parameter by which fitness is most easily assessed, and it is used for the elimination of unfit horses. We are interested in the heart rate at three different times: first, when the horse is resting; second, when it is working; and third, when it is recovering from exertion.

The 'normal' range for the horse's resting heart rate is widely quoted as being between 36 and 42 beats per minute. In fact, many horses suitable for endurance training have resting heart rates which are appreciably lower than 36 even before training. A slow resting heart rate usually indicates an efficient circulatory system: the heart does not have to work very hard to meet the body's normal requirement for energy. Physiologically, a horse with a naturally slow resting rate will probably have a comparatively large heart. The resting heart rate is important because, first, it indicates the horse's natural aptitude for the work, second, it provides a base parameter by which improvements brought about by training can be judged; and, third, it enables the time of recovery after exercise to be accurately measured.

Obtaining an accurate reading of your horse's resting heart rate is not as simple as it may at first seem as even a slight stimulus of excitement can elevate the rate by several beats, especially in the novice horse unaccustomed to having its heart rate taken. The initial reading at a pre-ride vetting, taken outdoors at a venue, after a horsebox journey and in the midst of the hurly burly of other horses and the ride start, is unlikely to be an accurate reflection of a horse's true resting rate. The most reliable way to discover your horse's true resting heart rate is to take it at home in the stable, ideally with a heart rate monitor which can be left on and read consistently over a period of time, repeating the exercise for two or three days. If a monitor is not available, a stethoscope can be used but several days will be needed to accustom the horse to the stethoscope to be sure of obtaining an accurate result. Also, the heart rate should be taken at the same time each day, at a time when the horse is quiet, before exercise and neither just before, nor after, feeding. The excitement of anticipation of a feed will certainly elevate the resting rate and it also rises in response to eating, to cater for the increased energy required for digestion.

The horse's heart rate when it is working is of interest because it can indicate to us whether the horse is working aerobically or anaerobically. Heart rate readings taken during exercise at varying speeds or efforts, in conjunction with tests for blood lactate levels, can tell us the anaerobic threshold for any particular horse. As we want to develop the horse's capacity for aerobic-energy production, we want it to work at a level where it is working as hard as possible aerobically (i.e. recruiting as many slow-twitch and type 2a fast-twitch muscle fibres as possible), but without reaching the point of bringing anaerobic-

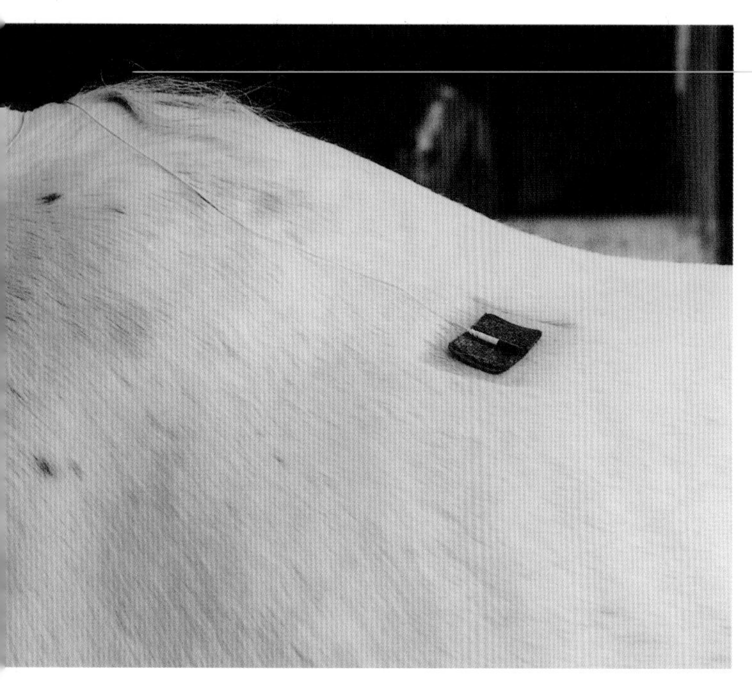

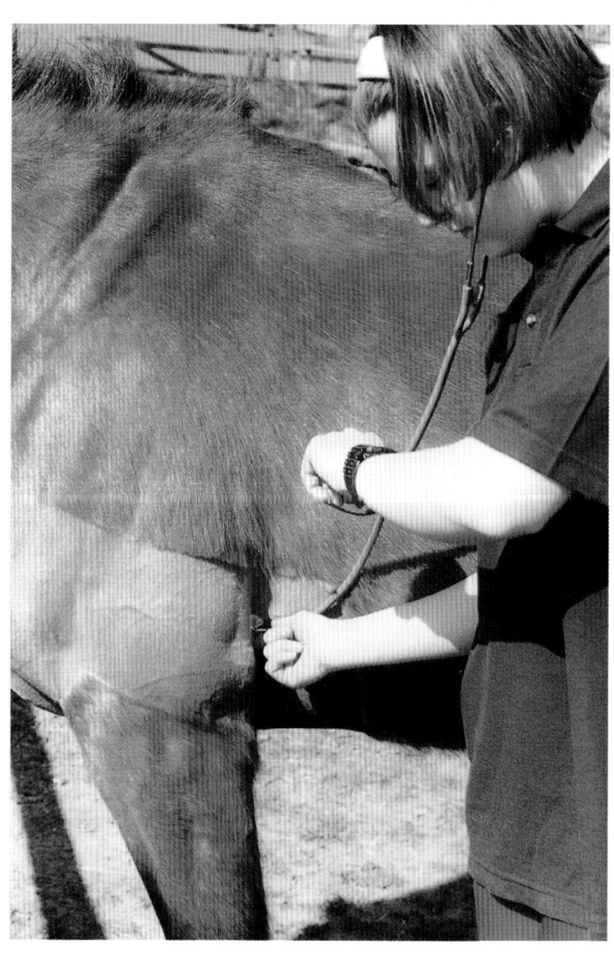

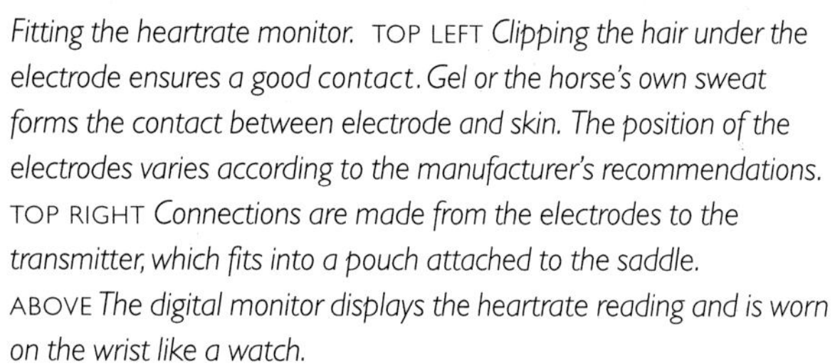

Fitting the heartrate monitor. TOP LEFT *Clipping the hair under the electrode ensures a good contact. Gel or the horse's own sweat forms the contact between electrode and skin. The position of the electrodes varies according to the manufacturer's recommendations.* TOP RIGHT *Connections are made from the electrodes to the transmitter, which fits into a pouch attached to the saddle.* ABOVE *The digital monitor displays the heartrate reading and is worn on the wrist like a watch.*

RIGHT *Taking the heart rate, or pulse, using a stethoscope. Each double 'lub-dup' sound counts as one beat.*

energy production (using the type 2b fibres) into play. The anaerobic threshold is variable for individual horses and, if training is properly carried out, will be raised as the horse becomes fitter. Scientifically, it is expressed as a measure of the level of lactate in the blood and researchers have generally suggested that the transition from aerobic to anaerobic work occurs when blood lactate falls within the range of 2–4 mmol/litre. In the resting horse the normal rate is about 1 mmol/litre.

How does the endurance rider, following a practical training programme, work a horse at the right level to improve its aerobic metabolism?

Muscle fibre recruitment is dictated by degree of effort and the most readily available 'meter' we have to gauge the amount of effort a horse is making is its heart rate which responds immediately to any demand for more energy. Heart rate will increase in relation to effort whether that effort involves greater speed or a greater challenge, such as climbing a hill or jumping. The change from aerobic- to anaerobic-energy production is progressive and is represented by a heart rate increasing from around 140 bpm (beats per minute) to a flat-out effort with a heart rate of 200+ bpm.

As the horse becomes fitter, it will be able to:

a. cover the same distance, at the same heart rate, faster
b. maintain the same speed at the same heart rate for a longer period of time
c. recover more quickly to normal from the same level of imposed stress.

Using a heart rate monitor during training provides an invaluable guide to progress. In the early stages, sustained work at a heart rate not exceeding 140 bpm ensures that the horse is working aerobically, using mainly slow-twitch muscle fibres and priming the body systems to perform in the desired way. This is known as long slow distance (LSD) work and it is the foundation of all endurance training.

Work at this level, carried out for an average of one to one and a half hours, covering between 5 to 10 miles (8–16 km) per session, four to five days a week over about eight weeks, will condition the average riding horse sufficiently to cope successfully with the basic-level qualifying competitions (for example, those found in Great Britain) of 20 to 30 miles (32–48 km) at speeds from 6 to $7\frac{1}{2}$ mph (9.6–12 kmph). In countries without qualifying levels of competitions, it will provide a sound basis for further training.

After three months of progressive LSD work, the horse should be capable of maintaining an average speed, over relatively level terrain and reasonable going, of 8 mph (12.8 kmph) during an hour's work. Do not worry too much about the speed of your workouts, however, unless your riding is all in flat country. Hillwork requires much greater effort, while producing much slower speeds. Walking up a steep hill might easily push a horse's heart rate up to the same level as a fast trot over level ground, but the average speed of the workout will obviously be much slower. What you are aiming for is improvement over your horse's initial performance, over a period of time.

Up to this point, the horse has been mainly utilising slow-twitch muscle fibres. In Chapter 9 we shall consider the next level of training and the methods of stimulating fast-twitch, high oxidative (type 2a) fibres to come into action. Before we leave the subject of basic conditioning, however, we must consider the third time when our horse's heart rate is of interest, i.e. when it is recovering from exertion.

When the vet takes your horse's heart rate 30 minutes after the finish of a competitive ride, he or she is checking to see whether it has recovered to an acceptable level within the normal range following exertion. The post-ride vetting time of 30 minutes, which is normally used, is an arbitrary one based on the long experience of endurance vets that if a horse has not recovered sufficiently in this time, then it is potentially in trouble. The pulse parameter of 64 bpm is also arbitrary and is, again, based on veterinary experience. In some countries and situations a lower or higher parameter might be used.

The heart rate for a horse working at a steady submaximal rate is likely to be in the region of 100–140 bpm. When the horse stops, the heart rate will fall within seconds to around 70–90 bpm. After ten minutes, the fit horse's heart rate should have dropped below the 64 parameter. The fitter the horse, the faster the fall in heart rate. A fit horse which is naturally adapted for the sport will reach a heart rate close to its resting rate by ten minutes or soon after.

A horse working at this level whose heart rate is still hovering around the 60 mark after 20 minutes is barely fit enough for the job, and if it has not reached 64 by the 30 minute time limit, it is either unfit, or suffering some illness or injury which has affected the heart rate.

CHAPTER 7

PREPARING FOR COMPETITION

WITH YOUR horse well on the way to achieving a basic level of competitive fitness, it is time to consider planning a programme of rides and preparing for your first competition.

Planning a Programme

First, develop an overview of where you would like to be by the end of the season. How much can your horse realistically achieve, given its age, condition, type, the time available for training, etc.? In some countries you will be limited by the national rules of the sport as to how much a first-season horse can do. In others, it is up to you but do bear in mind the premise that it takes three years to reach 100-mile (160 km) competitive standard if you want your horse to last.

In countries where the sport is well established, lower-distance competitive rides can be used as training rides towards bigger events. In some cases, a series of qualifying competitions may be compulsory. If you are not fortunate enough to be in this position, try to include one long ride of the appropriate distance in your training schedule, which you can ride in company with friends, at each relevant point during the season, i.e. about one per month. Ride a pre-arranged route in competitive style, aiming for a specific speed over the distance and note your horse's recovery heart rate after the finish, just as would happen in a real event. Doing this type of ride in company with friends will simulate competition experience and will encourage the horse to work more efficiently and enthusiastically than trying to train over long distances on your own. Excessively long, solitary training rides are as tedious for the horse as for the rider (unless you are a natural loner with wonderful riding country on your doorstep) and the horse can become soured before it ever arrives at a real competition.

If you do have a calendar of rides to choose from, aim, if possible, to compete once a month. This will give your horse competition experience and go a long way towards improving its fitness without imposing too much stress too frequently. During the course of the first season, you should aim to build up your competitive distance to finish with not more than a 30-mile (48 km) ride for a five-year-old and a 40- or 50-mile (64 or 80 km) ride for a six-year-old or older horse.

Sometimes, multi-day rides are on offer and these can be immensely valuable training exercises, ridden at a steady and not too demanding pace. Once your horse has successfully been introduced to competition at those distances in one-day rides, two or three days of up to 25 or 30 miles (40 or 48 km) per day will have a major effect on improving fitness and will also do wonders for the horse's mental maturity. The solid companionship and shared effort over a longer period in like-minded company really gives a horse the opportunity to settle down and learn what the job is all about, resulting in a calmer, more confident attitude. This type of event can also show up any chronic or deep-seated physical problems, as well as tack-fitting and rider problems, so it is altogether an enlightening experience!

Training Diary

Keeping a training diary can be a chore if you are busy but it is an invaluable way of keeping track of the work you actually manage to achieve in training, any problems encountered and overcome and of providing a record, for future reference, of your horse's progress. Two years on, it is easy to forget what your horse used to be like and how much hard work you have put in to achieve the level you have reached today.

The layout of the diary is up to you but whether you use an ordinary pocket book or a computer spreadsheet, your diary should contain the following information.

DAILY WORK

This should be divided between endurance training and other work. The endurance training section should note time spent, distance covered, speed, weather conditions, ground conditions, terrain, resting, working and recovery heart rates, the horse's attitude and any other relevant things you noticed.

The other work section should detail the type of work (such as schooling, jumping, lessons, lungeing, TEAM sessions), achievements, problems and general progress and should include a note of rest days. Also note time off for any other reason, such as illness or lost shoes, which interrupts the training programme.

Changes in feed

Note quantities by weight, any changes in quantity and additions or deletions of particular ingredients from the diet.

Changes in condition

Note changes in weight as measured by your weigh tape but be aware that the weigh tape will not give you the whole picture of condition. Remember that condition has two aspects – the actual weight gain or loss, plus the improvement in muscle delineation and tone as the horse gets fitter, resulting in an overall change in the horse's shape. Some people find it difficult to describe such changes in words and a photographic record of your horse's progress can be more useful.

Wear of shoes

Notice how your horse wears its shoes and how quickly. Make notes so that you can point out uneven wear to your farrier and keep a record of improvements or any adverse changes.

Health matters

Note the dates of vaccinations, teeth rasping and worming so that you can keep them up to date and plan any veterinary visits in good time.

Changes of equipment

Did you buy a new saddle or bit? What effect has it had on your horse?

A diary can become tedious and less valuable if it simply comprises a list of events, so, when you make changes which you have noted in the diary, relate later effects back to the original event. For example, if your horse has been losing weight and you make a change, such as adding oil to its diet or increasing its concentrates, note the effect a week later: 'weight loss stopped, energy improved'. Keep track of your horse's problems, for example: 'Changed to milder bit but still resisting, so made appointment for vet to check teeth and booked school lesson.' Later, you can note the results of the vet's visit and the lesson.

Equipment

During the weeks before your first competition, make sure all of your equipment is in good condition and fits the horse properly. The day of the ride is not the time to try out a new bit or saddle. Let us now take a look at the basic equipment you will need for a ride at this level.

As far as the horse is concerned, at this stage its usual riding tack will be appropriate, provided, of course, that it fits well. Even if you are certain that you are going to be committed to this sport, this is not the time to go out and buy a new endurance saddle or other specialist equipment. Until you have a season or so of competitive experience, you are not really in a position to decide what specialist gear will suit you and your horse. Buying the wrong saddle too soon is a very expensive mistake and it is quite possible to ride your first competitive rides on an ordinary GP or dressage saddle.

The saddle is the key to the comfort of both horse and rider so what do we mean by the words 'well fitting'? The obvious points are that the tree should be of the correct width so that the gullet clears the withers, leaving a clear channel of daylight along the horse's spine, and that the seat should not be so long that pressure is put on the loins. Many GP saddles, which fulfil these criteria and are apparently quite satisfactory for ordinary riding of limited duration, are used by aspiring endurance riders who are then surprised when problems arise. 'I had it restuffed; my saddler fitted it and says it is a good fit, so why is my horse getting pressure bumps?' is the usual complaint.

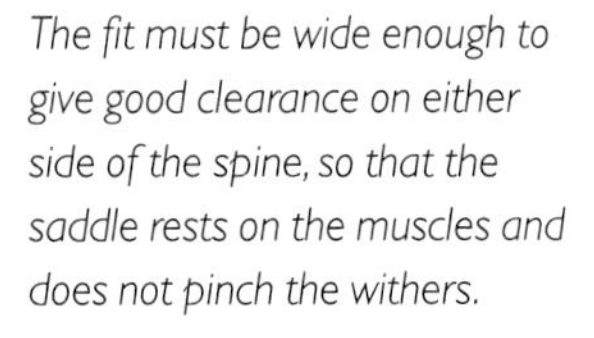

The fit must be wide enough to give good clearance on either side of the spine, so that the saddle rests on the muscles and does not pinch the withers.

The gullet must give clearance both from front to back and side to side.

The answer invariably lies in the distribution of weight on the horse's back and the fact that modern GP saddles often have 'continental' panels which are too narrow to spread the load sufficiently. The greatest weight is concentrated in a point load under the stirrup bar and, after many miles of trotting, the result is pressure bumps. The worst aspect of this problem is that by the time pressure bumps begin to occur – usually when the horse is competing at around the 40-mile (64 km) level – appreciable damage has already been done. The discomfort causes the horse to tighten its back muscles, preventing them from working freely to carry the rider in balance with good movement. However well you ride, if the horse is fighting against this discomfort in order to do what you ask, it cannot perform at its best. Its athletic scope is reduced and the risk of accidental injury and lameness is increased. Some horses try to escape saddle pain by evasion, resistance or, in extreme cases, by bucking or running away with the rider – have a good look at your saddle before you blame the horse for bad behaviour. Even where pressure bumps do not occur, over a period of time muscle wastage behind the withers may become evident. Sunken hollows in this region do not mean that your horse is getting lean and fit, they mean that its saddle is either too narrow or incorrectly balanced and too much pressure is being put on the forward end.

Most English GP saddles are designed to be ridden with a forward seat and riders also have a tendency to sit the saddle forward on the horse's back when saddling up. The stirrup bars are also often placed forward of centre. The result of all this is that when the rider starts to move the horse forward, the saddling

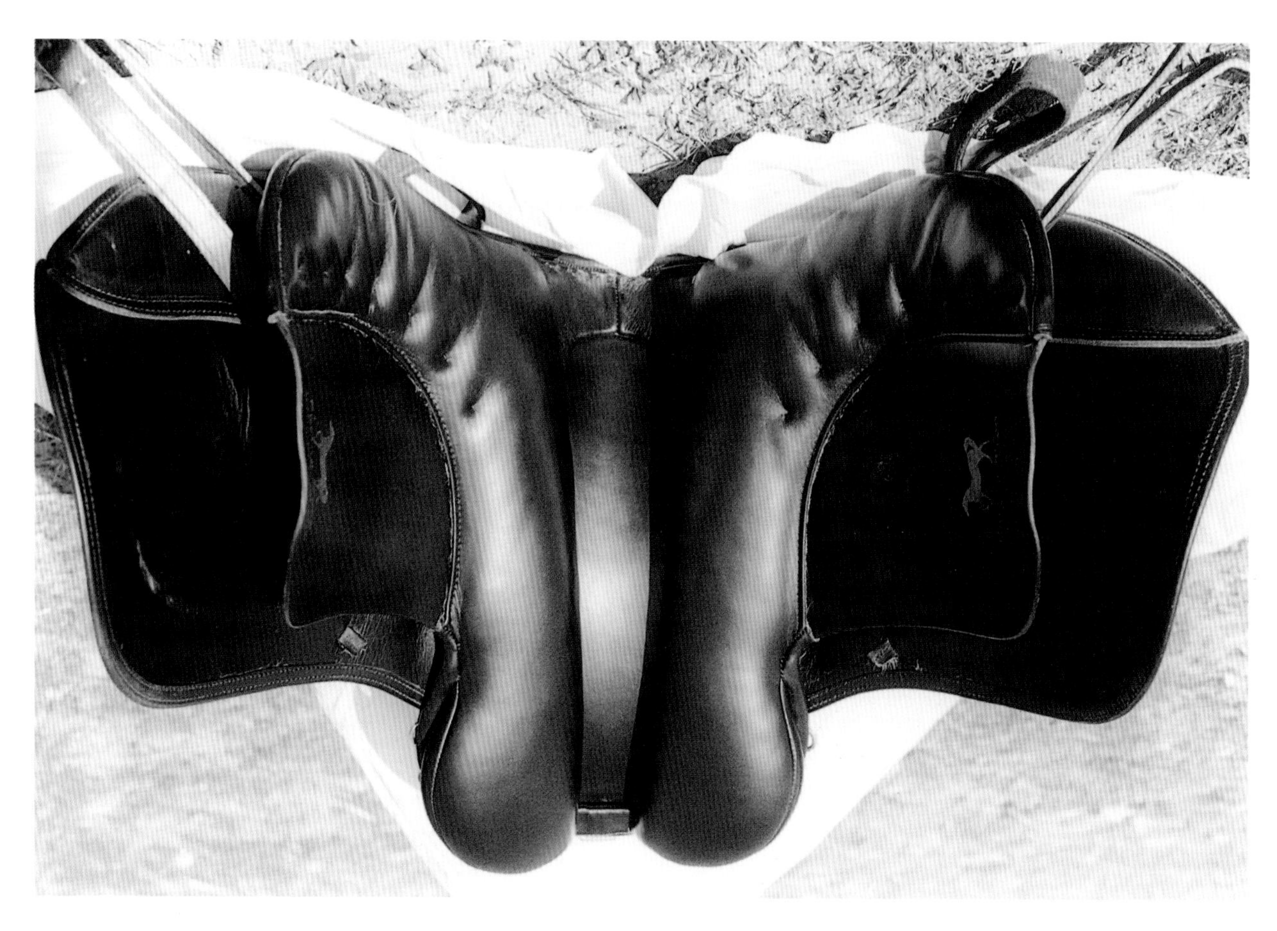

The Arabian endurance saddle has broad panels designed to spread the weight as far as possible over the horse's back.

system naturally places their weight forward, which is fine for hunting and jumping but not what you want for endurance riding.

Whatever saddle you are using when you first begin competitive distance riding, put it on your horse without a numnah, girth it up and take a critical look at the fit. First check the gullet. Is it both well clear of the top of the spine (at least three fingers' width) and wide enough to clear the sides of the spine and sit firmly on the back muscles? If it is too low, restuffing may solve the problem; if too narrow, you need a different saddle.

Next, stand to the side of the horse and check that you have placed the saddle in the centre of the horse's back, not forward on the withers. Is the seat level? On many GP saddles, this test will find the pommel lower than the cantle, so that the rider would be 'riding downhill'. This problem can be temporarily solved for lower-distance rides with judicious padding, using a wool blanket folded to give more lift at the front, or a purpose-designed pad that will lift the front, but in the latter case be sure that the pad extends well below the edges of the panels at the sides or the effect of pressure points will be exacerbated. Restuffing by a good saddler, to give more lift at the front or less at the back, depending on the saddle, is a more permanent solution, provided the basic design of the saddle is right for the horse, with an adequate area of weight distribution. The saddler will need to see the saddle on the horse, with you riding on it, to do an effective job.

Next, find the back of the horse's scapula (shoulder blade) with your fingers. Get someone to lift the horse's foreleg. Is the saddle clear of the scapula and your fingers? If not, the saddle is impinging on your horse's freedom of action and will cause bruising, pain and reduced performance. In these cases, switching to a dressage saddle, with a straight- instead of a forward-cut flap, may solve the problem.

ABOVE *The fitted saddle must be level to place the rider in the correct position. This saddle has a high knee/thigh roll for extra support and the stirrup hangs correctly in the centre of the flap. This is a Flex-ride stirrup with a broad base giving essential support for the ball of the foot.*

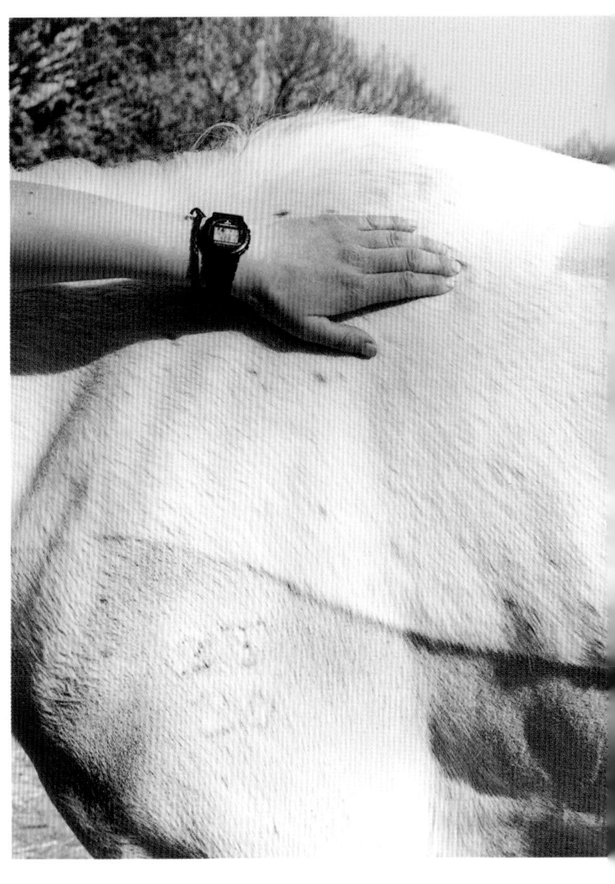

The bars of the saddle tree must not impinge on the scapula as it moves backwards. The back of the scapula can easily be found with your fingers and may be further back than you imagine.

Finally, notice the position of the stirrup bars and whether the stirrups hang centrally below the seat or forward of centre as in most GP saddles. If the latter, riding will be more tiring as it will take more muscular effort to maintain the correct position. You must be aware of the need to keep your position as upright as possible and avoid letting your horse fall on to its forehand.

Mount the horse and check all these points again with your weight in the saddle. Notice the difference in pressure on your horse's back, caused by your weight in the saddle. Imagine cantering downhill without the psychological 'comfort' of a numnah or saddle blanket. It should now begin to be clear how important it is that your saddle should be as comfortable as possible for your horse.

ABOVE *A plain snaffle bridle, well fitted. The noseband, fitted loosely, is not serving any functional purpose and could be left off. The Irish martingale is usually seen in racing and its main intention is to prevent the reins coming over the horse's head if the jockey has a fall!*

The other important items of tack to consider are your horse's bridle and bit. The critical factor is the extended length of time for which the horse wears the bridle, compared to other types of riding. A noseband which may rub out a coat hair or two in an hour's hack, can rub a raw wound in 40 or 50 miles (64–80 km). A slightly tight browband might be bearable for an hour or so, but can turn an equable horse into a crazy headshaker by the end of a long-distance ride. The design, fit and position of the bit in the horse's mouth can also make the difference between a trouble-free ride and pinched or rubbed corners or bruised bars, resulting in pain for the horse and penalties for you.

At Novice competitive ride level, your horse should go comfortably in the bit and bridle it normally wears for training. Later on, for endurance rides, changes may become necessary and we shall consider those in Chapter 9. The addition of any

A German hackamore, used here with a running martingale. The hackamore works on the nose, keeping the head down, so the martingale should be superfluous.

other restrictive tack should be avoided as far as possible – if the horse is not wearing it, it cannot cause a rub or sore. However, for a young or excitable horse, with the common tendency of throwing its head up, going above the bit and hollowing its back as an evasion in order to take off after other horses, a standing martingale fitted fairly short can be a useful precaution. As long as the horse is going correctly, this has no effect and when excitement does overcome concentration, it is a relatively gentle way of maintaining control, bringing pressure to bear on the nose at cavesson height, unlike the running martingale which causes a strong pull on the bit and interferes with the direct rein aids. Use the martingale only in competitions, otherwise the horse may become dependent on it. At home, concentrate on schooling the horse to go properly without it.

A happy horse and well-balanced rider. The standing martingale is useful with novice horses in early competitions.

Conformation dictates that many horses will need a breastplate in hilly country. This hunting breastplate is the most commonly used type.

The Aintree, or racing, breastplate is less often seen and needs careful fitting to avoid constricting the windpipe. Here, it is easy to see how sweating up under tack could cause a nasty rub on a long ride.

Novice endurance riders are often confused as to whether the horse should compete in protective boots. Some competitive ride rules preclude the wearing of boots, as judging includes the horse's ability to look after itself, with penalties for minor injuries. In an ideal world, a horse with perfectly straight action would never need to wear boots. However, young horses are prone to suffer self-inflicted injury until their muscles develop to give them better strength and balance. Many horses, even when mature and trained, do not move with straight action and may brush or otherwise be inclined to knock themselves. Therefore, when the rules allow, boots can be a sensible way of minimising injury. The design of the boots is all important. They must be lightweight, fit well, fasten securely and be of a material that does not rub – neoprene seems to work well. The rider must always be aware of the risk of grit or other foreign material working its way inside the boots and they should be removed and rinsed clean, and the horse's legs checked, as frequently as possible. In some types of going, such as sand or heavy clay, boots are obviously inadvisable for this very reason.

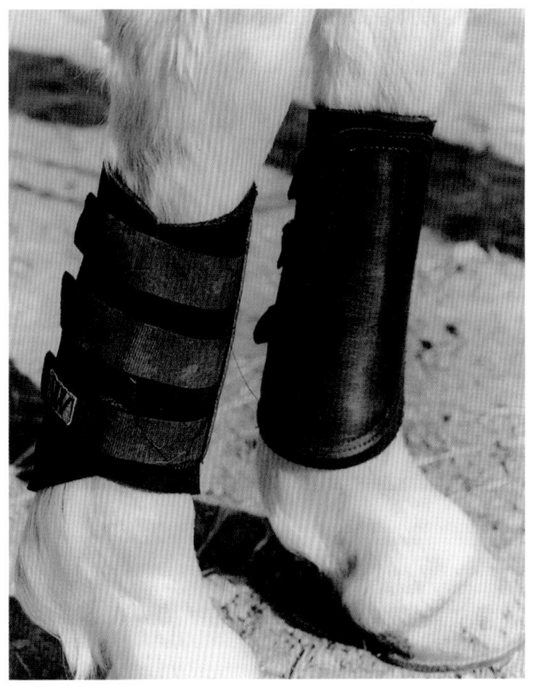

ABOVE *These Easyboots can be used instead of steel shoes if required, although they are most frequently carried for use in an emergency. They are also useful for a horse which needs to be kept in work while a hoof problem grows out, or as a poultice boot.*

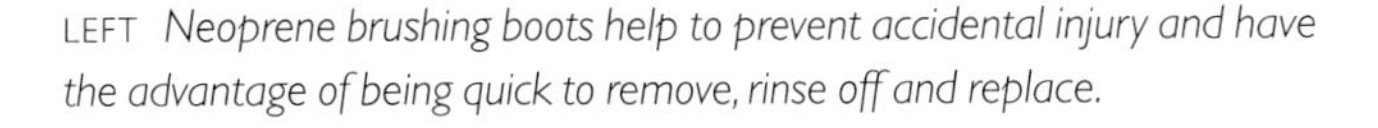

LEFT *Neoprene brushing boots help to prevent accidental injury and have the advantage of being quick to remove, rinse off and replace.*

Preparatory Tasks

Once you have decided on the date of your first competition, there are a number of tasks to be done in preparation for it.

Rides early in the season are often oversubscribed, especially in Great Britain, so send for schedules and submit your entry in good time. Be sure to provide all the information requested on your entry form. If your handwriting is not very legible, use block letters and always use your horse's registered name, not a stable name, to avoid any administrative confusion later – it is difficult trying to prove that the horse you qualified was called Sun Moon and Stars if you wrote Fred on the entry form! Also, don't forget to enclose your entry fee and a stamped, self-addressed envelope of the appropriate size for the return of ride information and maps.

If the ride is a special qualifier for a later event, make sure you have read, understood and fully complied with all the rules.

We considered basic conditioning in the last chapter and will take the subject further a little later. Allied with fitness training is the need to monitor your horse's diet, adding more energy-producing food as necessary and keeping a check on weight loss or gain, always remembering the basic priniciple of feeding good quality fibre.

Your first competition is most likely to be a set-speed event, where you have to complete the distance at an average speed within a minimum and maximum range, for example 20 miles (32 km) at not less than 6½ mph (10.4 kmph) nor more than 7½ mph (12 kmph). Ideally, allowing for variations in terrain, you will aim to ride consistently near the optimum mean of 7 mph (11.26 kmph) throughout the ride. There is no point in going as fast as possible for 19 miles (31 km) and then having an hour to spare for the last mile, nor in dawdling along gossiping with your friends then having to race for the finish to be in on time. In preparation, therefore, you will need to know how fast your horse travels in various gaits – different horses can have markedly different speeds in trot and canter – and you can work this out during training. Measure a stretch of reasonably level, good going, ideally a mile, although half a mile will do. When your horse is warmed up and going well, time how long it takes to cover the distance in each gait of walk, steady trot, fast trot and hand canter. Repeat the exercise several times on different days and you will have a good idea of your horse's natural average speed at the various gaits. In competition, making allowances for changes in going and gradient, you will still be able to judge with reasonable accuracy whether you are on time or not as you come to each distance marker or checkpoint.

Ideally, a horse should be shod between five days and a week before a competition. This ensures that there will be plenty of wear still in the shoes and they will be firmly attached, while giving the new shoes time to settle down and for any shoeing problems, such as a nail bind, to become evident and be rectified. Book your farriery appointment well in advance.

Any problems you have with your riding or your horse need to be worked on and ironed out if possible. For example, spend extra time practising opening and closing gates, riding in company or getting used to a particular hazard if these situations are causing difficulties.

Pre-ride Planning

The organisation of distance rides varies considerably. In Britain, for the price of a stamped, self-addressed envelope, you will receive a route map and details in advance of the competition. Elsewhere, a map may not be available until you arrive at the ride. If your map arrives in advance, you have time to work out the distances between checkpoints and the times you want to arrive at each one, and to study the terrain before you leave home. If not, you need to take a calculator with you, arrive early at the competition and get busy (or get your back-up crew to do it) before you get your horse ready for vetting.

The amount of preparation you need to do depends upon your personal confidence, self-reliance and determination under competition conditions. Some people arrive a day or more early, check out the route on foot or by car (if you do this, be careful that you do not infringe on private property where the route is open only to competitors on the day of the ride), buy full sets of local maps and make up copies of the route for competitor and crew and have their crew car packed with everything but the kitchen sink before feeding time on the previous day. Other people turn up at the last possible moment, don't even look at the photocopied map they have received until they are ready to start, grab the nearest available spare stranger to crew for them and set off confidently on their way.

For Novice competitions, the newcomer to the sport should be as well prepared as possible. Arriving the previous day is not necessary (unless you have a very long journey to the venue). The route for a 20- or 30-mile (32 or 48 km) set-speed ride should be sufficiently well marked for reconnaissance to be unnecessary but you would be well advised to obtain at least one copy of the relevant published local map – such as the Ordinance Survey Landranger or Pathfinder maps in Great Britain – and mark the route on it. The distances given for most organised rides are fairly accurate but if in doubt, you can check by using a measuring wheel – inexpensive, available from map shops and more accurate than a piece of string.

Note where the official checkpoints are and work out your riding times at the correct speed. Make sure your back-up crew is equipped with a note of the times so that they can work out when and where to meet you, and also make sure that you have these with you in an easily visible place when riding, such as written clearly on your map in a map carrier or even taped to your arm. As you pass any given checkpoint, you want to be able to check at a glance whether you have reached it on time. Your back-up crew will need a map which shows the road network for meeting you and you will need a map which shows landmarks on the route so that you can retrace your steps and find your way if you go wrong or if there is a marker problem. If possible, study the map before the start and notice any useful landmarks, such as main road or railway crossings, churches, public houses, telephone boxes, forest car parks, or anything else which has a symbol on the map. Get to know these symbols so that you can scan your surroundings and read a map quickly to pinpoint your position if you get lost.

Also study the map for changes in terrain. Get to know the changes in gradient depicted by the variation in the distance between contour lines. Be aware that forestry usually means hard but fairly fast going; work out how much roadwork is included; how much is open country and whether there are tracks; and look out for sections where the going looks good and others where you are likely to have to slow down. Is there a big hill near the start or finish, for example? How will it affect your tactics?

Building Up to the Ride

At Novice level, there is no need to make any changes to your horse's training or management routine during the days or weeks before the ride. Continue with basic training exactly as in the previous two months, maintaining your regular LSD work. Maintain a stable, high-fibre diet. Do not suddenly increase the amount of concentrates because you develop a conscience about the tremendous feat you are about to ask your horse to perform. Unnecessary extra high-energy food at this point will, at best, produce a hyperactive, overexcitable horse and, at worst, risk tying-up or other metabolic problems. Do not, in fact, change anything. Your horse should be able to produce the extra effort needed to complete 20 miles (32 km) in satisfactory time with ease if you have followed the guidelines of the previous chapters.

Crewing Equipment

For a Novice competition, assuming that you are going to the ride and home again the same day, the minimum of back-up equipment is needed. If your tack is in good order before the start, you should not need spares for a ride of this distance. For 20–30 miles (32–48 km), only one girth and numnah or saddle blanket are required. A spare set of horseshoes in the crew car is always advisable and it is worthwhile obtaining one of the proprietary plastic or rubber hoof boots which you can carry attached to your saddle in case your horse loses a shoe when you are out of touch with your crew.

For most rides of this distance, 5 gal (20–25 litres) of water in carriers, plus six or eight 'slosh bottles', a bucket and large sponge packed in the crew car will be enough. You will need another 5-gal carrier back at the finish if water is not provided on site, plus another water bucket. Take a full haynet, some soaked sugar beet and enough of the horse's usual concentrates for one feed – it will be ready for this after the final vetting.

Always take an anti-sweat rug plus a light cooler, a warm stable rug, a waterproof sheet (a New Zealand will double for this) and an extra warm blanket or rug in case of need. Take leg wraps or bandages and gamgee, which can be used for warmth or support or used over ice packs in the rare event of a tendon injury.

Carry a hoofpick with you *en route* and make sure your crew car has one too. You will need a large sponge and sweat scraper for washing down and a towel is always useful. Brushes and a curry comb to remove dried mud and tidy up the mane and tail for the final vetting are the least essential items. You will need your stethoscope to check the heart rate before the final vetting.

Having provided for your horse, don't forget that you and your crew also need sustenance. You cannot ride your best if you have been too nervous to eat breakfast and then don't eat or drink throughout the competition. Hydration is particularly important. Remember the rule that if you don't drink before you feel thirsty, you have left it too late. Becoming even slightly dehydrated can affect your concentration and energy level. Many novice distance riders fail to realise this until they begin to wonder why they always feel sick, headachy and exhausted after a ride, while other people don't.

So pack a picnic box with the type of foods that might appeal to you and give you energy. Bananas, muesli bars, nuts and raisins and yoghurt are some suggestions, but it is really a matter of personal choice. Do heed a word of warning about chocolate – it will give immediate energy but is followed by a corresponding 'low', so save it until after the competition. Isotonic drinks are popular and so, increasingly, are the high-carbohydrate mixtures formulated especially for athletes but, at this level, plain water is as good as anything. The important thing is to top up before you start and avoid anything that is likely to provoke a tummy upset while riding, such as too much fruit juice or coffee.

The final thing to pack is a basic first aid kit. The contents may vary, but suggestions include:

- antiseptic or antibiotic wound dressing
- cotton wool
- gauze dressings
- poultice dressing
- three or four 4-inch (10 cm) wide elastic bandages
- scissors/sticky tape/Elastoplast
- arnica ointment/tablets
- petroleum jelly
- wound ointment
- headache/painkilling and indigestion tablets
- antiseptic ointment

Also on this subject, the effects of sun and wind can be harsh on your skin when riding for several hours, so use a good moisturiser or sun-protection cream and lipsalve before you start.

Rider Clothing

If your clothing is uncomfortable, you will continually change your position to ease the discomfort, thus unbalancing your horse and impairing its performance. So, what should you wear?

International rules for endurance riding have set a certain standard of dress and in the interests of the public image of the sport these should be adhered to as far as possible. They require protective headgear, adequately secured; breeches and high boots, or breeches with gaiters or high socks and ankle boots or running shoes, or jodhpurs with ankle boots or running shoes; a shirt with a collar. Within these limitations is a huge variation of choice of materials and there is no restriction on colours.

Starting from the top, your headgear should conform to an internationally approved standard and if it is a jockey skull cap, it should be covered with a silk. A collar has the practical function of helping to protect the back of your neck from sunburn, as well as looking smarter than a T-shirt. A scarf or bandana provides further protection and can also be used to keep out dust if necessary or as an emergency bandage. A sweatshirt or jersey in toning colour with your silk is smart and workmanlike. Breeches or jodhpurs need to be carefully chosen if they are not to rub when worn for long distances, so avoid those with inner seams. Many riders are now happier with lycra riding tights, in either traditional colours or colours that tone with the rest of the outfit. Bright colours have a place in endurance riding from a safety point of view – they are easier to spot if you are lost in bad weather conditions or have had a fall *en route*, and when things are going well your back-up crew can pick you out of a group of riders from a distance, register how well you are doing and be prepared when you arrive.

Most long boots are too hot for distance riding and are not designed for running if you want to dismount and give your horse a break by running alongside. A suitably designed short boot, with a thick, non-slip, but not ridged, sole and adequate ankle support, worn with half chaps, is the choice for most riders. Riding 'trainers' are popular but if you choose a walking boot or trainer without a heel, then caged stirrups must be used. For Novice rides, until you begin to acquire specialist equipment, ordinary jodhpur boots with thick socks are fine.

Travelling to the Ride

The most important thing for the newcomer to remember is to allow plenty of time. Nerves are much less frayed if you do not have to panic to make your pre-ride vetting on time. It is much better to arrive early and have an extra ten minutes for a final check of the map and something to eat and drink.

Your horse should be trained to load without fuss. Most keen endurance horses learn to look forward to going in the lorry or trailer as a prelude to an exciting event and change in routine. If you have loading problems, get some experienced help and take time to work them out. Often, horses that are reluctant to load have become that way because they have not been given a good journey last time they travelled, so ensure that your horse is driven with care and consideration, with no sudden stops and starts, nor swings round corners and roundabouts. Endurance horses spend a great deal of time travelling to and from events, so their welfare while travelling is important. A bad journey can easily destroy your chances of successfully completing the ride.

Make sure your horse has had plenty of chance to drink before setting off and give it a haynet while travelling. Eating hay on the way to the ride won't detract from its performance – remember the emphasis on a high-fibre diet and the difference between distance riding and flat racing.

Travel the horse in clothing appropriate for the weather conditions and the way it travels – an anti-sweat rug and cooler or light rug if it tends to sweat up; warmer rug on a cold day; or summer sheet or no rug at all on a hot day.

Don't forget to pack your ride information, maps, horse identification and vaccination certificate if needed, any club membership documents or similar essentials, and you are ready for the experience of your first competitive ride.

CHAPTER 8

COMPETING AT NOVICE LEVEL

ON ARRIVING at the ride venue, check that your horse has travelled well and is happy, then collect your number from the secretary and check the notice board for any important information or route changes. Make sure your crew knows about these too.

Unload your horse, remove its travelling boots and tail bandage and, if you have come a long way, see if it wants a drink. Your horse should be trained to stay quietly tied up to your trailer or lorry so that you and your crew can get on with organising things without one person having to hold the horse. However, for its first ride or two, if it is really excited by all that is going on, it might be better for one of you to take it for a walk to help settle it down. Remember the rule that a stallion or kicker should have a red ribbon on its tail and a green horse a green ribbon. Steer clear of any of these that you see and if you are worried about how your novice horse will behave in company, put a green ribbon on its tail as a warning to others. In any case, always be aware of where your horse is in relation to others and avoid going so close as to risk a kick. If your horse gets kicked because you led it a hair's breadth past someone else's rear, it is your fault, not theirs.

When you are ready and your horse is settled and tidy, go for your pre-ride vetting and remember that you may get penalty marks if you are not on time. The horse should be presented unsaddled, with clean legs and feet and in either a bridle or headcollar, depending upon the rules of the organising body. Do not oil its hooves – the vet will not appreciate having to pick up oily feet. If you have been sent a vet sheet in advance of the ride, be sure that you have filled in the necessary details legibly and fully. If the ride is a competitive one where penalties may be awarded and you are required to declare any injuries or blemishes, declare everything, even old scars and brushing marks. Less experienced ride vets have been known to give penalties at the finish for anything not on the vet sheet at the start and it can be difficult to argue that a particular scratch was incurred before the ride day if it hasn't been noted on your vet sheet.

The pre-ride vetting will take two or three minutes. The vet writer should check that the details of horse and rider are correct, then the vet will take your horse's heart rate (pulse) with a stethoscope. If taken over a full minute, as required for some competitive rides where grading is based on heart rate, this can seem to go on forever – a minute is a long time when you are waiting for it to pass. If the vet takes the reading for less than a minute, he or she will use a multiplication factor to arrive at the number of beats per minute. When the

The veterinary surgeon takes the heartrate, or pulse, using a stethoscope and stopwatch.

heart rate is close to the maximum permitted parameter, however, the reading should always be taken for a full minute to give the horse a full and fair opportunity to pass.

The horse's pre-ride heart rate in an open-air venue is likely to be higher than the resting heart rate you have established at home. The journey, the busy atmosphere of the venue, anticipation of what is to come and general excitement all have the effect of elevating the heart rate. An experienced horse's heart may be only a couple of beats higher than its normal resting rate. An inexperienced novice may have a much higher rate and, in a few cases, a horse which is really overexcited might have a reading well over the maximum permitted parameter of 64. If this should happen with your horse and the vet is kind, he or she will tell you to take it away and settle it down, then try again. The vet may even move away from the general vetting area to a quieter spot, if there is time, or he or she may take the view that the true heart rate cannot be read because of excitement and allow you to start anyway, with a caution to ride carefully. If, however, the vet decides you cannot start because he cannot get a reading under 64, that decision is final and there is nothing you can do about it, except look at your horse and work out why it is overexcitable. Insufficient work, too much high-energy food and insufficient education in company are the usual reasons.

The mouth is checked for injuries.

Once the heart rate is noted, the vet will examine your horse for 'lumps and bumps', also noting anything you have declared. He or she will open the mouth to check for bruising or sores, look for girth and saddle sores, check your horse's back, examine its legs and should also pick up and check its feet. The vet may also pull down an eyelid to look at the mucous membrane and exert pressure on the gums with a finger to test capillary refill time. Healthy mucous membranes are salmon pink in colour; they become red and congested when a horse is dehydrated or overstressed. The capillary refill time – the time it takes for blood to flow back into the gum after it has been squeezed out by thumb pressure – should be no more than three seconds. Any longer and a degree of dehydration is indicated. The 'pinch test' is also used to provide a basic dehydration parameter. The vet takes a 'pinch' or fold of

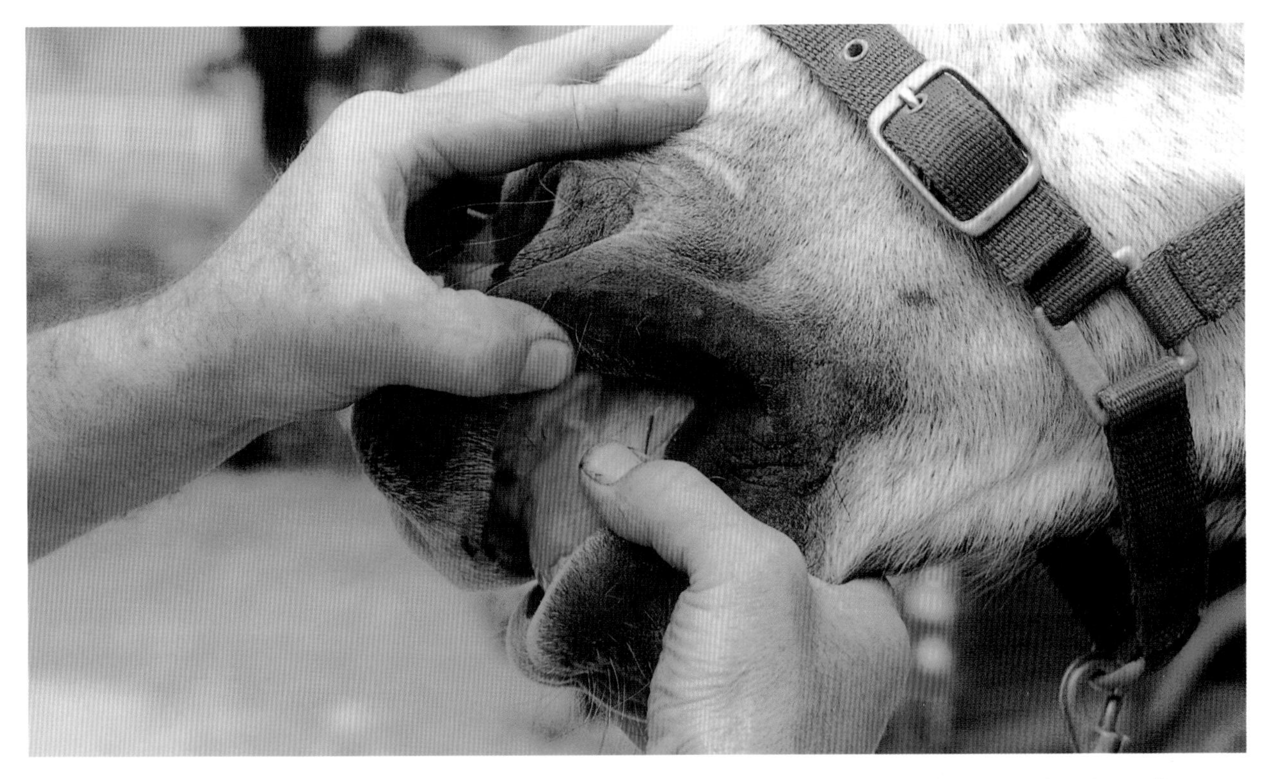

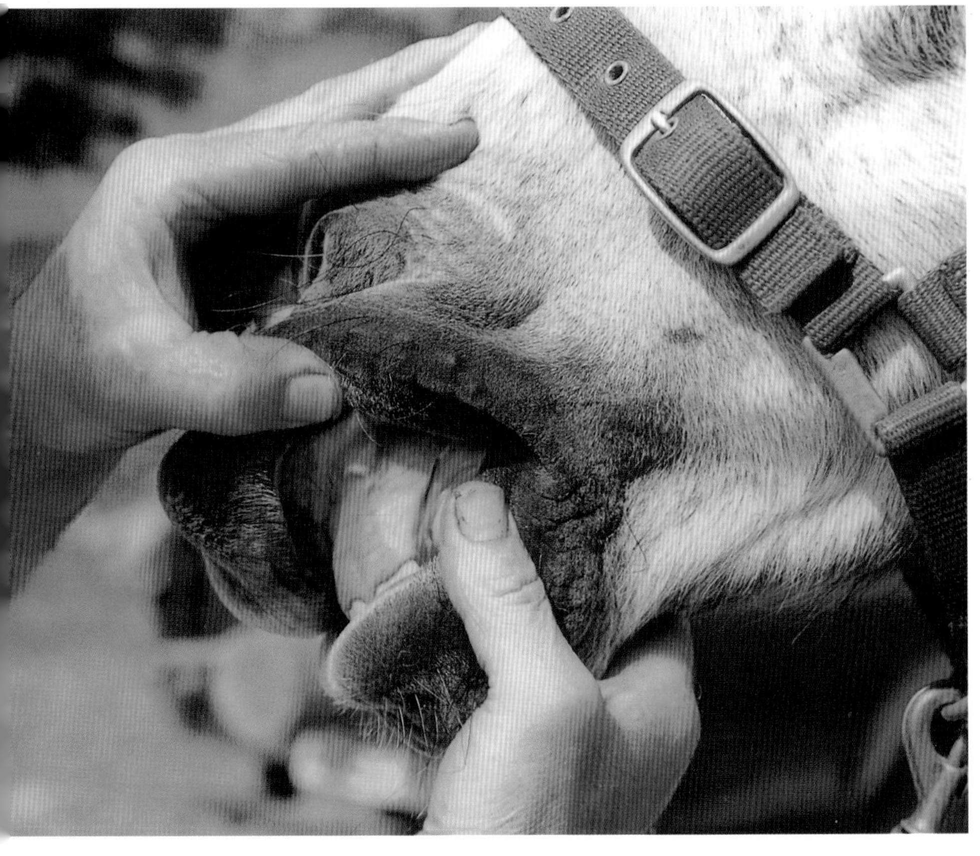

ABOVE *A capillary refill test to assess dehydration is done by pressing on the gum with the thumb and* LEFT *counting the seconds until the circulation returns to normal. The imprint of the thumb mark can be seen in this picture.*

about three-quarters of an inch of skin between finger and thumb at the point of the shoulder, then, without pulling, releases it. The time the skin takes to flatten out is counted in seconds and recorded on the vet sheet. For most horses at the pre-ride vetting, a figure from 0–3 will be recorded. In later stages of a ride, a pinch test score of five or more seconds indicates serious dehydration.

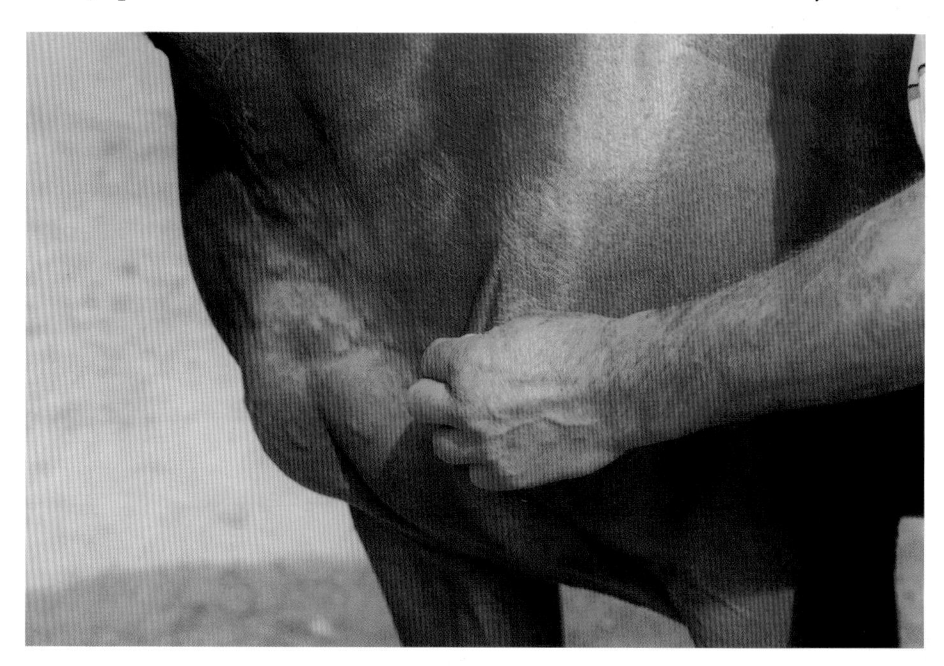

The pinch test, shown here, is another method of assessing dehydration. The fold of skin at the point of the shoulder is grasped without pulling, released, and the seconds counted while the skin returns to normal.

Finally, the horse will be trotted up to check for soundness. There is an art to trotting out a horse for distance ride vetting, which is completely different from trotting out at a show. Learn to do it properly and teach your horse to do it well. Take the reins or leadrope about a foot (30 cm) from the head in your right hand, with the slack in your left hand. Ask the horse to trot smartly out in a straight line away from the vet. You are not allowed to carry a whip, so make sure your horse has learned this at home and will trot on command. Once the horse is trotting well, drop your right hand from the reins so that the horse's head is free. Run straight and look straight ahead, not at the horse. Slow down as you reach the turn, stop, turn to the right so that the horse is between you and the vet and trot back in the same manner, slowing down as you reach the vet, unless he or she indicates that you should continue straight past. Where possible, the trot up will take place on hard, smooth ground. If the vetting has to be on grass, you may be asked to trot a figure of eight instead of a straight line.

Some rides have inspections of your horse's shoes and tack, so be sure that all are in good order. Once the pre-ride vetting is over, tack your horse up, making sure everything is well secured and comfortable. A 'bum bag' is useful for carrying essentials such as a hoofpick, bandage and carton of drink and don't forget to take your route map. A few minutes before you are due to start, mount up

The rider is asked to trot the horse away 30–40 metres and back.

and warm up your horse with a brisk walk and a trot. If there is enough space, trot some circles and changes of rein to get your horse balanced and supple. Be at the start in good time and check your watch (and your crew's) with the starter. Smile when your crew waves goodbye, relax and enjoy your ride.

How you ride the first part of the course depends on the going and terrain. If it is good and level or undulating, you can settle straightaway into a steady, working trot. Don't let your horse extend its trot or canter until it is well warmed up and settled. The extra speed is unnecessary and going faster only excites an unsettled horse even more. It also wastes a considerable amount of energy and increases the risk of muscle damage and tying-up. Provided you don't waste time at meeting points, a good working trot will see you round most 20-mile (32 km) courses at an average speed of between $6\frac{1}{2}$ and 7 mph (10.5–11.3 kmph), which is all that is required.

If the early going is a steep climb, don't push the horse to go faster than it can easily manage. Let it walk, but not dawdle, until you reach easier ground.

You may soon catch up other riders, or others may catch and overtake you. Don't worry about them but concentrate on settling your own horse into its own stride and paces. Above all, don't be towed along by horses going faster than your settled pace, however enthusiastic your horse may be about the idea. At this stage, training your horse to listen to you and developing the partnership between you is much more important than whether you get your rosette at the finish. If you find yourself in the common situation where two or three others overtake you then promptly slow down in front of you or maintain a position 50 yards ahead and just in view and your horse is becoming excitable or taking too strong a hold, slow down until they are out of sight. Come back to a walk or even dismount. Your horse must not get the idea that it is all right to chase every tail in front of it, until and unless you ask it to.

Begin to train your eye to find markers on the trail ahead and to notice landmarks on the route. In open country, try to develop your appreciation of the topography and of distance in relation to visibility. If you do miss your way, it helps if you can pinpoint a visible hill, wood or church spire on your map. Most courses are well marked but even the best-marked route can suffer from the accidental, or sometimes deliberate, destruction of markers, so your map is your failsafe and you must learn to read it accurately.

If possible, try to have your crew meet you for the first time in about 3 to 5 miles (5–8 km) from the start, just to make sure that the horse has settled and everything is going as it should. If your crew has gone 10 miles (16 km) down the track and your horse loses a shoe in the first half hour, you haven't a hope of getting back on course and finishing on time.

It becomes second nature to endurance riders to encourage their horses to drink water at every available opportunity and newcomers to the sport are often perplexed and confused by this as they have grown up with the traditional stable manager's rule of never letting a hot horse drink cold water and of restricting water intake before strenuous exertion. What are the facts?

A horse working continuously for several hours (anything from three to 24 in an endurance ride) loses a considerable amount – gallons rather than pints – of water and essential salts (electrolytes) in sweat. This needs to be replaced on a continuous basis to enable the horse to continue to work efficiently and, ultimately, to prevent dehydration and the associated problems of exhaustion and possibly colic. The amount the horse needs to drink depends upon the weather conditions, the distance and the speed of the competition. Most horses have enough reserves to cope with 20 or 30 miles (32–48 km) at the relatively low speeds of Novice competitions without needing to drink, so if your horse

The horse should be encouraged to drink whenever the opportunity arises.

drinks when offered water that is fine, but if not, don't worry. Dosing with electrolytes at this level is certainly unnecessary and could cause a harmful imbalance. The horse will be able to replace any loss from its normal food after the ride. It is good practice, however, for your crew to offer the horse a drink of plain water immediately you arrive at the meeting point. If this becomes a habit, the horse will learn to drink when it does need water in future competitions.

If a horse which needs to drink is prevented from doing so, it will become progressively dehydrated and performance will deteriorate. If, through inexperienced management, a horse reaches this condition by the end of a long ride, its water intake should be monitored, allowing about a quarter of a bucket at a time, with several minutes between drinks. A severely dehydrated horse may be too exhausted and disinterested to drink at all and in these serious circumstances immediate veterinary attention and intravenous fluid therapy are essential.

Back on your first ride, once a drink has been offered, your crew should have a 'slosh bottle' ready to hand up to you, with the cap off! The slosh bottle is a plastic water bottle – usually a recycled orange juice bottle or similar – of about $3\frac{1}{2}$pt (2 litres) capacity, filled with water which you pour over your horse's neck and shoulders to cool it down. Evaporation of sweat is the primary means of cooling for a working horse, so wetting the skin assists heat dissipation by conduction, reduces the need to sweat and minimises dehydration. It also freshens up a tiring horse remarkably well. Do not pour water over the horse's hindquarters; at this level and speed of competition the large muscles must be kept warm and working and sudden chilling can result in cramps.

The number of slosh bottles needed obviously depends on the weather conditions on the day. If it is freezing cold and raining, you won't need any, but if it is mild and muggy, you will use at least one every time you meet your crew. The more humid the conditions, the more necessary the slosh bottles. Also be aware that windy conditions can be very drying and sweat can evaporate so quickly that you may not realise that your horse is sweating at all. As long as your horse is moving on at a steady pace, it is better to slosh than not.

Always have the bottle handed up and do the sloshing yourself; don't be tempted to let your crew do it from the ground. When you progress to bigger rides you will slosh your horse on the move and the horse must get used to you pouring water over it from above. Also, under some rules only the rider may actually do anything to the horse *en route* (although the crew may hold up a bucket for the horse to drink) and anything else may be construed as forbidden outside assistance. Your horse will probably be surprised the first time a cascade of water falls around it and may spin around, trying to evade it, so give yourself plenty of room. Most horses quickly get used to the idea and soon accept it as part of the routine.

Next, have a drink yourself. Develop the habit of always taking some liquid

ABOVE *Making use of a river crossing to wash the horse down. Standing in the water for a few minutes will also help cool his feet.*

Sloshing on the run. This competitor in the early stages of a major French ride keeps going as he cools his horse. Experience will tell the rider when and where to stop and for how long.

whenever you meet your crew, even if you don't feel thirsty and it is only a few mouthfuls. That way, you will avoid becoming dehydrated and fatigued. Remember, if your energy is depleted, you become a liability, not a help, to your horse. While you have your drink, your crew can quickly check your horse's legs and shoes, then you should be on your way. All of this should have taken no more than a couple of minutes and the only aspect that cannot be hurried is if your horse wants to drink, when he should be allowed all the time he needs to drink his fill.

How many times your crew manages to meet you depends on the accessibility of the route by road and the driver and navigator's skill in getting to the various access points. On a 20-mile (32 km) ride, three or four meets are ample and, in general, on longer rides, you will be lucky to be met every 6 or 7 miles (9.5–11.25 km). Being met more frequently than this is usually detrimental as it interrupts your rhythm and takes up too much of your riding time.

On a set-speed ride, keep track of your time at checkpoints.

Under most rules, it is your responsibility to make sure the checkpoint stewards have taken your number, so take care not to miss any checkpoints, call your number to the steward and make sure he or she has it right before you ride on. Check your speed, using the times you worked out earlier, as you pass each checkpoint. There are two ways of monitoring time – actual time of day or hours and minutes from the start. You either set your watch to the right time by the timekeeper's clock, or to 1200 and note the times for each checkpoint accordingly.

If you are down on time, don't panic. Hurrying along often results in not spotting markers, missing turnings and wasting even more time. Instead, concentrate on your riding and the going. On time or not, always guide your horse on to the best ground, to minimise concussion and wear and tear on its legs and feet and to give yourself the best chance of completing with a sound horse. With practice, your horse will respond to neck reining and a minimal weight aid from you. Very experienced horses will ultimately learn to choose the best going for themselves. If time is short, canter where you can, for example down the grassy centre of a hard track. When you cannot canter, make the best time possible by maintaining balance and rhythm in your trot. A rhythmic pace is far less tiring for your horse than a stop and go one. In trot, make it an automatic habit to change diagonals frequently. While concentrating on your riding, don't forget to look for markers. It is easy, when in a good rapport with your horse, to become oblivious to everything else.

If you are short of time and your horse is showing its tiredness by reluctance and wanting to slow down, don't push it. You will have to accept the fact that your horse just isn't fit enough for the job in hand and train some more for another day. Unless your horse is seriously overweight or ill prepared, however, this is unlikely to happen on a Novice ride.

If you are in good time, perhaps even at risk of finishing faster than the maximum permitted speed, you can slow down and take it easy for the final stretch of the ride. In good weather, you can allow your horse to relax and walk in to the finish with the best chance of passing the final vetting. If it is cold, take care that your horse does not become chilled through slowing down to a walk – it is better to trot back along the track for a short distance and keep moving than to arrive with a cold and shivering horse with stiffening muscles.

What do you do if something goes wrong during the ride, such as a lost shoe, or your horse going lame?

The first and most important rule is that you do not leave the ride route. Obviously, if the problem is a lost shoe (or a similar difficulty but not serious), you walk your horse (dismounting only if you deem it necessary) on to the next accessible point, send a message via another rider or a steward to your crew and the ride farrier and hope that your horse will be reshod before you run out of time. If your horse needs veterinary assistance, however, you must not move from your reported position, even if you think your horse is better and can walk on, say, to a road for a lift back to the venue. Once you have called for a vet, you are deemed to have retired from the ride and must stay put until the vet arrives. The vet does not want to spend hours driving round the countryside, maybe walking some considerable distance, looking for a sick horse which has vanished. Apart from worrying about the horse, he or she needs to find you as quickly as possible so that they can deal with your horse and get back to their other duties. The smooth running of the ride and the safety of other horses may depend on this.

With good fortune, however, you won't be in this position and will arrive back at the venue with your horse going well and having enjoyed your ride. Now it is time to think about the final vetting.

As soon as you cross the finish line, dismount and give your horse's back a rest. Collect your vet time card from the timekeeper and walk your horse back to your box or trailer. Remove the bit, loosen the girth *one* hole and offer the horse a drink. Unless it is a very hot day, throw an appropriate rug over the hindquarters – a cooler on a warm day, cooler or anti-sweat plus a thicker rug on a cold day.

Next, sponge down the neck and legs, removing sweat and mud and helping the horse to cool down. If the weather is cold, or if the horse is clean and dry

At the finish, loosen your girth one hole at a time, to avoid pressure bumps.

anyway, sponging will not be necessary. In cold weather, brush mud off the legs once they are dry or, if you do sponge them, towel them dry. Sticky clay, which contains fine particles which irritate the skin and can cause mud fever, should always be washed off as soon as possible and a squirt of mildly medicated wash in the water will help to remove the dirt and soothe any abrasions.

Loosen the girth another hole and pick out the horse's feet. Check the heart rate with your stethoscope. By now you will have been in for several minutes and the heart rate should be dropping steadily. If it is over 70 bpm, sponge more cool water over the horse's neck and legs. Remove the saddle. The reason for loosening the girth gradually and not removing the saddle immediately is to avoid pressure bumps as the circulation returns to the skin which has been compressed. If pressure bumps do occur, you need to look at the design and fit of your saddle (see previous chapter). Sponge away saddle marks and sweat, using the minimum of water. The back muscles can be gently massaged to help to restore circulation.

Offer another drink. Keep the bucket in front of the horse and it will probably reach for it when it does want to drink. By now the horse should be relaxed and calm. If it is still tense and excited, take it for a walk and let it graze a little if it wants to. Recheck the heart rate. If all is well, it should now be well under the 64 bpm parameter for elimination. If not, you will have to assess the reason. Is it overexcitment? Is the horse too warm still and needs more cooling (this is unlikely on a Novice ride except in very hot weather conditions)? Is it actually more fatigued than you thought? In the latter two cases, you can try to speed recovery with more water cooling to help to dissipate excess heat more quickly. The areas to sponge are the neck and inside the legs, where large veins are close to the body surface. If it is fatigued, you can still walk the horse to help the circulatory system to remove the waste products of energy production from the muscles, or massage the major muscles for the same effect and use TEAM skin massage techniques to help the horse to relax. However, if a horse has become so fatigued at Novice level that the heart rate is still over 64 after 30 minutes, it is usually the result of inadequate training and preparation of a horse which is basically unsuited to the work – native ponies and cobs, with thick, unclipped coats, are often in this category.

Stop your horse from eating, if it has been grazing, at least five minutes before your vetting time, as eating uses energy which slightly increases the heart rate. If it has been standing still, walk it gently for five minutes, to make sure it has not stiffened up, before presenting it to the vet.

The veterinary inspection will follow a similar procedure to the pre-ride vetting but may also include a Ridgway, or 'minute', test. First, the heart rate will be taken in the usual way. Next, you will be asked to trot the horse up for a distance, ideally of 44 yd (40 m) (but more usually 33 yd (30 m) due to the difficulty of finding venues with sufficiently hard trotting areas) and back and, as you begin the trot, a stopwatch will be started. When you return, the vet will continue his or her inspection until one minute has passed. He or she will then take the heart rate a second time and the reading in a horse which is 'fit to continue' will be the same or lower than the first reading. If the second reading is more than three or four beats higher than the first, but still under the elimination parameter, the horse may be starting to tire but not yet have reached a stage where there is cause for concern. At your Novice ride final vetting, such a reading can be taken as an indication that your horse was only just fit enough for the competition and needs more work, or more competitions at the same level, before progressing to the next stage.

If the second reading exceeds the elimination parameter, the horse has reached the stage of being at risk and should not be ridden further. Under some countries' and organisations' rules, this would mean elimination at the final vetting; under others, the reading may be taken in conjunction with other clinical observations to arrive at a decision. In a few cases, a higher second reading may be attributable purely to excitement, especially with a novice horse, and an experienced vet will be able to use their judgement to decide whether to pass the horse if all other parameters are normal and the horse is obviously fit and well.

The trot up during the Ridgway test will be observed to check the horse for soundness. If the vet has no doubt that a horse is lame, he or she may eliminate it; if they are uncertain after the first trot, they may ask a colleague to observe a second trot. If both vets cannot agree, a third vet may be asked, to obtain a majority opinion. No horse should be asked to trot more than three times and where there is doubt the horse should be given the benefit of it. If the vet, or vets, decides to eliminate the horse for lameness or any other reason, their decision is final and there is no appeal.

When trotting a horse up for lameness during a competition, the vet is not expected to make a diagnosis but merely to decide whether a horse is lame or not. Most vets are happy to be consulted after the finish of the competition as to the reason for the lameness but are too busy with their work during the actual ride to make the necessary thorough examination or discuss your horse with you there and then, so be patient and wait until they have finished their ride duties.

The final vetting will also include a check for injuries, especially saddle and girth sores and mouth bruising. These are seldom serious enough to incur elimination, although that is possible in extreme cases, but may well incur penalties in competitive rides, which will lower your grading or award.

Once the final vetting is over, while the organisation works out your speed, veterinary results and final award, there is time to look after your horse and yourself before the journey home.

Most horses like to graze if grass is available. Offer a small feed, including some easily digestible, soaked sugar beet which is often palatable to a tired horse. Sliced apples or carrots are also often well received. Walking gently while grazing is the best way for your horse to relax and recover from the exertion of the ride and it may well now urinate if it has not done so before. Offer water again and make sure it has every chance to drink its fill before being loaded.

Some people like to bandage a horse's legs with cooling paste after a ride and whether you do this is a matter of personal preference. Veterinary, as well as lay, opinion differs on the value of such treatment and it should be considered in the context of the overall management of the horse. If, on arrival home, the horse will be turned out with the freedom to move around, preventing tired muscles from stiffening and giving the circulation the maximum chance to carry away waste products of energy production, bandaging is unlikely to be of much value. If, however, the horse must be stabled, with all the restrictions on its natural inclinations that involves, then bandaging may help to prevent filling of the legs and inflammation resulting from the stress of exercise. It is much

The vet checks the back for soreness.

more important to check the legs and feet thoroughly the next morning for any signs of damage.

When you have had something to eat and drink, consider how you feel yourself. Do you have any aches and pains? Where are they and what caused them? Backache is often caused by trying to maintain an uncomfortable riding position, so check whether your saddle enables you to ride in the desirable balanced position. Asymmetrical aches or sores indicate that you have been riding in a one-sided way. Investigate the cause and rectify it – it could be anything from a weakness in one knee or ankle, requiring physiotherapy or support, to a basic riding fault which can be ironed out with some lessons. Was your clothing comfortable or did the extra hours in the saddle throw light on something that needs to be changed for next time? Blistered hands, heels and toes, bruises on shins or behind the knees, rubs caused by unsuitable underwear – all can be prevented with a little thought.

What about your horse? Did the tack serve its purpose or not? Check for rubs and sores, especially around the face and everywhere under the saddle.

Give your horse at least half an hour after the final vetting before loading up to go home, and check to be sure that nothing untoward has happened in the interim when you put on its travelling gear. Is it relaxed and comfortable? If in doubt, seek veterinary advice before you start on the road, especially if you have a long way to travel. If everything is well, give it a haynet to munch on and to help to pass the journey time. If the weather is cold, make sure the travelling rug is warm enough.

At home, ideally, the horse should be turned out, rugged if necessary, according to the weather. A feed may be given but some horses will prefer just to go off and graze. Next morning, check the horse over thoroughly and, all being well, continue with your usual routine. Take particular note of any loss of condition and, if it is marked, give the horse a few days off, turned out, to recover to normal before progressing further with its work. In most cases, no more than the usual rest day should be required and a 'change' rather than a 'loss' of condition should be noted. The change should be part of the progress towards fitness, with perhaps some loss of excess weight, improved vitality and the beginning of improved muscle development. These changes are often more noticeable as a result of actual competition, rather than in training at home.

Also check the amount of wear on the shoes and whether the ride has produced any deviation from the usual pattern of wear. If so, point it out to your farrier on his next visit.

With your first competition behind you, you are now ready to progress to a more regular competitive schedule and from there to the intermediate levels of distance riding.

The farrier will check the horse's shoes before the start.

CHAPTER 9

COMPETING AT INTERMEDIATE LEVEL

AS A HORSE progresses through the levels of set-speed, lower-distance qualifying or competitive trail rides, regular competition will enhance the fitness developed through the training programme at home. If the horse is going to make an endurance horse, the effect will be psychological as well as physical and the horse will learn to anticipate what is ahead and concentrate its mind on the job. At first this may include rather too much excitement but, as time passes, the good prospect will settle down and have an attitude of calm but eager and willing co-operation. Good behaviour and trust in the rider and crew should become second nature.

Progressive Fitness Training *(see also Chapters 6 and 11)*

Physical fitness is fine-tuned by the concentrated effort of competition, while work at home continues to build on the basic groundwork of muscle development, improving balance, rhythm, strength and suppleness. At this stage of the horse's endurance career, the respective stresses of training and competition bring about comparatively rapid physical changes and it is as easy to allow incorrect development, with associated weaknesses, as it is to ensure correct development and progressive strength. Long-distance competition actively encourages horses to go long and low, stretched out, with their weight on the forehand, hocks out behind them, using the speed of their forward motion as a means of balancing themselves as a racehorse does. The racehorse, however, is working for only a short time and on prepared ground, usually carrying the minimum of weight. If the endurance rider allows his or her horse to adopt the racehorse technique – and it happens just as easily in trot as in canter – there is a risk of sudden injury on rough or uneven terrain, as well as the long-term accumulation of an assortment of lameness problems involving muscles, ligaments and bones. Therefore, a regular programme of flatwork and lungeing is essential to counteract the effects of competition on the horse's way of going, to rebalance it and to continue to encourage correct and efficient physical development.

A horse which is unbalanced and on its forehand frequently has a shortened, hurried stride. The balanced horse, however, can be taught to lengthen its stride so that, although the pace may feel slower, more ground per stride is actually being covered – an important consideration when the horse has 50 miles (80 km) or more to go. If the horse is balanced and trained to be responsive to the aids, the whole business of manoeuvring over varying terrain becomes easier, with the horse lengthening or shortening, picking its way to the best going and avoiding dangers such as rocks or rabbit holes with the minimum of effort and guidance from the rider. Far less energy is wasted by both horse and rider and the likelihood of a successful result to the ride is immeasurably increased.

The incredibly powerful trot of the Standardbred. As a general rule, however, the extended trot is too energy consuming to be kept up for long.

Your first, short-distance competition will have been ridden perhaps three months after you began training, but bear in mind that it takes at least two years to fully condition bones and, although muscles become 'fit' quite rapidly, their development, in terms of strength, bulk, suppleness and tone, is a long-term process.

From now on the horse is going to build up its fitness to tackle increasingly longer rides at moderately faster speeds and this requires the imposition of increasing amounts of stress, but in a controlled way. LSD work (described in Chapter 6), using mainly the long, lean, slow-twitch muscle fibres continues, augmented by work at a stronger pace, aimed at recruiting the fast-twitch, high-oxidative muscle fibres. Remember that there are two types of fast-twitch fibres – type 2a fibres with an ability to use oxygen, which can be improved by training, and type 2b fibres which cannot use oxygen and are recruited last for fast sprinting. The former are recruited as the demand for energy exceeds the ability of the slow-twitch muscles to supply it and the extent to which they can function aerobically, as opposed to anaerobically, can be increased with training.

Research has not yet fully explored the role of the various muscle types and how they are developed. A new theory suggests that, contrary to former belief, not all muscle fibres have a genetically pre-determined role, but that the direction they may take is a response to stimuli or stresses imposed early in life. If this is the case, an adult horse which raced as a two-year-old, for example, could be expected to have more muscle fibres adapted for sprinting than a similar horse left in the field until four or five. The implications of this as regards endurance work remain to be discovered and it must always be remembered that any beneficial effect on muscle fibre development gained from training very young horses must be weighed against the possible disadvantages of wear and tear on bones and ligaments.

Meanwhile, it is accepted that appropriate training of the mature horse results in improved oxidative function of the type 2a fibres, enabling the horse to travel further at a faster speed before fatigue sets in.

How do you incorporate this aspect of fitness into your training?

It is easy to be confused by the varying advice given in books on fitness training, which goes into great detail but often differs considerably in terms of the actual programme of frequency, duration and intensity of work. So let us set out some specific basic principles for training the endurance horse.

1 LSD work (see Chapter 6) is the first essential. It must be maintained regularly during the first two years of training, initially four or five days a week, reducing to two or three days a week by the end of the two years.

2 After about three months, more strenuous work, aimed at increasing the oxidative capacity of type 2a muscle fibres, is introduced. This should be included in the training programme two or three times a week, by adapting some of the purely LSD sessions.

3 When the horse reaches the stage of being prepared for major endurance race rides, a limited amount of anaerobic work, to recruit the type 2b muscle fibres, is advisable to 'tune' the horse to cope with sudden demands for extra energy, which may form part of the tactics of this level of ride.

4 Once or twice a week, schooling and lungeing should be incorporated into the programme, for correct muscle development, balance, suppleness and obedience to the rider's aids.

5 The horse should work five or six days a week during its training or conditioning periods over these first two years. One or two days should be rest days, and the horse should either live out or be turned out every day for some relaxation and freedom.

6 A break from fitness work, of six to eight weeks, during the winter is advisable for seasoned horses, to give body tissues a period of healing, rest and recuperation. However, a novice horse can be kept working, with more concentration on schooling, lungeing and an occasional ride out, but less fitness work, during this time.

7 At any time when the horse is showing signs of overstress, in body condition, impaired action or mental attitude, it should be turned out and rested until back to normal. You cannot improve a horse which has been overfaced in any way with more of the same treatment!

We shall now look at the fitness training, outlined in (**2**) above, which is necessary for the horse to progress through Intermediate level competitions from 30 to 50 miles (48–80 km) at speeds of 7–8 mph (11.25–12.8 kmph).

The basic principle is to increase the intensity at which the horse is working to a point where the slow-twitch muscle fibres cannot supply all the energy required and the type 2a fibres are called into play, using the remaining available oxygen which has been transported from the lungs via the circulatory system. Obviously, the ability of these muscle fibres to supply energy is limited by the amount of oxygen available and the work the horse will now do also has the effect of increasing the capacity of the respiratory and circulatory systems.

For practical purposes, the desired effect is achieved when the horse's heart rate averages around 160 bpm. Some authorities try to define set exercises as a way of controlling the amount of stress imposed, both for this work and for anaerobic work, for example 'x minutes of cantering at y speed, repeated z times'. This type of regimented training is usually referred to as 'interval training', based on the idea that the stress is applied on a repetitive format with varying 'intervals' between efforts. There is no set rule for the number of repetitions, speed or time of the stress efforts, which are conducted at canter, nor for the length of time of the intervals and whether they are conducted at walk or trot. Different trainers work out different programmes for individual horses, taking account of the task for which they are being trained. Some trainers, particularly with regard to event horses, have reduced interval training to a fine art, directly relating their speeds and times to what is required in the competition, for example on the steeplechase and the cross country course.

If you have the use of suitable facilities, this can be a very effective way of training the horse to higher levels of fitness. Most endurance riders, however, have to adapt their training to use the nearby surrounding countryside in the time available and time is also often limited if you work outside the world of horses, as many endurance riders do. Also, the specific performance demands on an endurance horse, in terms of speed, time and distance, cover a much broader spectrum than in racing or eventing and vary according to the tactics and conditions of a particular ride, so your training must be equally varied in scope.

When you begin to step up your horse's work to this level, there are a few basic points to bear in mind.

1 Every horse is an individual. Ride any two horses up the same hill at the same speed in the same conditions and the graph of the rise and fall of their heart rates will vary.

2 Type 2a muscle fibres will be recruited when the horse is working at heart rates between 140 and 180 bpm (average 160 bpm).

3 Improvement is effected by repeatedly reaching this level of intensity of effort for short periods, followed by periods of recovery, not by trying to maintain it continuously over one long period. In fact, the horse will only be able to maintain this level of energy output for a short time initially. If it is forced to continue, the heart rate will rise, anaerobic respiration will come into play, fatigue will quickly necessitate the horse being pulled up and an 'oxygen debt' will be created, which the horse must repay during recovery. Repeated stimulation of the fast-twitch, high-oxidative fibres, however, develops their capacity to produce energy so that, over time, the horse can maintain a higher level of aerobic energy output for longer periods, delaying the time or raising the heart rate at which the 'anaerobic threshold' is reached. This is the essential aspect of fitness training which turns a riding horse into an endurance horse.

In approaching this training, the tools the endurance rider usually has available are the local terrain and a series of well-worn riding routes, varying ground and weather conditions, varying amounts of time, a means of measurement of the horse's heart rate, and his or her own experience and knowledge of the horse concerned.

Terrain

This may vary from flat to mountainous; both have advantages and disadvantages and the trainer must adapt their methods accordingly. If your training locale is flat, your horse is going to have to work faster over longer distances to achieve the same training effect as a horse which is trained in a mountainous area. It will be quite easy for you to work out your horse's natural speed at the various gaits, but you will have more problems of wear and tear on your horse's legs and would be well advised to box to hillier ground for your LSD work as often as possible. Without the strengthening effect of hillwork, schooling to build up balance, strength and muscle power becomes even more important.

If you are based in a hilly or mountainous area, fitness will be much easier to achieve, although care must be taken not to overstress young horses and it is more difficult to assess your horse's base parameters at the various speeds and gaits unless you can find some level ground for the purpose.

On level ground it is relatively easy to maintain a steady heart rate, although with some horses it will be difficult to achieve a high enough heart rate for this intermediate training without a considerable increase in speed. You therefore need good going, such as downland turf, racing gallops or even a safe beach, for the faster work.

Treadmill researchers have found that the imposition of even a slight gradient increases the energy demand on the horse many times, and the trainer will find that even walking at a good pace up an appreciable hill will push a horse's heart rate up to the level required.

On flat ground, the trainer must impose the repetitions of effort by working the horse up to the required level, maintaining it for a short time, then allowing a recovery period before repeating the exercise. In this situation studying formal methods of interval training will help in deciding the number and duration of repetitions, commensurate with the individual horse's condition and level of fitness.

The trainer in hill country can use the terrain as an aid, building up the heart rate on uphill stretches and recovering on the downhill sections of regular training routes.

Using Established Routes

You will know from your LSD work how long a particular training route takes to complete and at what average speed your horse covers it. Average speeds will be markedly slower in hilly country than on the flat and will also be affected by stretches of bad going and the number of gates. You will also know, if you use a heart rate monitor, how the varying terrain affects your horse's heart rate. Asking your horse to work harder at appropriate points on the ride, such as trotting instead of walking up a particular hill, or cantering along a track for a specific distance, is an easy way of increasing the stress imposed by a controlled and quantifiable amount. Over the course of a ride of, say, 10 miles (16 km), there will be enough repetitions to achieve the desired effect.

Varying Ground and Weather Conditions

These are limiting factors which must be considered when assessing the effect of training and a measure of common sense must be employed when the conditions are unsuitable for the work you want to do. The horse must be trained to cope with rough going but this does not involve riding over it flat-out and leaving the horse to fall on its nose or worse (see Chapter 5). For fitness purposes, avoid bad going for faster work and let any such tracks on your training routes be negotiated during the 'recovery' phase of the work. Endurance horses must learn to move comparatively fast downhill but, again, do not attempt to ride fast work for fitness training and monitoring downhill. You will not reach high enough heart rates and the strain on the horse's joints is excessive.

Be aware of the effects of temperature and humidity on your horse's ability to perform. In cool, damp weather the average heart rate for a given amount of work will be appreciably lower than on a hot, humid day. Endurance horses can

Mist clearing on an autumn morning. These cool, damp conditions are ideal for the horse.

A horse under pressure in the heat. Stephane Fleury and Roc'h of France on their way to the bronze medal at the 1994 World Games at the Hague.

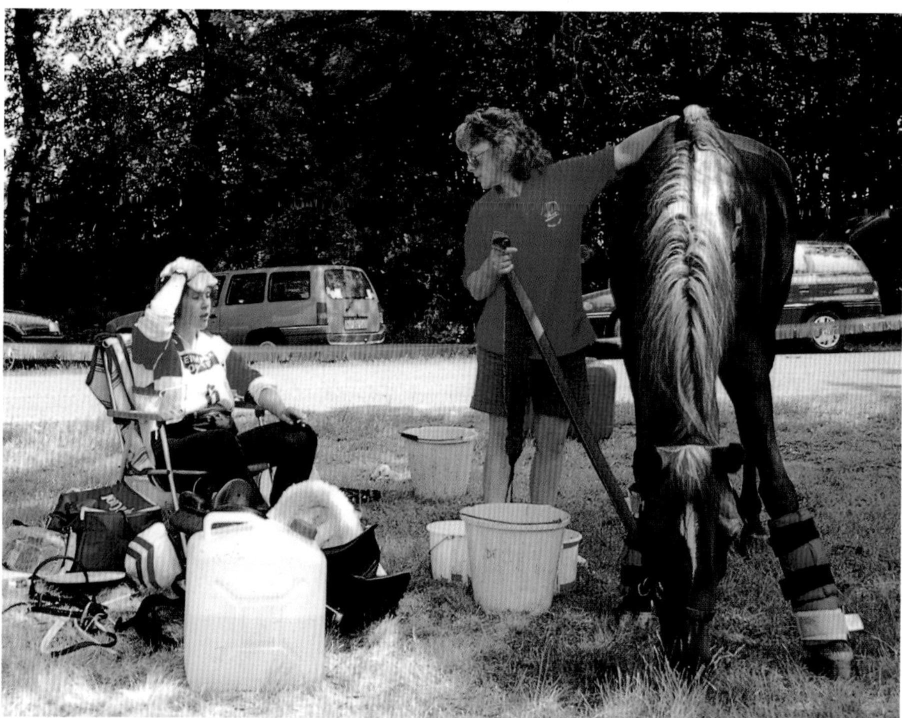

Heat affects the rider too. This race in Holland was run in temperatures over 90°F. The winner, Denise Falsetta, cools out with an ice pack during a veterinary hold, while her horse Soneri has ice packs on her legs.

and do perform successfully in very hot and humid conditions but they are aided by constant crewing and veterinary monitoring and should also be performing within the level of ability to which they have been trained. The training process, however, seeks to extend the horse's level of ability by taking it beyond what it is accustomed to do. The production of energy also generates heat which has to be dissipated and if heat is produced faster than the horse is able to get rid of it, there is a risk of heat exhaustion. It is unwise to ask a horse to achieve new levels of effort in adverse conditions of heat and humidity and although this is unlikely to be a problem in northern Europe, it can be a serious risk in less temperate climates. Conversely, you should also be aware of the risk of chills and muscle cramps after strenuous work in cold weather and if you have to hack home after a workout, you should keep the horse moving briskly. If boxing home, rug it up well.

The waterproof sheet is useful when waiting for the start, or on a tired horse coping with really cold, wet weather.

Time Availability

If your time is limited by working hours or other commitments, try to think of your training programme in terms of a weekly, rather than a daily, achievement. During the first two years of the endurance horse's career, steady miles under the girth are important, but it does not matter whether they are achieved on a six-day-a-week or a four-day-a-week programme. Riding on alternate days will not do your horse any harm and may even be better for it than a regular daily grind, provided that the work is of good quality, so ride as well as you can and ensure that the horse works actively.

The *fartlek* system is a good one for those with limited riding time. *Fartlek* is a Swedish word which means 'speed play' and it basically involves combining a mixture of different types of work – trots, canters and short gallops – making use of your local terrain. This ensures that the horse gets a mixture of steady and faster work, the trotting and cantering stimulating the type 2a muscle fibres and the gallops introducing anaerobic work, bringing in the type 2b muscle fibres.

Heart Rate Measurement

Obviously, a heart rate monitor is invaluable in assessing the horse's ability to cope with faster work and in ensuring that it is, in fact, working hard enough to reach the desired level of applied stress. The use of a monitor also provides more information than can be detected with a stethoscope alone. Some horses have relatively erratic heart rates which rise and fall rapidly as the level of work increases or decreases. Other horses have heart rates which rise and fall more slowly and maintain a steadier working beat. When a horse begins to work, its heart rate may rise to a higher rate, or be more erratic, than when it has warmed up and has been working for half an hour or more. The warming up process is vital to get all the body systems working efficiently and no fast work should be attempted for at least half an hour after beginning your ride. If you have used a monitor for your LSD work, you will have begun to get to know your own horse's pattern and should be able to spot any unexpected deviations from the norm, which may indicate that something is wrong, such as an incipient virus or response to pain which is a prelude to lameness.

Once your horse has warmed up, you can push its work level up to the point where its heart rate averages around 160 bpm. On flat ground, it should be fairly easy to maintain this heart rate for a brief time, say, no more than one minute to begin with, then allow a recovery to between 80 and 100 bpm before repeating the exercise. Three repeats will be enough initially.

On hilly or undulating ground it will be more difficult to maintain the heart rate at a consistent 160 bpm. Trotting uphill, for example, might produce an increasing scale from, say, 90 at the bottom to 180 at the top. This is further complicated by the fact that most monitors require a steady beat for a few seconds in order to register a change, so your monitor might continue to register 90 until you slow down at the top of the hill, when it will suddenly jump to a much higher figure. As you work more and more with a particular monitor, you will become accustomed to its peculiarities and be able to allow for them. Meanwhile, do not worry that your horse is going to be exhausted because its pulse has gone up to 180 or more. If the periods of asking for the effort are kept short and the horse is happy to keep going at a steady walk when it is allowed to slow down, you are achieving the desired effect. The anaerobic threshold is different for each horse and also changes as the horse gets fitter, so there is no magic number to be used as an absolute guide. Simply use the figures of increased heart rate which the monitor registers as indicators of the level of intensity of work which your horse has reached.

Of more importance are the recovery figures when the horse slows down or stops, and the time taken to reach them. These can be monitored, with a little more trouble, with a stethoscope as well as a heart rate monitor. The advantage of the monitor here is that it gives the maximum heart rate which has been reached and the extent of the fall within seconds of slowing down or stopping, which is considerable. For example, if you have trotted uphill for two or three minutes and the horse's heart rate has risen to, say, 175 bpm, when you pause at the top to make a recovery check, the rate is likely to fall to around 100 bpm within about ten seconds.

If you want to record a series of recovery heart rates for successive stress efforts, wait two minutes after stopping each time and note the reading. The recovery time will depend upon the duration of the working time and the horse's fitness level, but if you have been trotting at working pace for anything up to ten minutes, your two-minute recovery rate should be not more than somewhere between 80–120 bpm. As a further check, if you have time, you can do a ten-minute recovery check and this should always be below the competition elimination parameter of 64 bpm. It may be more practical, however, to do two-minute recovery readings during your training session and add a ten-minute one when you arrive back home, or at the end of the session, as appropriate.

As the heart rate falls so rapidly when you slow down or stop, there is no point in doing an immediate check with a stethoscope. Wait two minutes and then do your check. It is possible to take a horse's heart rate without dismounting, with your fingers on a pulse point near the withers, but the point is quite difficult to find, even if you can persuade your horse to stand still for 15 seconds while you count.

If your horse does not recover to the parameters suggested above in the specified time, something is wrong. Either the horse has been pushed too hard and you need to step down your level of training to a point where the horse can cope with it more easily, or there is another reason, such as impending illness or lameness. Never push your horse on to another effort until it has recovered sufficiently from the previous one. If, after ten minutes, the heart rate is still over 64, walk the horse quietly home, check for other problems and if there are none, rest it for a couple of days before recommencing training at a more moderate level.

Over a period of several months, you should begin to notice a decrease in recovery times or, in other words, recovery to a lower rate in the specified time. This signifies an increase in fitness, with a commensurate rise of the anaerobic threshold. As you notice this improvement occurring, you can increase the duration and intensity of work to an appropriate degree. When your horse is capable of maintaining a steady pace, over varied terrain, with the heart rate in the range 140–180, it is fit enough to compete in 50-mile-plus (80 km+) endurance rides. This may take up to two years to achieve with a young horse which begins as a complete novice.

From this point onwards, a limited amount of anaerobic work, ideally in the form of interval training, can be introduced and we shall consider this in Chapter 10.

The Trainer's Personal Knowledge of the Horse

The heart rate monitor and other training tools are wonderful aids but it is the horse which remains the focal point of all training and you ignore what your horse tells you, regardless of scientific trappings, at your peril.

For years, horse trainers have followed their own intuition, on the basis of a horse's condition, attitude and willingness to work, to decide how and when to train. The good rider or trainer knows how to work the horse within itself and decides from the way the horse feels when to ask for that little bit more effort that takes the horse beyond what it can easily accomplish, adds the element of controlled stress and pushes the horse on to a new level of fitness. How the horse 'feels' also tells the trainer when to stop. Nothing but experience and thoughtful observation can teach this ability and turn a rider into a horseman. It applies to every subject associated with training as well as to the actual work the horse is doing and we shall now look at some of the points you need to consider and maybe change while your horse progresses through this intermediate level of training and competition.

Soundness

We have seen that fitness is achieved by the imposition of controlled amounts of stress which cause changes in the body systems. However, there is a very fine dividing line between enough and too much stress and you must be constantly vigilant to ensure that your horse is not being asked to do too much within too short a space of time.

Check the legs carefully every day, watching for any signs of heat, inflammation and swelling of tendons, puffy swellings around joints, sore spots or tenderness, knocks and bruises to bones. Treat heat, swelling, inflammation and bruising with cold packs immediately – preventing lameness is better than curing it. Arnica ointment is an excellent natural remedy to speed the healing of bruises and many riders use homoeopathic arnica treatment too. Joint inflammation and sore shins require rest and you must back off training until the symptoms subside. Appropriate therapeutic treatment prescribed by your vet may be helpful in some cases.

Check the feet daily to note the wear of shoes. More work means more frequent shoeing and you should be particularly careful that the hoof is not allowed to grow over the outside of the shoe at the heels as corns, once started, can become a chronic and frustrating problem. Insist on good heel support when your horse is shod (see Chapter 3); the extra work required at this stage can wreck the feet of an inadequately shod horse.

Condition

The muscles of an unfit horse in good condition (for example, on summer grass) are soft, almost blancmange-like in texture. The average riding horse develops firmer, more resilient muscles, but most are still covered with an appreciable layer of fat and the general appearance of the horse is rounded or well covered. As a horse of this level of fitness is trained upwards for endurance, the fat cover diminishes and the shape of the muscles becomes more clearly outlined. The muscle texture becomes harder and more strongly resilient to pressure. The reduction of fat cover reduces the cushioning effect between the muscles and nerves and the saddle so that the fit of the saddle becomes critical. Pressure points that were not evident before now begin to cause problems as pressure prevents the nerves from sending necessary messages to the muscles, which then begin to atrophy. This muscle-wasting effect is seen in the hollows which develop behind the withers or on either side of the spine under a badly fitting saddle. A saddle which was a good fit on the semi-fit horse may cease to fit properly as the horse's shape changes, so keep a constant check on the condition of your horse's back. Gentle palpation with your fingers can elicit a pain response from the horse at any sore points. (You will sometimes see people – even some vets – dig sharply along either side of the spine with finger and thumb and, of course, the horse flinches! This does not show evidence of a sore back, just that the person has hurt the horse and is completely unaware of how sensitive the animal is. Remember that a horse can feel a fly land on its skin and conduct your examination accordingly!) With the flat of your hand, feel for any areas of heat or raised skin; these are early warning signs that damage is already occurring and prompt action needs to be taken.

As the fat disappears, your horse will also become leaner. This must not be confused with thin and you do not want to see its ribs when the horse is standing still. The endurance horse, while much sparer in appearance than the average eventer, for example, still needs a good covering of muscle and a fraction too much weight is far better than not enough, especially at this stage of training. These bodily reserves are needed to help to build and develop power and strength in the muscles and to meet extra energy demands during competition. Some horses will lose a lot of weight during competition, others very little. Much depends upon the temperament and individual metabolism of the horse and on the conditions on the day. Highly strung, finicky feeders are more difficult to keep in good condition – although they may be good performers – than more placid individuals.

Feeding

This is directly related to condition and you must work out a diet and feeding regime that suits your horse in order to keep it in the right condition for the work it is doing. Appetite tempters, such as molasses, can be given in moderation. Herbal products or a good vitamin and mineral supplement can also help to improve appetite. Experiment to find out what your horse likes, but beware of giving a deluge of different additives all at the same time and, as far as possible, keep to natural products. Garlic, honey and cider vinegar may encourage appetite or disguise the taste of something the horse doesn't like, such as the water in a different district while competing away from home.

If your horse's appetite is fine but it is losing too much weight or lacking energy, gradually increase the amount of concentrates given, but also continue to feed as much high quality fibre as the horse will eat. Ease up on the workload until the horse's condition has stabilised.

Equipment

If you have reached the stage of regular competition at 40- and 50-mile (64 and 80 km) level, now is the time to consider whether to invest in more specialist equipment. There are many endurance saddles on the market, all with different features. No matter which one you choose, the principles of fitting for the horse must be as previously discussed. As far as comfort for the rider is concerned, see Chapter 5 on endurance equitation.

Numnahs must be chosen to minimise friction and the build up of heat under the saddle and natural wool or sheepskin remain the most popular, although medical fleece works well and synthetics are continually improving. Girths must also be chosen to minimise friction and natural fibres or neoprene girth covers are best.

The classic endurance bridle is the combination design which can be converted from bridle to headcollar simply by unclipping the cheekpieces to remove the bit. The noseband has a headcollar ring for the attachment of a leadrope. These make life very easy for your back-up crew during competition and mean that the horse can be given a drink with the bit removed within seconds. They are available in leather or synthetics such as nylon or biothane. The nylon type can be machine-washed, while the biothane simply rinses clean and also causes the minimum of friction and rubbing when worn.

If your horse is becoming increasingly strong in competitions as it becomes fitter, you may need to consider a different bit from that used for training at home and for schooling. Whatever bit you choose, the prime object is to avoid getting into a pulling match. The horse must respond and the rider must reciprocate through the principle of give and take, not just hang on. The inability of many riders to do this is the reason why the use of stronger bits is often discouraged by so-called experts and instructors. Paradoxically, the horse's ability to ignore even strong pressure on a mild bit is frequently the excuse for a rider

A Western reining bit which can be used as a snaffle, or with a curb chain. The copper rollers encourage salivation and help to make this a mild but effective bit.

to switch to stronger 'brakes', which he or she then wields with similar and more painful force, having completely failed to understand the basic principles of the rein aids.

Riding 40- and 50-mile (64 and 80 km) Set-speed Competitions

Your approach to these should be the same as for the lower mileages. The two essential differences are that you will probably be riding at a faster average speed to achieve the required result or qualification and there will be a halfway halt with a vet check.

The problem of riding faster takes care of itself provided you have done your training well and the conditions on the day are reasonable. You work out your checkpoint times in exactly the same way as for lower-distance rides and should, by now, be able to judge the speed your horse is making over given terrain at any particular gait, pace and rhythm.

Even on a cool day, the horse becomes warm and sweats when moving at speed, so sloshing is still necessary.

The halfway halt generally consists of a specified rest period, usually 30 minutes, during which you must present the horse for a veterinary inspection, typically 20 minutes after arrival. After the inspection, you have just about enough time to tack up and be on your way, so any care and attention to the horse, such as allowing it to drink and, if necessary, eat, and checking feet and shoes must be done before the vetting. Change your girth and numnah for clean, dry ones, too. Some competitive rides have a vet check without a rest period, in which case time spent in caring for the horse will come out of your riding time. Be aware of this but don't stint on the horse's needs.

From Set Speed to Endurance – the Next Step

There are some people who will happily ride numerous 50- or 60-mile (80 or 97 km) competitive rides, but quail at the unknown terrors and pitfalls of competing over the same distance in an endurance or so-called 'race' ride. The only real difference is that, in the latter, the element of competition against other horses and riders is introduced in addition to the test of distance, terrain, conditions and individual fitness of horse and rider. The competition procedures have been adapted to accommodate this factor, so that we have mass starts, highly skilled back-up crews and the 'vetgate and hold' system of veterinary inspection.

The lower-distance (50-mile or 80-km) endurance rides are usually won by very determined riders who get a kick out of the fast speeds attainable over this distance on comparatively tall, long-striding horses. These horses are not necessarily always good at the longer-distance endurance competitions. Many of the other competitors in the 50-mile endurance class, however, will be riders using the distance as a stepping stone to longer rides or, in the case of more experienced riders and horses, as a training ride for a major endurance competition. They will ride keenly but with circumspection and regard to their horses' welfare and future aims. The competitive rider with a horse ready to progress should therefore not be deterred by the fear that a 50-mile (80 km) endurance ride will be an uncontrolled free-for-all. In the next chapter we shall look at how to approach endurance riding, the differences in procedures and the job of the back-up crew, from basic level up to the 100-mile (160 km), one-day ride.

CHAPTER 10

COMPETING AT ADVANCED LEVEL

THE PROGRESSION from lower-distance, set-speed or competitive trail rides to 50-mile-plus (80 km+) endurance rides is really the point of graduation from the training levels of Novice and Intermediate competition to the senior, Open division of the sport. There are some higher-distance, top-level, set-speed rides, but these require a different approach from rides 'against the clock' and will be considered separately. First, we shall look at those rides which commonly fall within the worldwide definition of endurance, sometimes called 'race rides' or 'gated rides' and which culminate in the classic championship distance of 100 miles (160 km) in one day.

The horse and rider who have successfully competed in a range of lower-distance classes are ready to tackle a 50-mile (80 km) endurance ride – not to win, but to learn. If your horse is fit enough for a 50-mile CTR, it is fit enough for a 50-mile endurance ride, tackled sensibly. The fitness gained in early endurance rides will carry the horse forward to the next stage, supplemented by some adjustments to the training programme, which we shall consider later.

At this level of competition, having the right equipment in the right place at the right time begins to be a critical factor. Appendix 4 is a checklist of items which it is advisable to have for your horse, crew car and overnight stays.

The Competition

THE MASS START

The earlier the ride starts, the more difficult it is to persuade your body to wake up and tune in to what is expected of it. The prospect of riding 100 miles

The mass start at the Hague.

(160 km), starting at 3.30 am can seem a much crazier idea than that of riding 50 miles (80 km) starting at 9 am. Fortunately, in most countries the aspiring endurance rider can begin with the latter and, as most endurance rides begin reasonably early, there isn't too much time to be nervous. Most 50-milers will be one-day events, with the pre-ride vetting on the morning of the ride so, by the time you have registered, checked the notice board for route changes or collected your map and had your horse vetted, you will probably have only half an hour in which to tack up and warm up your horse before the start.

In competitive rides it is possible to warm up your horse *en route*, by starting out at a steady and moderate pace. In an endurance ride, however well intentioned you may be to start slowly, it is as well to be prepared and warm your horse up thoroughly before the start. Use the available time to work in, trotting some circles, gaining the horse's concentration, suppling it up, stretching its muscles and getting its circulation going. After ten minutes or so at trot, do some canter work, then drop back down to trot to calm the horse before the start. If the horse is excitable, take it away from the starting area, behind some horseboxes or to any quieter spot, to do this work. It is essential that your horse is listening to you at the start and not to the other equine competitors. If you have persevered with your flatwork over the past two years as advised, its value will be apparent now, if not before.

First-time competitors often view the idea of the mass start with trepidation but it need not be a traumatic experience if you keep your head and take a few sensible precautions. Most horses are too busy taking everything in to misbehave, or else are so accustomed to ride venues by now that they take the proceedings in their stride. Obviously, there are more horses milling about in a group than usual, so take special care to avoid putting your horse in a position where it can be kicked. If your horse is likely to lash out, resort to the red ribbon warning. (In some countries mass starts are the norm for qualifying and training rides, as well as for race rides.)

Ideally, set out in the second half of the field, allowing the faster, experienced horses to get away in a leading group and settling your horse down with the more steady-paced competitors. Do not interpret the fact that your horse

Early sun strikes this group of riders setting out on the World Championship ride. Third from the left is three times champion Becky Hart with R. O. Grand Sultan.

wants to speed off from the start to mean that it is a natural 'front runner'. Very few horses are truly front runners, especially in the context of endurance riding, when the front runner is likely to be an exhausted horse halfway through the competition! Of course, if your horse is a good endurance prospect, with a competitive nature, it is very likely to want to go faster than it should at the start. It is your job to settle and control it at the speed at which you feel it *should* go. If the horse is playing up and your only recourse is to pull back to a walk or get off and let everyone else clear off out of sight, so be it. You can always catch up later.

Some competitors prefer not even to start until the main field has departed from view and then trot out quietly behind. This can work if it is absolutely essential, for example if your horse is so hyper-excitable that you really can't control it in a group of fresh horses together. However, it does not teach the horse anything and it could become a disadvantage in later competitions. As long as your horse is not an actual danger to itself or others, take some deep breaths to relax yourself, start with the rest and sort your horse out on the trail.

The speed of the start depends upon the terrain over which the route runs. A big hill will quickly sort out the fit and well prepared from the less fit horses. Some, going too fast, may succumb to metabolic problems. A green motorway, on the other hand, will encourage a fast getaway *en masse*. Whatever confronts you, keep your wits about you and ride *your* horse, according to *your* plan, not somebody else's. Study your map well in advance so that you know what to expect and are prepared.

RIDING THE COMPETITION

Everything seems to happen faster in an endurance ride. Try to arrange for your crew to meet you within 5 miles (8 km) of the start so that they can cope with any unanticipated early problems. Thereafter, crew meeting points will be where the organisers permit or where the route is accessible. Some crews are much better than others at finding accessible places. You need a good driver and a good map reader and navigator. The crew must also be able to work out how long it will take by road to reach the places on the ride route where you want them to meet you. There is no point in your crew trying to meet you every other mile if they are going to be there too late. Missing the horse at the one vital checkpoint between inaccessible sections of route is even worse and could endanger the horse. A meet every 5 to 8 ridden miles (8–13 km) should be possible on most rides. Experience shows that the horse that is well and frequently crewed has a far better chance of success than the horse which is left to cover many miles between meets. Crewing must not delay the horse, however, and an experienced crew will know when and how often to stop their horse to offer a drink or otherwise minister to it and when it is sufficient to pass up a couple of slosh bottles on the run.

The crew should have all necessary equipment out of the back-up vehicle and ready for the horse before it reaches the meeting point. Usually this includes slosh bottles with caps off, a bucket of drinking water for the horse and a drink for the rider. These should be ready whether the horse and rider want them or not and the rider should have a drink whenever the horse stops – remember that by the time you are thirsty you are already dehydrated, so drink whenever the opportunity presents itself.

If the horse is making a fast average speed and the day is warm or humid, electrolytes may be offered, diluted in a separate bucket according to the manufacturer's instructions. If offering electrolytes, always also offer plain water and let the horse take its choice. Electrolytes are also available in syringes in paste form and can be given in this way provided the horse is already drinking well. Never give concentrated electrolytes to a horse which is showing signs of dehydration. (See Appendix 3 for more information about the use and misuse of electrolytes.)

Extra crew members can be positioned further along the route with additional slosh bottles. The rider should practise taking the slosh bottles while the horse is on the move and can discard them once emptied over the horse's neck. The crew then retrieve the empties for refilling. Do not leave empty bottles scattered around the countryside – you will not be welcomed back!

At the last meet before a vetgate or the finish, it can be helpful to stop the horse for a more thorough wash down, minimising the work and time required before presenting the horse in the vetgate by helping it to come in cool. This may not be possible on a fast ride if you are in hot contention but is good practice on your early endurance rides where your aim is a good completion, or on longer-distance rides where a few seconds spent in freshening up your horse may well be worth several minutes *en route* or in a vetgate.

Crewing should become more frequent as the ride progresses. Towards the end of a 100-mile (160 km) ride, every couple of miles is not too often if the route is accessible and if the rules allow. There is nothing more encouraging to a tired horse and rider than the sight of a friendly face waving a slosh bottle or drinking flask and cheering you on. The crew must, however, be sure to leave enough time to arrive at vetgates and the finish ahead of the horse. In most top-level rides, crewing is not permitted within the last $1\frac{1}{4}$ miles (2 km) before a vetgate.

In early endurance rides, your tactics should be simply to get your horse home safe, sound and having performed to the best of its ability. To conserve glycogen for later energy production, it is advisable to ride your horse well within its aerobic capacity for at least half an hour at the start of shorter endurance rides and for up to an hour on longer rides. This also continues the warming-up process, minimises lactic acid build-up and reduces any risk of metabolic stress (tying up) in the early stages. If you can ride with a heart rate monitor, aim to keep the heart rate under 140 bpm for this period. This can be

Australia's Brook Sample decides that getting off and running with your horse is the best way to tackle the traffic at the approach to a vetgate in the Hague.

very difficult, especially with an inexperienced endurance horse, as the heart rate is likely to rise rapidly if the pace is quick or if there is a strong pull uphill. Don't worry too much, but ease back whenever you notice your horse's heart rate rising over the 140 bpm mark.

After half an hour or so, on a 50-mile (80 km) ride, you can aim to ride with the heart rate around 150–160 bpm on good going for a horse beginning endurance competition. Obviously, the heart rate will fall when you have to slow down for stretches of bad going or if you are on level ground and this gives the horse a chance to recover so that it is not working at a level of maximum sustainable energy output throughout the ride. Developing a horse's

Running alongside your horse needs practice at home!

stride length and a rhythmic way of going helps it to cover ground economically and fast. However, this should be done within the respective gaits and paces, not persistently at a one-speed, extended trot. It has frequently been observed that changes of gait and pace at regular intervals, including changing diagonals at the trot, minimise the risk of muscle strain and delay the onset of fatigue.

Fitter, more seasoned horses will have a higher anaerobic threshold and can therefore safely make higher average speeds. In an endurance ride, unlike set-speed rides, you do not have the restriction of having to ride within a particular speed range, but are free to make the best possible time having regard to your horse's fitness and performance ability relative to the terrain and weather conditions on the day. Your skill in managing these four factors is at the heart of endurance riding. We shall look at how tactical riding can influence the competition in Chapters 11 and 12.

VETGATES

The principal difference between the vetgate system and other veterinary inspections is that the rider and crew decide when to present the horse for vetting and the time taken between arrival at the vetgate and presentation of the horse is included in your riding time. Therefore, the quicker you are able to have your horse ready for inspection, the greater the advantage that can be gained over fellow competitors who may have less fit horses or less skilled crews.

The average time taken by individual horses varies tremendously. Some fit horses with exceptionally good recovery rates are able to present almost immediately; others take anything up to 20 minutes. The maximum time after arrival in which you are allowed to present before being eliminated is usually 30 minutes. However, a horse well conditioned for the job should not take more than ten minutes for its heart rate to fall to the required maximum parameter. Between ten and 20 minutes is still acceptable but if a horse has not recovered sufficiently after 20 minutes, it is unlikely to do so within a further ten minutes. If it does, it may still fail the Ridgway test and, in any case, such a long recovery period is indicative of approaching fatigue and should be taken as a warning for the horse to slow down even if it is not eliminated.

Several factors can influence the time taken to present, apart from the horse's basic fitness level.

1 Speed of approach to the vetgate Ideally you want to arrive at a vetgate with the horse's heart rate already falling. It is therefore a good idea to slow down for the last stretch of trail into the gate. How far before the gate you slow down, and whether you slow to a jog, a walk or even dismount, is something you can learn only from experience with your particular horse. A heart rate monitor is an invaluable guide here as you can slow your horse's pace to arrive with an appropriate recovery rate, for example around 80–90 bpm, which, by the time you have dismounted and untacked, will have dropped again to near the required parameter. If you don't have a heart rate monitor but have kept a record of your horse's recovery rates during training, you should be able to make a fair guess at how much you will need to slow down for the heart rate to be falling steadily.

2 Crewing area within the vetgate layout Some vetgates are well organised, with plenty of space; more often space is limited and the vetgate area will be very busy. The ideal crewing spot is under a shady tree, close to the entrance to the actual vetting area but away from other competitors! On a hot day, finding a shady spot for your horse will help it to cool out faster. However, you must then be careful that the heart rate does not rise again if you have to stand in the sun waiting for your turn to vet. If your spot is close to the entrance of the vetting area, you can keep an eye on proceedings and present your horse when no one else is queueing up; there is also less chance of the heart rate creeping back up than if you had a longer walk to the vet. Choosing a spot away from others helps an excitable horse to keep calm, especially at vetgates

5
9

early in the ride when the horse is still fresh. It can take a long time to get this type of horse's heart down, the problem having nothing to do with tiredness but caused simply by excitement.

3 Weather conditions The production of energy for work also results in the conversion of a high proportion of energy to heat – a wasteful byproduct which must be dissipated to maintain the correct body temperature essential for the efficient functioning of vital body systems. The harder a horse works, the more heat it produces.

There are two principal ways in which the horse gets rid of this excess heat: first, by the evaporation of sweat and, second, in water vapour lost during exhalation. Both methods involve water loss and, ultimately, dehydration if the required fluid level is not restored. They also involve the loss of essential salts, particularly through sweating, which need to be replaced (see Appendix 3 on electrolytes).

In a situation of average exercise, in comfortable temperatures, the horse is able to replace any lost fluid and electrolytes by its usual eating and drinking routines. The extra energy required for endurance work, however, produces extra heat, more sweating, faster respiration and increased fluid and electrolyte loss. The extent to which this happens is regulated not only by the horse's individual type, muscle structure, body mass in relation to skin surface area and fitness, but by the external weather conditions. A cool breeze will help the dissipation of heat by convection. If it is raining as well, conduction comes into the equation and reduces the horse's need to sweat. The hotter the weather, the more the horse sweats; the higher the relative humidity, the less effective is the process of evaporation. On a chilly day, therefore, little or no mechanical cooling out by applying water is needed and a fit horse's heart rate should fall quickly. In environmental conditions which adversely affect the horse's ability to get rid of excess heat, the crew's help is needed.

4 Cooling out for vetting This procedure is often misunderstood and, consequently, is tackled ineffectively, sometimes with detrimental results for the horse.

On arrival at the vetgate, the horse should first be offered a drink. If it is too tense or stressed to drink immediately, the bucket should be offered again after a minute or two when the horse has begun to calm down and recover. Drinking replaces lost fluid, which helps to maintain the correct volume of blood for efficient circulation. If blood volume is reduced, the supply to the vital organs is maintained at the expense of other parts of the body. However,

OPPOSITE ABOVE *Crystal Calif, a top British horse, on his way to winning the 1988 National Championship ridden by Janet Maddock. International rider Denise Passant follows on Seagull.*

OPPOSITE BELOW *The British team finds a shady spot at the first vetgate on this ride in France.*

circulation to these areas – from the muscles to the skin – is needed to carry heat from the body core to the outside and a horse which drinks well in hot weather will have far less difficulty in maintaining normal body temperature, and will require less external cooling, than one which does not.

Cooling out 1994 Red Dragon winner, Warren's Hill Rustam, before the vetting.

The crew should then sum up the situation in terms of the heart rate reading, the horse's general appearance and attitude and the external conditions. The method and extent of cooling out should be decided on this information.

Aggressive cooling out with large amounts of water is unnecessary in moderate climatic conditions, even on race rides. The shock to the horse's system is often more detrimental to performance than the loss of a few minutes while the horse recovers more naturally. If there is even a slight breeze or the air is cool, the quarters should be rugged as soon as the horse is stopped on arrival at the vetgate, in order to keep the big muscles warm and prevent stiffening. Cool water can be applied intermittently to the large veins to assist the cooling process over a period of several minutes, while the crew also slacken the girth, monitor the heart rate, wash down the lower legs, pick out the feet and check for injuries. After a few minutes, removing the saddle will also help cooling by allowing more air to get to the skin. Massaging the large muscles will also assist circulation and TEAM work will help the horse to relax. Gentle walking may help recovery in some cases and, in any event, the horse should be walked for a few minutes before vetting to loosen up muscles which may be stiffening.

In most conditions, the water used for cooling should be cool but not so cold as to constrict the blood vessels near the surface of the body, which would have the effect of reducing the circulation and preventing heat transference to the surface. The water should be applied to areas where the large blood vessels are close to the surface – the underside of the neck, inside the front legs and between the thighs. The best method of application is a slow, steady stream, either by repeated sponging or hosing at moderate pressure.

Sponging the big veins inside the hind legs helps cool a horse down faster.

Where high relative humidity prevents effective evaporation, the water, once applied, should be scraped off to allow effective reapplication. In extremely hot and humid conditions, ice can be added to the water to keep it colder than the surrounding air.

The application of cold water to the large muscle masses of a stationary horse will result in cramps and stiffness and is to be avoided. Water sloshed on to these areas by the rider on a moving horse will help the horse to keep cool in very humid conditions, but is otherwise unnecessary and detrimental.

Water cooling can only remove heat from the body as fast as the blood circulation can carry it to the skin's surface. Once a horse begins to suffer from fatigue, both heart rate and respiration are elevated in a necessary attempt to keep the supplies of oxygen and nutrients going and to remove waste products. A fit horse, however, will intersperse normal deep breathing with shallow panting, in order to assist heat dissipation.

A back-up crew hard at work at a vetgate on a hot day.

Even in conditions of adverse heat and humidity, a fit horse should be ready to pass the veterinary parameters after about ten minutes of cooling out. If, after 20 minutes of continuous cooling, the heart rate is still too high, further cooling with water is likely to be ineffective. Even if the first reading is low enough, the second reading after a Ridgway trot will probably be elevated, indicating that the horse should be pulled. A high respiration rate and body core temperature are further indications of fatigue.

The most frequent error made by inexperienced crews, however, is that horses are drenched repeatedly in too much cold water in conditions which do not warrant it, in an attempt to bring the heart rate down too fast. The result is a chilled and shivering horse whose heart rate promptly rises again in an effort to keep warm!

5 Stage of ride and fitness of horse As a ride progresses and a horse becomes more tired, it is logical that it will take longer to recover at each successive vetgate. This tends to be especially true of a horse that is new to longer-distance endurance rides, whose fitness and acclimatisation to the work is not yet established, and the rider must be ready to slow down if the horse is not recovering as well as anticipated. The same thing does not necessarily happen with more experienced horses, however, as other factors intervene, such as varying difficulty of terrain, changing weather conditions and the rider's tactics. As already mentioned, some horses will take longer at the first vetgate due to nervous excitement. A particularly difficult stretch of track, with major hills, may tire horses more than a slower section later in the ride. Sometimes, good going can catch riders out, when riding at higher speed results in a longer recovery time. The rider's skill is required to interpret the situation and to ride the horse appropriately for the conditions.

THE VETERINARY INSPECTION

The procedure of the actual inspection will be similar to that for other rides. However, there are further aspects to consider. From the moment the horse is presented to the vet steward, the riding time stops and the hold time begins, whether or not there is a vet free to see the horse immediately. Hold times will vary from ten minutes to a full hour, depending upon the stage of the ride, the overall distance and the conditions on the day. However, every horse has the same hold time at any specific vetgate.

When the horse is taken to present, have a rug over its quarters and, if it is hot, a helper can take a bucket of water and a sponge along in case of a wait. The person presenting the horse should check the heart rate immediately before presentation as sometimes even a short walk on a hot day can send the heart rate up again. If there is a queue inside the presentation area, a decision must be taken whether to present immediately and join the queue or wait a few minutes, as further cooling may not be allowed once you have presented. At this point, it is vital to know the individual horse. Some horses have excellent recovery rates which never cause problems. Others may experience a fall, followed by a rise, while some may simply be slow to recover. Horses which are on the borderline of being fit enough for the task in hand often have fluctuating heart rates. Under most rules, heart rate monitors must be removed before presentation to the vet.

If the horse fails the vetting because of a high heart rate, a representation may be allowed, but this may not be any later than 30 minutes after the initial arrival time at the vetgate. If the horse passes the vetting, it will be directed to a hold area, where it can be attended by the back-up crew during the remainder of the hold time. If the hold is 15 minutes or less, there will be time only to tack up, with clean girth and numnah, and get ready to set off on the next stage. During a longer hold, the horse can be offered a feed and given a chance to rest while the rider also rests and has something to eat and drink. Before leaving, the heart rate should be checked again and the horse should be offered a last drink. The rider should check the tack before mounting and that he or she has

Brook Sample's crew checks Sharahd Cavalier's heartrate before presenting to the vet at the second vetgate at the Hague.

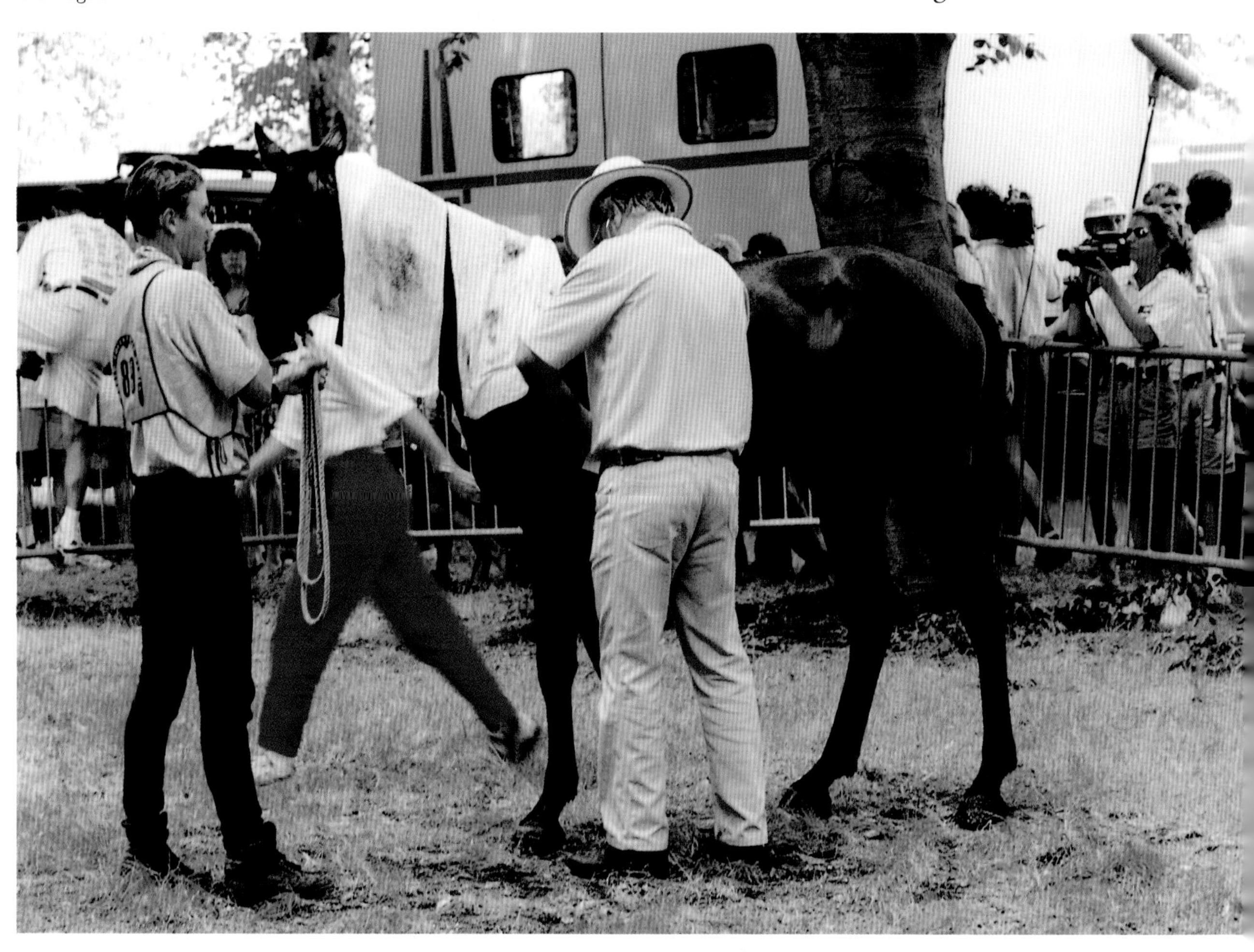

the rider card if one has to be carried. The horse's neck should be sponged or sloshed just prior to departure to delay the onset of sweating.

Learning to cope with vetgates – for horse, rider and back-up crew – will take a little practice, but it is an important aspect of the sport to learn in preparation for more serious competition.

The final vetting will be either 30 minutes after the horse finishes or, sometimes, at the rider's discretion at any time within 30 minutes of finishing. However, there is no representation this time, so, if presenting early, it is essential to be sure that the horse is ready.

Extending the Training/Competition Programme

If all has gone well with the training programme, the horse should have reached this level by the end of its second season or early in its third season, depending on age (perhaps earlier for mature horses which previously competed in other sports). It will be developing strength and stamina and will have learned the job fairly well. Regular competition will enhance physical and mental fitness and fewer miles will need to be covered in training at home. A balance must now be struck between enough work to maintain condition and too much wear and tear on the limbs. The trainer must observe the horse on a daily basis and make adjustments to the programme as necessary.

The options for competitions between the 50-mile (80 km) and the one-day 100-mile (160 km) ride are varied. Over the course of a season you can set up a progressive programme to gain more experience which could include one-day rides of 50–80 miles (80–129 km), or multi-day rides of varying distances, from the two-day 75 (121 km) or 100 miles (160 km), to three- or four-day competitions. It is preferable to tackle some of these longer rides than to do too many 50-milers. At this stage, if you want your horse to have a long and successful endurance career, you should aim to add distance to the equation, not speed, and once your horse is capable of going 50 miles (80 km) the temptation simply to do the same thing faster is quite great. This is a good way to wreck a promising young prospect. If you consider that 50-mile rides are often won at speeds in excess of 12 mph (19 kmph), whereas the winning speed for most 100-mile (160 km) rides is likely to be between 8 and 10 mph (13–16 kmph) (except for major championships held on the flatter courses), you will see that this extra speed puts considerably more stress on the legs than extra distance, so why risk everything you have worked for.

Endurance riding is a game of horsemanship and 'thinking' riding, not a flat-out free for all. Also try to include some more difficult courses and some easier ones in your programme – the more difficult ones to provide a harder test, the easier routes to give the horse a mental break.

Competition plans must be flexible to allow for unforeseen setbacks but, basically, you should plan for one serious competition every month to six weeks. Increase the difficulty of the test on a progressive basis. A shorter-distance competition, such as a 30- or 40-mile (48 or 64 km) set-speed ride, can be included between the bigger rides as part of your training programme.

It's all team work! Jo Trego, Oliver's Taboo and supporters after taking second place and best condition at the British National Championship in 1994.

Multi-day Rides

Multi-day rides are fun and are a good means of preparing horse and rider for the longer-distance one-day events. The horse has the benefit of an overnight rest between stages but is asked to perform again next day and this is an excellent way of adding fitness without excessive stress. It is sometimes suggested that multi-day rides are more difficult because of the risk of the horse stiffening up overnight. Provided the horse is well managed, this will not happen. At the end of each day's work the horse should be walked to allow the muscles to get rid of waste products, and then allowed to graze and relax before being stabled. Outside corralling is preferable, if possible. Legs and backs must be carefully checked for injuries, minor wounds treated appropriately and ice-packs used for any heat or swelling. As always, massage is recommended. A small feed can be given when the horse is put away, and another late in the evening, plus the usual ration of good quality forage. The horse should be checked several times during the evening, just as it should after any long ride.

Next morning, check the horse over in the box, then take it out in good time to walk it out or lunge it before the morning vetting, to allow muscles a chance to stretch and warm up.

Multi-day rides are also good for the rider, as they condition the riding muscles to cope with longer periods of work! The rider should, by now, be fairly fit but the additional time in the saddle will, initially, take its toll. As with any form of unaccustomed sporting activity, the third consecutive day is usually the worst, as tired muscles lose their elasticity.

Multi-day rides can be either race rides or set-speed rides. The race type are tackled as any other race ride, the only difference being that, after the first day, there may be the usual mass start with times adjusted for the previous day's finishing times, or there may be a staggered start, taking account of the previous day's finishing times. Both have disadvantages. In the former case, it can be difficult to know where you stand in the placings; in the latter, riders can become very spread out and you may have to ride on your own for miles.

The set-speed rides pose a different problem as a relatively high average speed has to be maintained, and the horse must not collect any veterinary penalties, to obtain the highest award. If the terrain and weather conditions are also tough, this can prove an impossible task and the effort for the horse can be even greater than for a race ride, where you can at least adjust your speed to suit the conditions and competition on the day. Once again, knowing your horse is all important and you must be prepared, at any stage during the ride, to drop your speed to a lower classification if indications that your horse is tiring appear, before it is too late and fatigue sets in. We shall deal with signs of tiredness in the next chapter.

From now on, both horse and rider will be put under greater mental pressure as the day in the saddle becomes longer and new distance barriers are broken. Increasing the distance of your competitions progressively will help you to cope with this and we are now ready to move on and prepare for the ultimate challenge – the one-day, 100-mile (160 km) ride.

CHAPTER 11

THE ONE-DAY 100

THE ONE-DAY 100-mile (160 km) ride is the greatest challenge in the sport of endurance, no less for the first-time contender, hoping just to complete the distance with a fit, sound horse, than for the seasoned competitor out to win on an experienced horse. How do you prepare for such a challenge?

Fine-tuning Fitness

There is a certain amount of truth in the adage that if you only train a horse over long, slow distances, you will have one that is capable only of going a long way slowly! This may even be sufficient for the rider whose only aim is to get round, but for the true endurance enthusiast that is not enough. Throughout the long period of training from inexperienced novice to fully fledged endurance horse, each new challenge must be treated with respect. At any point on the way, the rider can opt to stay at that level and not aim higher but for the committed endurance rider all the shorter-distance competitions are a means of preparation for major rides. Once the horse has successfully completed a major event, it is time to think about getting placed or even winning.

The training and competition programme outlined so far has conditioned the horse to cope with extended distance at a good average speed, using mainly the aerobic energy metabolism (see Chapters 6 and 9).

The capacity to produce energy anaerobically for very short periods, recruiting the fast-twitch, low-oxidative muscle fibres, will, however, have been used whenever the situation has demanded a sudden surge of effort, for example when tackling a short, steep slope or in a sprint to the finish against another competitor. Although the horse will use aerobic energy production for the majority of a ride, the ability to extend its capacity for anaerobic energy production can be enhanced by training and will be useful when it reaches a level where outpacing a rival contender comes into the tactical equation. This type of training should be regarded as a 'top up' to the principal aerobic work and must be limited to no more than once a week in the final build-up to a major ride. If too much fast work is done, the aerobic capacity will suffer, with consequent loss of stamina.

Once the horse begins to gain experience in race riding, this fast work can be introduced in the form of interval training. It must not be attempted until the horse has reached this stage and has the basic groundwork of aerobic conditioning and physical adaptation to minimise the risk of strain. The aim of this work is to push the heart rate up to between 180 and 200 bpm for about two minutes. This is followed by a similar recovery period, during which the heart rate should fall quickly to around 100. If the horse takes longer to recover, then too much has been asked and the work should be waived until the horse is fitter. If the horse recovers well, the number of efforts can be progressively increased over several weeks to no more than four or five intervals in one session.

When undertaking this form of training, it is essential to keep a close check on the horse's legs and stop immediately if any heat or swelling becomes apparent. The horse must be rested and treated with the appropriate method of therapy until all symptoms have disappeared, when it can slowly be brought back into work. Carefully monitored and judiciously scheduled fast work will enhance physical strength and resilience as well as improving the capacity for anaerobic energy production, but overstress at this level can result in irreparable damage or, at the least, damage that will take a long period of rest to cure.

It can be difficult to achieve the intensity of effort required to produce heart rates of 180+ unless you have a racetrack to work on. Utilising hills or carrying weight can help to achieve the desired effect but do be sure that the going underfoot is safe for galloping.

The Countdown to the Ride

The first one-day, 100-mile (160 km) ride will be the major feature on the season's calendar and although allowance must be made for setbacks and each ride must be taken as it comes, it is not unreasonable to plan your programme towards this achievement. Work backwards from the big day and allow for at least two other serious competitions as potential warm-ups. How much work you need to do in preparation for these will depend upon the type of ride, distance and dates relative to the beginning of the season and the date of the 100-miler. No hard rule can be laid down. By this stage the individual competitor should know his or her horse well enough to plan its basic programme of competition and training. The 100-mile event should simply follow as a natural progression.

Horses also vary in the amount of time off they need between competitions. Some riders allow a few days after a ride before bringing the horse back into work; others may allow as much as a fortnight or, if the event has been particularly hard, three weeks. It is also necessary to decide whether the horse should have time off before a major competition. Ideally, the build-up programme will end about a week before the big event and the horse will need only to be kept ticking over in the final days with a couple of leg-stretching hacks and perhaps a schooling session or some lungeing. By this stage it is certainly too late to do more fitness training and a couple of days' break during the week before the ride gives an opportunity for the horse to relax and get rid of any tension or stiffness.

During the weeks prior to the ride, fitness training will concentrate mainly on tuning up the muscles and body systems with fast work once a week, interspersed with schooling and some relaxational sessions of a mixture of work (*fartlek*). Basic aerobic work will have been taken care of during the early part of the season, consolidated with shorter-distance competitions, building up to the bigger warm-up events in preparation for the 100-miler (160 km).

The further the horse progresses in endurance competition, the more critical the various aspects of management become and attention must again be paid to the following:

DIET

Additional work requires additional fuel for energy and although the basis of the diet must remain good quality fibre, the ration of concentrates will need to be progressively increased, commensurate with the work. At this stage it is easy to overfeed, so do not increase the level of feed too quickly but be alert for any slight falling off in condition or loss of enthusiasm for work. Early in this season is also the time to think of including a higher ratio of fat in the horse's diet, to provide more energy without notably increasing the volume of the feed. Any form of vegetable oil may be used and your regular vitamin and mineral supplement may need to be changed for one with appropriately higher levels of vitamin E and selenium which are necessary when feeding a high-fat diet (see Chapter 4).

HEALTH

A fit, highly tuned animal that is subject to the repetitive stresses of training and competition may actually become more vulnerable to infections and health problems than a horse working at a lower level, or at least be more severely affected in terms of performance and peaking for a particular event. Routine health treatments, such as worming and vaccinations, must not be neglected and the trainer should also be aware of problems induced by stress and travelling and should monitor vital signs, including temperature, provide any appropriate treatment and allow the horse suitable time for acclimatisation and rest as applicable. If there is any doubt concerning any of these matters, veterinary advice should be sought.

The horse's general health should also be under constant observation. For example, it may suffer due to overtraining, adverse environmental effects, changes in routine, variation in the quality of feed, particularly forage, changes in management or equine companions, or any number of other things. Overtraining, in particular, may be characterised by loss of muscle bulk, tightening of the skin and a loss of the shine seen in a healthy coat, coupled with listlessness, loss of stamina or general unwillingness to work and susceptibility to metabolic problems. The only cure is a complete break from competition and training while the horse recovers its lost condition and basic health.

FEET

Competing over longer distances will accentuate any problems of foot balance or asymmetrical action and the level of wear on the shoes should be noted and corrective action taken if necessary. Wider-web shoes, which cover more of the sole, offer more support and better protection than the standard size which varies depending upon hoof size.

RECORD KEEPING

At this level of competition, records of performance data are even more useful than during basic training and Novice competition. They enable a complete picture of the horse's performance history to be built up and sometimes a pattern of events can be detected which gives a clue to an apparently insoluble problem. They are also useful for reference when discussing problems with the vet or farrier and can help the trainer to prevent mistakes or problems recurring.

Rider Factors

It should not be forgotten that the rider is an equal part of the competitive combination and as much attention needs to be paid to the health, fitness, comfort and preparedness of the rider as of the horse. The rider's fitness is discussed in Chapter 5 but, in preparing for a major competition, health and diet should also be taken into account.

Enough sleep is an essential prerequisite to peak performance. The body needs sleep for both mental and physical relaxation and to repair body tissues. This does not just mean an early night before the ride but, ideally, no late nights for several days.

A basic healthy diet is integral to athletic fitness. However, to prepare for a specific event, the principle of 'carbohydrate loading' can be utilised. There are several variations on this idea, but the basic method is to increase intake of carbohydrate foods in regular small amounts for several days prior to an event to build up energy reserves. Advice from a qualified nutritionist should be sought before making any drastic changes to your diet.

Human performance can be seriously limited by dehydration and it is advisable for the rider not only to start the competition well hydrated but to avoid substances which have a dehydrating effect, such as coffee and alcohol, in the last day or so before the event.

Attention should be paid to comfort as extra distance will turn slight rubs into painful sores or bruises, and the fit of all clothing needs to be checked. This applies equally to the horse – don't use anything new and untried.

The Ride

If you can arrive early and reconnoitre some of the route and vetgates, so much the better. Be sure that you have the best available map of the area, with copies for both rider and crew. Load the crew vehicle in good time and check that nothing has been forgotten. A rider and crew member should go to the briefing and be sure to note any late route changes, where the crew may and may not go or other information not already provided.

Pre-ride veterinary examinations are often conducted in the stables, so there may be little chance to warm the horse up for the trot up but it should be walked briskly or given a short trot to ensure that it is moving freely before it is trotted in front of the veterinary panel. At a major ride the trot up will usually be watched by the entire veterinary panel so that they can all establish in their own minds how each horse that they will judge later is moving before the start of the ride.

When everything is as prepared as it can be, a crew member should be detailed to give the horse its late and early feeds and the rest should turn in early. Tomorrow will be a long day!

The Start

The start of a one-day, 100-mile (160 km) ride may be any time from 3.30 am onwards, depending on the time of year and location of the ride. Most people

It is important to keep the horse straight when trotting up for the vet.

do not feel like breakfast at such an hour but the rider should eat something. Organising your own food the night before and leaving it ready is probably better than trying to eat something the ride organisation may provide and which you may not be able to face. The crew can take food with them and eat while waiting at a checkpoint. It is vital that the crew refuel themselves with food and drink regularly during the day. Crewing is hard work and it is easy to forget to eat.

There is often a morning trot up before the start, with the horse tacked up and ready to go. Get up early enough to be on time without rushing and to allow time to warm up the horse – remember that its body systems also slow down during the night while it is resting.

The horse should be at the start several minutes before the off, well warmed up, so that the rider can choose a suitable position in the field. For the first 100-mile (160 km) attempt this is likely to be about two-thirds of the way down the pack, where the horse can be settled, stay out of trouble and avoid being towed too fast by the leaders. The start is usually a spoken countdown, sometimes ending with the words 'The route is now open for competition'. Sometimes, the horses will be led for the first stretch by a car or motorbike, especially if it is along a roadway. At a given point the vehicle will peel off and the route will be open.

Early Stages

Near the back of the pack, in semi-darkness, the rider may not see much for the first few miles except the tail of the horse in front. Some riders like to wear a helmet-mounted light, others prefer to let their eyes become accustomed to the dim light naturally, especially as the horse's ability to see where it is going can be disturbed by artificial lighting. The same applies if it gets dark before you reach the finish.

How to ride the early part of the race depends greatly on the terrain. In open country the light will be better. If there are hills, the horses will settle and spread out more quickly. If there are narrow tracks, with overhanging trees, it will be darker and the horses will bunch together more, especially if the terrain is flat. In this situation, the rider must concentrate on keeping a fresh horse out of trouble, not treading on the one in front and staying clear of the one behind.

Now is also the time for the rider to sort out his or her own tension and settle into the ride. Pre-race nerves should quickly disappear but it is easy to stay tense and tight in the hurly burly of the start. Try to relax. Take deep, 'centred' breaths to help this. Think how you are riding and run a checklist through your mind: shoulders, back, hips, knees, ankles, wrists, hands. Are they all supple and relaxed? You will not last 100 miles (160 km) in relative comfort if they are screwed up tight. Also, if you can relax and ride well, it will help your horse to relax, carry itself efficiently and conserve energy.

How fast should you be going at this stage?

Every rider should know their own horse and what it has proved capable of in the past and this should give you a good idea of the speed you can expect to start out at, relative to the overall demands of the competition, bearing in mind weather conditions and terrain. A useful guide is to cover the early miles at roughly the average speed you expect to make for the whole competition. Fit, experienced horses and others with less wise riders will go faster, but if you do that on your first 100, you are not going to make the finish. Go much slower,

Horses grouped together in the fast early stages of the ride. Have your horse under control, your wits about you and watch your back!

on the other hand, and you will leave yourself a hard task in making up the lost ground. Obviously, if there is a big hill or some other problem, allowances have to be made.

If you are using a heart rate monitor, aim to keep the heart rate under 140 bpm for the first hour. This may sometimes seem too slow but it will pay dividends later. Also remember that your first 100-miler is a learning process; you are not there to win. You will learn more and arm yourself with much more knowledge for the future if you ride prudently now and finish the ride, than if you burn out your horse's reserves before the end.

Psychological Factors

The thought of riding 100 miles (160 km) can be daunting for the fittest rider and there are different ways of coping with the idea. One of the most effective is to think of the ride in stages. For example, think of each phase between vet-gates as a 25-mile (40 km) CTR. You know you can cope with that and when the first is behind you, all you have to do is cope with the next one.

Sometimes there is a known hazard or difficulty to be encountered on the route, for example a big climb in the third stage. The way to cope with this is to study the rest of the route in advance, using your map if you can't actually reconnoitre and plan how you will ride the whole thing, making an allowance

British international rider Kate McIver and Silver Rabba at Nancy in France.

for this difficult section. Find out where the good going is and plan to make up time on that. Plan to have your crew meet you at the best point to help your horse over this testing section. In this way, major obstacles can be kept in perspective.

First Vetgate

The first vetgate will probably seem to arrive very quickly. Fit, experienced horses will pass in a few minutes; excitable ones will have problems and unfit or overridden horses will be found out here. Aim to come in at a slowing pace on a falling heart rate. Ideally, by now the rider should have a seasoned crew and will have enough confidence in them to let them take over. Early vetgates are usually chilly so the horse needs a rug over its quarters straightaway, even though it may be steaming from exertion in the cool morning air. Treat the vetgate like a normal one in any other shorter ride.

The hold will probably be fairly short, 20 minutes in good or cool conditions, perhaps longer if it is hot. Sloppy sugar beet or water with soaked sugar beet added is a good choice to offer here; a separate bucket with electrolytes added can also be offered if the horse has been sweating heavily, but make sure that plain water is also available. Concentrates may be offered but, unless it is habitually greedy, the horse is unlikely to be very interested at this stage. If grass is available, let the horse graze.

The crew must be ready to take the horse over as soon as the rider dismounts. Here, Becky Hart's crew take charge of R. O. Grand Sultan as he arrives at a vetgate.

Becky Hart trots up R. O. Grand Sultan at a vetgate in the Hague.

The Second Stage

By now, it will be full daylight, the rider and horse should have settled into the race and the field will have been sorted into better order by the vetgate. There will probably be a strong leading group, with the rest in smaller groups at varying speeds, and a few stragglers. If all has gone well, the first-time competitor on a well-prepared horse will be somewhere between half and two-thirds of the way down the field, or perhaps a bit better placed if there are very few entries or if the horse has gone through the vetting quickly. It is amazing how many places can be made up by good vetgate technique.

It is easy now to settle into company with one or a group of other competitors and simply ride with them. However, that is not a course to be recommended. Horses often naturally adjust their paces to stay together, following the herd instinct; even the leader of a group will tend to maintain a speed that keeps it just in front of the rest. The rider must stay alert and *ride* the horse. Do you want to be going this fast or this slow? Can you make better speed on this particular ground? Are the others risking lameness by going too fast over a bad stretch? If your horse is good at going up- or downhill, there may be an opportunity to break away from this group and gain an advantage of several places. Also, the horse should travel at a speed which suits its own paces and stride length, not one which is adapted to fall in with other horses.

Courtesy to other competitors and, even more importantly, to other users and owners of the land over which you are riding is vital to the continuance of the sport. For example, if another horse is the only one left drinking when yours has finished, you should wait until the other horse has drunk its fill, however impatient you are to be away. Walkers, cyclists and private landowners are not in the race and do not want to be mown down by speeding horses. Slow down as you pass – to walk if the track is narrow – give a polite greeting and thank them if they have moved aside for you.

In British rides, dealing with gates often causes complaint. The idea that the person who opens the gate should also shut it, although technically correct, is impractical where there is a group of riders, especially if there are a number of gates in quick succession. It is common practice for the first rider to open the gate and ask the following riders to close it as the alternatives are to allow the rest to pass or to shut the gate in their faces. It is then incumbent on the last two to wait for each other while one of them latches the gate. Galloping off and leaving one person to close a gate is extremely bad manners. If you are in a situation where there is a short gap between your horse and others going through gates ahead of you, but still within calling distance, they should, technically, shut the gate in front of you. They may, however, leave it for you, provided they have indicated that that is what they are doing and you have confirmed that you will shut it and provided there is no risk of livestock escaping in the meantime. However, in these circumstances you cannot expect them to wait for you to catch up.

At this stage of the competition the horse should be able to work maintaining a heart rate of around 160 bpm, with breaks for slower going.

Second Vetgate

The horse has now done an appreciable amount of work and is halfway through the ride. The speed with which it passes the vetting and the heart rates at the Ridgway trot will indicate how well it is coping. If it passes in less than ten minutes and the heart rates are under 60, with the second reading the same or lower than the first, everything is under control and the horse has the all clear to continue the ride according to planned tactics.

If the horse takes longer than ten minutes to present but less than 20 and the heart rates are in the 50s with the second pulse lower than the first, then all is well, but perhaps the pre-presentation crewing could have been better managed and the horse presented sooner.

Vetgates at international rides can be stressful and crowded. Here the crew get to work on European Champion Jill Thomas's Egyptian Khalifa.

This hay bag is one of many useful items devised for endurance riders.

If the horse takes longer than 20 minutes to present, or if both heart rates are 60+, or if they are lower but the second reading is more than four beats higher than the first, then the horse is tiring and the rider should slow the pace sufficiently to allow the horse time to recover. Careful management is needed during the hold to give the horse the best chance of continuing to the finish.

Cathy Brown trots up her 1992 ELDRIC Champion, King Minos, at the Barcelona World Championships.

This crew have devised a shower system to cool their horse.

At this stage of a 100-mile (160 km) ride, all horses should be offered a small, moist feed of concentrates. It is as well to take a variety, say coarse mix plus oats or barley, as a horse's tastes can change during the course of a ride. Sliced carrots or apples may tempt the horse to eat and the usual soaked sugar beet is invariably acceptable.

Proprietary carbohydrate 'boosters', basically comprising a combination of partially pre-digested starch and fructose, are gaining in popularity and may be given before and during competition, according to the manufacturers' instructions. However, the middle of your first 100-miler is not the time to experiment. Try them out, if you wish, on a testing but less important ride (see Appendix 2).

Electrolytes may be offered, as before.

Remember to refuel the rider! Tiring riders often refuse to eat and it is the crew's job to make sure that they do, to keep energy levels up. Stick to carbohydrate snacks, either proprietary sporting bars, drinks or gel sachets, or cereal bars and bananas. Avoid chocolate and too much sugar.

The Third Stage

From now on, the crew should meet the horse as often as possible, as moral encouragement for both horse and rider becomes increasingly important. Now is the time when fit horses will move up the field and the less fit will slow down. If your horse is going well, take advantage of good going.

Continue to think about your riding. As you become tired, muscles tense up or contract, so consciously relax them. Also take care to stay balanced and help your horse as much as possible. A fit horse should be able to continue at the same heart rates as before, a tiring one needs to drop speed to keep to these heart rates and to slow further to recover energy resources.

A fit rider can help a tiring horse by dismounting to run down hills and walk up them. The removal of the rider's weight from the horse's back makes an appreciable difference to the effort a horse has to make and the heart rate will fall commensurately. The rider's ability to do this can easily make the difference between finishing a competition or not finishing it and between finishing with a good placing or not. Walking or running for a while also gives the rider's muscles a break and gets rid of tension or stiffness.

The Third Vetgate

This is usually approached with a feeling of relief. Only 25 miles (40 km) to go and you are still in the race!

All the points mentioned concerning presentation at the previous vetgate also apply here. This is the stage at which the first-time 100-mile (160 km) horse is most likely to reach a tiredness threshold and take longer to present. The results of the vetting must be interpreted and taken into account when deciding tactics for the last stage. Also consider the horse's attitude. Is it happy, eating and drinking or wanting to graze? Or is it dull and listless? Keep a check on the heart rate during the hold and consult a vet if it rises or if there are any other worrying signs, such as reluctance to move or colicky symptoms. Better to pull out now than have a sick horse on your hands.

A tiring horse feels the cold more quickly and stiffens up more quickly, so make sure it is kept warm during the hold. Use massage to help the circulation and encourage relaxation. Give the rider one too! Offer another feed and plenty of water. Allow as much time to rest as possible but have the horse tacked up in time to walk around and stretch its muscles before setting off again.

ABOVE *When the weather is chilly, the horse must be kept warm for the vetting.*

ABOVE RIGHT *Rest and refreshment are essential for the rider during the holds.*

RIGHT *At the 1991 European Championships international vet Franz Arts checks Jane Donovan's Ibriz, placed fourth.*

The Last 25 Miles

Horses have a wonderful ability to recognise landmarks and also a strong sense of direction. If the last part of the route is the same as the first, but ridden in reverse, the horse will soon realise that it is on its way home and may well perk up considerably. Even if the actual route is different, if the finish is at the same place as the start, the horse will know that that is where it is heading for.

One danger to be aware of here is that a strongly competitive horse, full of adrenalin, may well continue at a faster speed than its resources can support. A close watch needs to be kept on the heart rate, on the horse's general appearance and on how it is going, and if the horse appears to be doing better than predicted by its performance at the previous vetgate, the rider should be warned to proceed with care. Such a horse might well trot cheerfully through the finish and then succumb to exhaustion, requiring prompt and aggressive veterinary treatment.

Sometimes the front runners in a major 100-mile (160 km) ride will speed up considerably in the last phase and it can be a hard decision not to try to keep pace with more experienced and stronger horses. A horse is entitled to be tired after 100 miles but the aim is that it should pass the final vetting in good condition and that will not happen if tiredness develops into fatigue. Therefore, it is important for the rider to be aware of the early signs of tiredness, which may not have been encountered previously in shorter-distance competitions.

Things the rider is likely to notice include increased respiration, with occasional deep, sighing breaths as the horse attempts to increase its oxygen intake. Some horses, particularly Arabs, may also try to stretch their necks forward and down for the same purpose. Horses may change legs more frequently at the canter, try with more determination to shift the rider to the favoured diagonal at the trot, or change gait between trot and canter more often. Stumbling and inattention to the going, loss of interest in keeping up with overtaking horses and slowing more quickly to a walk when going uphill, are all indications that the horse is beginning to tire physically. Slowing down now should prevent further trouble.

Physiological signs obviously include a higher heart rate to maintain the same effort, slower recovery rates when the effort is reduced, raised respiration rate, raised temperature, reduced gut sounds and signs of dehydration. The latter is symptomised by decreased skin elasticity, as shown by the pinch test, decreased sweating and evidence of dried salt deposits on the coat, slow capillary refill, reddened mucous membranes (instead of pink) and darker-coloured urine. A horse showing any of these symptoms must be given as much opportunity to rehydrate as possible and, if it continues, must slow right down, even to a walk if necessary, for the final stages. The vet at the previous vetgate will have noted the horse's degree of tiredness and if he or she considers the horse is still fit to continue, may well warn the rider to proceed slowly. If there is a combination of too many of these clinical signs, the vet will eliminate the horse.

A hot day in Holland. Rick Wiggans and Rani Tarina receive attention from their crew en route.

Mental tiredness is typified by 'switching off'. The horse simply loses interest in what is happening and becomes dull to ride. It is likely to be reluctant to lead a group or another horse, prefering to tuck its nose in behind and be 'towed' along. Riders often complain that other riders have used them 'to get a tow'. A horse in this situation may be genuinely tired and the heart rate is the best clue to this. However, it might simply be mentally overwhelmed or be going through what is usually called 'the wall'. This is the point where the readily available energy resources from food and nutrients in its system have been used up and the horse has to switch to another source, that of stored fat, or rest until the nutrients available from food have been replenished.

If all the signs, except the horse's attitude, are good, it is fairly safe to assume that this is the case and to give the horse a breather but continue in the ride. Once the alternative supply of fuel begins to reach the muscles, the horse should recover its enthusiasm and be ready to move on faster. The utilisation of a high-fat diet and the use of carbohydrate boosters are both aimed at prolonging the horse's capacity to work before reaching this 'wall', ideally beyond the distance of the competition. Getting a 'tow' from another competitor can be a useful tactic for a horse going through this temporary condition but you will not be popular if you use it to excess.

There is invariably a final vetgate between 5 and 10 miles (8–16 km) from the finish, which will pick up really tired horses. Fortunately, today the veterinary control standards of major rides ensure the maximum protection of all competing horses and serious casualties through overstress are very rare.

Keeping yourself and your horse going when you may be totally alone for many miles is both a challenge and a joy of endurance riding. As you help each other towards that distant finish line, the sense of comradeship between horse and rider is unsurpassable, and when the end is finally in sight, the knowledge of what you have achieved together (with the help of a supportive back-up crew) will soothe away all the aches and pains.

The Final Vetting

This can be unbelievably nerve-wracking but, provided the horse has been well managed and is sound, should not pose any problems. If your horse does get eliminated, ask yourself why. We shall deal with some of those problems, and their solutions, in the final chapter.

Aftercare

This should be the same as for other long rides, but more so. Make sure the horse has cooled out properly and is relaxed and happy before it is put up for the night. The horse will have few reserves of energy for keeping warm, so make sure it is adequately rugged. Give two or three small, moist feeds over the next few hours, rather than one large one, provide plenty of fresh clean plain water, plus some with electrolytes, and replenish the haynet as the horse empties it. Treat legs according to your normal practice. Leave the horse to rest but check on it every hour until you are certain all is well, then once or twice during the night.

At top rides, best condition judging may take place the day after the ride. Here is a fit, well-muscled horse ready for judging.

In best-condition judging, the vet will take the horse's attitude and bodily condition into account, as well as soundness, injuries and final heart recovery rates.

CHAPTER 12

ASPECTS OF WINNING – AND LOSING!

THE WHOLE ethic of endurance riding is based on the premise of rider, horse and horsemanship against terrain, time and conditions. The idea of competing against other riders to win or earn a top-ten placing preoccupies a relatively small group of people. However, insofar as public imagination is gripped at all by the sport, this is the aspect which gains publicity and which has taken endurance riding to recognised international level. Fortunately, there is room for both types of competitor. In fact, the so-called élite could not exist without the interest and support of the hundreds of riders whose sole aim is the personal satisfaction of doing the best job possible with the horse they happen to own.

If, however, your aim is to join that élite band of competitors who regularly make the highest placings in the major rides, and perhaps compete internationally, you will have to bring a number of extra factors into your personal equation.

First, time spent and dedication must increase. Instead of fitting your training around other commitments, your horse's needs become paramount. If that means getting up two hours earlier in the morning to train before work, ask yourself how much you really want to do this.

Secondly, you must work at extending your knowledge of horse management and train your powers of observation of your horse to recognise to the finest degree if something is going wrong before it actually happens. You must also know what to do to put it right before it becomes a serious, performance-threatening problem. A patch of roughed-up hair under the saddle, a barely noticeable spot of heat in a leg, a slight shortening of front action, a higher than usual resting heart rate or temperature, and minimal loss of weight are all examples of potential trouble which can be averted by taking prompt action.

ABOVE *The victorious Irish team at the 1993 Home International endurance ride, smartly turned out.*

Former ELDRIC Champions and World Silver Medallists, Jane Donovan and Ibriz.

Some riders start competing in race rides, reach a certain level and can get no further even with basic good management. Either the horse or the riding technique is simply not up to the task. As far as the horse is concerned, different horses are capable of different jobs. A horse may be a brilliant all-round family horse, capable of doing lower-level endurance rides among its other achievements, but simply may not have the physiology, paces, conformation and attitude necessary for top-level endurance work. In this situation, if you want to excel in endurance, the only answer is to get the right type of horse for the job (see Chapters 1 and 2).

Endurance is a thinking sport and if you have thought about your experiences along the way and learned from them, if you have trained and built up your horse's performance ability on a progressive basis and if the horse has not yet reached its limit in terms of ability or age, you should now be ready to aim for placings or even to win.

Focus your programme between events on the build up to peak at the right time. The best athletes may be difficult to live with but they are single-minded about what they are doing. Nothing gets in the way of the plan. The idea of psyching yourself up to a ride is no less applicable than for a boxer psyching himself up for a fight. Get out your maps or visit the route if that is possible and permitted, get to know the terrain and going and rehearse how you will ride it. Know where you can make up time, where slow down. Know how fast you

En route at the 1991 European Championships, Montelimar, are Cathy Brown and Naquib.

want to start, given the ground over which you will be riding and knowing that your horse will not be operating at maximum efficiency for up to an hour after the start, even though it has been well worked in.

You probably know some if not all of the other competitors. What will they be doing? Imagine how they will ride this route. Who will override their horse at the start? Who is a careful, steady competitor who nearly always finishes well? Who is likely to win and how does your horse compare with theirs?

Take yourself through the whole ride. How experienced is your crew? How will they cope at the vetgates and what will you need to do yourself? How will you ride your horse into each vetgate? What if there is a racing finish? How will you ride it?

Overall, imagine the situation – in detail, not in some vague, fuzzy way – as it will be with your horse going well.

Once away from the start, it is imperative to get your horse settled as quickly as possible. Most good horses are competitive and likely to fight to get to the front. You have a choice of either pulling right back and letting the speed merchants go, getting off and running with your horse if that is a less energy-consuming way of controlling it than riding, or you can let your horse run on and hope it will settle fairly quickly. A big hill will provide the necessary incentive for a horse to settle into its work. On flat ground, the speed will not abate but pulse rates won't be so high either. The important thing is not to let your horse run so far and so fast that its energy reserves are fading before you are halfway through the race. The horse's energy must be monitored throughout. If you ignore minimal signs of glycogen depletion, however competitive the horse is, your chances will be blown.

Tackling a qualifier on Dartmoor for the Golden Horseshoe in 1986 are Val Long and the incomparable Tarim, sire of many successful endurance horses, with Jill Thomas and a young Egyptian Khalifa.

The hurly burly of the first few miles is also the most dangerous from the point of view of injury. Horses with their eyes set on the horse in front are not choosing their going and a silly accident now will also put you out of the race. It may be easier to control your horse right at the front if you can cope with being a pace setter. If horses behind are constantly pushing, however, holding the lead is probably pushing your horse faster than it ought to go. You can try switching positions, sometimes in front, sometimes dropping back.

However you cope with the early stages, remember that the race is never won in the first 25 miles (40 km). Good vetgate technique, always useful, now becomes vital. You cannot afford to lose minutes in pre-presentation, nor be late for the off. If you come into a gate too slow, the heart rate might rise again or be slower to recover. You need to know your horse's optimum speed from which it can make the fastest recovery. Often a horse will recover more quickly by slowing in the last mile from a relatively strong pace, than from having gone too slowly from too far out.

On the trail again, remember that if your aim is to win, you really are on your own out there. It might suit your purpose to ride with another competitor for part of the way but don't stay with them if it is not to your advantage. You can catch up on the gossip later.

Winners take every opportunity to gain a tactical advantage, but do this within the bounds of the rules, common sense and the spirit of sportsmanship on which endurance riding is based. If someone else is in trouble on the trail, however, you must stop and help no matter how well you are doing.

Look to your own and your horse's resources to gain ground where you can. Is your horse particularly good going up- or downhill and does this afford opportunities for overtaking and leaving the opposition behind. Where are your horse's weaknesses and how can you help it to overcome them, for example by giving it a few minutes' rest or by dismounting. Most horses perform better on some kinds of going than others, so plan to make up time where your horse is happy to go on and make allowances for going it dislikes. While thinking about covering ground in the most efficient way for your particular horse, remember to change gaits and diagonals regularly. If the going is all much the same, it is easy to continue at the same pace, in the same gait, for miles on end and this ultimately builds up tension and stiffness in the horse. Changing gait helps the horse in the same way that dismounting and running or walking for a stretch helps the rider.

If you are going to overtake, gauge your timing so that you can leave the other horse well behind if possible. This means choosing a point where your horse can perform on the ground and terrain better than the horse you want to pass.

Competitive riders will try to lose one another in the miles before the finish and if good management has got them to this point, the strongest, fittest, best ridden horses will have the advantage. However good you are, sometimes there

Val Long and Tarim after winning the Summer Solstice 100-mile ride for a record third time.

Jill Thomas and Egyptian Khalifa on Exmoor, where they have won several gold medals.

will be a better horse out there which has been equally well trained and ridden. If there is nothing much to choose, it may well come to a racing finish – a phenomenon which fills endurance enthusiasts with emotion and outsiders with amazement.

How do you ride a racing finish? Ideally, with the minimum effort necessary to keep your nose in front. If you know the other horse is stronger, you may have to settle for second rather than be eliminated at the final vetting. A galloping finish on a tired horse is also an invitation to injury and lameness. In the heat of the moment, however, the temptation just to go for it is overpowering and if you can keep your head, keep your horse balanced on its legs and have assessed and accepted the risks, then all you need is luck, win or lose, to see you through 'fit to continue'.

Causes of Elimination or Retirement

Each successful ride would be less satisfying were it not for the knowledge of the things that can, and sometimes do, go wrong. There are two main causes of elimination: metabolic problems or lameness.

METABOLIC PROBLEMS

Paradoxically, the improvement in veterinary controls has so greatly reduced the incidence of horses suffering serious metabolic problems that many ride vets have never had to cope with a horse needing rigorous treatment during competition. If a horse does become dangerously compromised due to exhaustion, dehydration or rhabdomyolysis (tying-up), it is vital that immediate and adequate fluid replacement therapy is carried out. Delay or insufficient treatment can result in fatal renal failure. Laminitis (founder), while normally associated with diet, can also originate in exhaustion or excessive traumatic stress. Treatment within hours of onset is essential in the effort to prevent drastic separation of the laminae and rotation of the pedal bone. Horses can and do recover from severe traumatic laminitis but the recovery period is long and painful, requiring intensive nursing, and it is also expensive.

In the previous chapter we noted signs of tiredness that may occur during competition. If these are ignored, more serious fatigue and, ultimately, exhaustion result. Rhabdomyolysis may occur in a fatigued horse but it also occurs in many other situations. Much research has been carried out as to its causes and some progress has been made but the physiology of the syndrome is extremely complex and no absolute conclusions as to its causes have been made.

In endurance competition, it tends to occur in one of two situations, either early in the ride or later, when fatigue becomes part of the equation.

In the first case, it is a classic response to the 'carbohydrate overload' theory, the basis of the old 'Monday morning disease'. What happens is that the horse, which has had its exercise restricted, without a corresponding reduction in concentrate feed and is then asked for a sudden, strenuous work effort, experiences chemical changes within the muscles, causing cell damage which results in the horse tying-up. For many years, this was attributed to a sudden build-up of lactic acid due to anaerobic energy production. More recently, research has indicated that the role of lactate in energy metabolism is more complicated. Some horses, for example, can tolerate much higher lactate levels than others and lactate can also be burnt as an energy-producing fuel.

Despite lack of knowledge of the precise cause, the effect can be prevented in practice by good management. For example, assume that a stabled horse is given a rest day, then travelled most of the following day to a ride where it is stabled overnight and competed next day. With the rigours of the ride in mind, the trainer has continued with the normal diet, forgetting that the horse's exercise has been limited for two days. Then assume that the rider, through inexperience or the horse's excessive freshness, sets off too fast while the horse is still not properly warmed up. Insufficient oxygen is reaching the muscles to maintain aerobic-energy production and the anaerobic metabolism comes into play. Within a few miles this can no longer be sustained, the muscle cells suffer damage and the circulatory systems become clogged with the detritus of waste products and damaged tissue. The congested muscle masses stiffen and swell, becoming hard and painful. The horse stops, obviously distressed and unable to continue. Veterinary attention must be sought immediately. Meanwhile, the horse must be blanketed to keep it warm and minimise shock. If it is willing and able to move, gentle walking will help the muscles to begin to get rid of the accumulated debris. Myoglobin, which transports oxygen within the muscles, is released when the cells are damaged and is excreted with other waste in the urine. The colour of the urine, varying from reddish-yellow to dark brown according to the amount of myoglobin present, is an indicator of the severity of the attack. Flecks of tissue may also appear.

What could have prevented this scenario? Firstly, the trainer could have ensured that the horse was exercised or turned out the day before the journey and could have lunged, corralled or walked out the horse instead of stabling it on arrival at the venue. Secondly, the concentrate portion of the diet could have been reduced on the days when exercise was restricted. Thirdly, the rider could have spent up to half an hour quietly warming up the horse before the start of the ride and could have started out at a more restrained pace, ensuring that the horse worked aerobically instead of anaerobically.

In some cases, repeated tying-up has been linked with an electrolyte imbalance but such cases need individual investigation and are not necessarily related to endurance riding.

Rhabdomyolysis, in conjunction with exhausted horse syndrome, is less likely to occur today because of the superior veterinary controls mentioned above, but may occur when an apparently keen horse, running on adrenalin which disguises the fact that it is tiring, makes an extra effort towards the end of a ride. This may be in terms of speed, an increase in difficulty of the terrain or, in the case of the less experienced horse, simply the extra distance in conjunction with its level of fitness.

A fatigued horse follows the symptoms of tiredness with loss of appetite, unwillingness to continue and some loss of muscle control, apparent as trembling when movement stops. Provided the horse stops at this point and the correct care is given, a full and fairly rapid recovery usually results. However, if the fatigue is not recognised and the horse is asked to continue, it will become exhausted to a life-threatening degree.

In the exhausted horse muscle damage is due to excessive depletion of fuel reserves combined with electrolyte depletion and the consequent inability of the muscles to continue working efficiently. Dehydration is frequently a further cause of exhaustion, the lack of body fluid reducing the volume available for circulation of the blood and also reducing gut motility. Colic is a further complication of this.

The horse's ability to dissipate heat and maintain an acceptable core temperature is compromised by hard work in conditions of high external heat, humidity and solar radiation. Once the temperature rises above 40°C (104°F), the body systems are in danger of failing.

Occasionally horses are eliminated from competition with 'thumps' or synchronous diaphragmatic flutter. The condition is seen in tired, sometimes dehydrated horses as a regular muscular twitch of the flanks, synchronised with the heart rate, which is the result of involuntary contractions of the diaphragm. The exact cause is still unknown, although an intracellular calcium imbalance is involved. Mild cases often improve quickly without treatment but the treatment vet will administer fluids containing calcium for more severe attacks.

LAMENESS

Lameness is by far the most common reason for failure and elimination of horses in endurance rides. Unlike other sports, the basis of veterinary judging means that lameness is quickly detected and the horse stopped from further competition. In addition, as horses may not compete in endurance under the influence of painkilling drugs, there is, fortunately, no possibility of disguising lameness. These aspects, plus the rules for elimination which are designed to ensure the welfare of the horse, mean that lameness in endurance horses is fully documented, whereas in other sports, such as racing and eventing, it goes unperceived by the general public.

There are many causes of lameness, with results of varying severity. The majority of lamenesses incurring elimination in endurance rides are caused by minor injuries such as foot bruising, overreach and muscle strain. They are seldom serious and are usually resolved fairly quickly with rest. They can be considered a normal hazard of athletic performance, similar to the minor problems that may be experienced by the human athlete.

Tendon strain, the bane of the racehorse, is comparatively rare in endurance horses. Splints, spavins or curbs occasionally occur during the development of the horse's career, due to overstrain or trauma. Serious accidental injury seldom happens. In the older horse, it is the accumulated effects of concussion which most frequently result in lameness, due to bony changes and arthritis in the joints.

How can the incidence of lameness be minimised?

The nature of the sport at top level means that the horse will be asked to maintain the fastest practical pace over a variety of terrain – pavement, baked clay, rutted chalk, sand, turf, mud, peat moor, sharp flints – any of these might be encountered in the course of 100 miles (160 km). The immediate reaction, therefore, is to find some means of protecting the foot. However, protection is seldom effective on a horse which already has basic foot problems. For example, fitting pads to poor feet usually results in lost shoes. It is sometimes wise to use pads if the terrain warrants it, for example a route that is known to have a preponderance of sharp stones. In this case, the pads must be expertly fitted by a farrier who understands the specific needs of the sport, and the packing material used to prevent the ingress of mud and stones under the pads must be smoothly and accurately inserted, with the pad finished level. Any pressure caused by uneven packing will result in bruising. The most commonly used packing material is silicone but this is not wholly satisfactory as it can sometimes break up and work its way out. Tow and Stockholm tar or other materials are sometimes used. The pads themselves are usually synthetic, of varying types of plastic. They must be capable of some expansion and of maintaining the nails firmly in place so that the shoe is not loosened. Leather pads are sometimes used, but tend to wear out quickly on stony tracks and become soft and inefficient once they get wet.

Fitting pads changes the horse's way of going and if they are to be used in competition, the horse needs a chance to get used to them beforehand. However, it is unwise to leave pads on for more than a few days or the sole will begin to soften. The use of pads is fraught with difficulty and although they are used as a matter of course in some countries where rough going is prevalent, this is not recommended in Britain where wet going and mud are more often encountered.

An alternative to pads and an excellent way of providing extra support and protection for the foot is the use of wide-web shoes which cover more of the sole than a standard shoe and tend to wear longer and more evenly. Beware the loss of grip, however, on hard, slippery ground such as tarmac and dry grass; the use of stud nails will counteract this problem.

Foot protection is a guard against the common problem of bruising but won't prevent other types of injury which cause lameness.

It is much more important to ensure that the horse's feet are correctly balanced and that it is well shod, with plenty of heel support. The importance of correct farriery has been stressed in earlier chapters and its effect on the alignment of limbs and joints can resolve many lameness problems including brushing, speedy cutting, overreach, muscular strain and overall poor action which is the cause of all of these faults. Careful, knowledgeable farriery can even help to relieve conformational asymmetry, enabling a horse to compete better than it otherwise would. However well shod the horse, unbalanced riding will contribute to the risk of injury and lameness (see Chapter 5).

Finally, lameness can arise out of conformational or developmental weakness. If a horse has been unsympathetically trained and its ability to carry a rider undeveloped, its physique will succumb more easily to strain. Similarly, if the basic conformation is at fault, the horse will have to compensate for this in action and will be less able to accommodate the stress of continuing strenuous work. Lameness can be partially prevented, therefore, by the selection and breeding of the right type of horse for the sport.

Kay Trigg and the 14.1hh Brookhouse Maestro, winners of many top British National titles.

Lilla Wall and Alfie, the British 'secret weapon' who helped to win team gold at the Stockholm World Equestrian Games.

12

New Frontiers

Endurance riding is the sport of the pioneer, the seeker of adventure and challenge. It arose from the desire of people to take their partnership with the horse to new limits of achievement. At international competitive level it has seen the introduction of many techniques aimed at beating the other teams – in particular, the professional expertise of the back-up crews – but at the purest level it is the challenge of horse and rider against the natural elements. As a sport, it has also pushed back the frontiers of veterinary knowledge and horsemastership but there are still many questions unanswered and research will continue to probe them. What really causes thumps? Why does a tired horse still have plenty of energy reserves in its muscle cells? Why are some horses more prone to azoturia than others?

ABOVE *At the end of 100 miles: the author on Rani Tarina (nearest camera) finishing second in the Summer Solstice. The other horse, Cocky Socks, was sadly eliminated for lameness.*

OPPOSITE PAGE *One of Britain's top combinations of the mid 1990s, Jo Trego with Oliver's Taboo.*

Every horse and rider combination has its own problems to overcome and as long as there is country to ride over, endurance riders will continue to rise to the challenge – one horse, one hundred miles, one day.

There's always another race, another day.

APPENDIX 1

Endurance Organisations

Australia

Australian Endurance Riders Association, B. Timms, Box 144, Nanango, Queensland 4615, Australia. Tel: (61 71) 631 568

Canada

Canadian Long Distance Riding Association, Joan Spiker, Box 160, Jarvie, Alberta, TOG IHO, Canada.
Tel: (1403) 954 2152

Europe

European Long Distance Rides Conference (ELDRIC), Secretary: Dr Georg F. Riedler, Sonnenterrasse 25, CH-6030, Ebikon, Switzerland. Secretariat: Bureau Perfect Services, Beatrix P. Schnüriger Gotthardstrasse 52, CH-8002 Zürich.
Tel: (411) 281 2050 Fax (411) 281 1456.

France

CNREE, J. Robin, Logis de Seneuil, F-79410 Cherveux, France. Tel: (33 49) 75 02 25; Fax: (33 49) 75 05 71

Great Britain

British Horse Society Endurance Riding Group, British Equestrian Centre, Stoneleigh, Kenilworth, Warwickshire, CV8 2LR, England

Endurance Horse and Pony Society of GB, Mill House, Mill Lane, Stoke Bruerne, Northants, NN12 7SH, England

Scottish Endurance Riding Club, L. Wilson, 9 Elliott Road, Jedburgh, Roxburghshire, Scotland. Tel: 0835 863823

New Zealand

NZETRA, Ray Tylee, Tiverton Downs Road, RD 1, Reporoa, New Zealand. Tel: (64 7) 333 8013

South Africa

Endurance Riders Association of South Africa, Dr Louwtjie Viljoen, PO Box 142, Honeydew 2040, South Africa. Tel: (41 41) 33 2087

United States

American Endurance Rides Conference, 701 High Street, Suite 216, Auburn, CA 95603 USA. Tel: (1 916) 823 2260; Fax: (1 916) 823 7805

APPENDIX 2

Additives and Supplements

WHAT IS THE DIFFERENCE?

A supplement is a substance included to achieve the desired balance of nutrients in the diet. An additive is a substance given for its anticipated effect on health or performance, but is not in itself of nutritional value.

ARE THEY NECESSARY?

In certain circumstances, supplements are required to balance the nutrients provided in the diet, for example where the basic ingredients are deficient in certain respects, or where one ingredient is needed to counterbalance the effects of another, for example, maintaining the correct calcium:phosphorus ratio. Additives for performance horses are used with the aim of enhancing or stabilising digestive function, to contribute to the achievement of peak performance.

Constituents of Common Supplements

VITAMINS:

Fat-soluble Vitamins

Vitamins A, D and K These do not normally need extra supplementation in the diets of performance horses.

Vitamin E A basic broad-spectrum vitamin supplement will provide adequate vitamin E unless a high-fat diet is fed, when extra vitamin E is required to counteract the oxydising effect of fatty acids on the vitamin. Different authorities quote enormously varying requirements for vitamin E in the diet, ranging from 200 mg per day for maintenance to 2,000 mg per day in work for a 500 kg horse. How much extra vitamin E should be given to horses on high-fat diets has not been scientifically established and recommendations vary from 5–30 mg/kg of feed, for each 1 per cent increase of fat in the diet. Both proprietory compound high-fat feeds and high-performance vitamin supplements take the need for extra vitamin E into account but it is necessary to read the individual product analyses to ascertain the degree of supplementation. The trace element selenium works in conjunction with vitamin E but the amount required does not increase with extra work. Adequate levels will be provided in proprietary high-performance horse supplements. Specific selenium supplementation is required only where a geographic soil deficiency of the trace element occurs. Selenium is toxic if overfed, so care must be taken not to 'double up' on these supplements.

Water-soluble Vitamins

B complex, including B1 (thiamine), B2 (riboflavin), B12 (cyanocobalamin); folic acid; C (ascorbic acid) These vitamins are synthesised in the horse's gut and deficiencies are rare, except in permanently stabled horses. Horses on a high-fibre diet should not need supplementation and the common practice of supplementing racehorses with injections of B12 (required in the production of red blood cells) is unlikely to be of value.

Biotin A more recently discovered vitamin, required for protein, fat and carbohydrate metabolisation, which also has a role in horn growth and development. In some cases biotin supplementation, together with the amino acids lysine and methionine, plus sulphur and zinc, may improve poor feet.

Essential amino acids: lysine and methionine These are frequently included in performance supplements on the basis that traditional cereal diets are deficient in lysine, while methionine is known to be involved in several essential functions.

TRACE ELEMENTS:

Copper, zinc, manganese, iron, iodine, selenium*, cobalt

Sufficient quantities usually available in the basic diet. Suspected deficiencies require individual investigation; frequently due to localised soil deficiencies.

*Selenium: toxicity may also occur – see vitamin E above.

APPROXIMATE REQUIREMENTS FOR MAJOR MINERALS

Mineral	Daily Requirement (1000 lb or 454 kg horse)	
Calcium Cereals	23 g min.	Available in forages, especially alfalfa. Cereals are deficient in calcium. A fully stabled, hard-working horse may need additional supplementation to that provided in a broad-spectrum supplement.
Phosphorus	14 g min.	High levels in cereals. It is essential that phosphorus in the diet does not exceed the ratio of calcium 2:phosphorus 1.5.
Magnesium	4 – 6.5 g	Adequate in good basic diet.
Sodium & Chloride	40 g	Sodium low in common foods. Supplementation required.See Appendix 3.
Potassium	45 g	High levels available in forage. See Appendix 3.

ELECTROLYTE PREPARATIONS: SODIUM, POTASSIUM, CHLORIDE, CALCIUM AND MAGNESIUM (SEE APPENDIX 3)

HERBS

Herbs are deep-rooted, slow-growing plants found among the natural flora of the countryside. They provide a wide range of nutrient and therapeutic substances and herbal medicine has a well-established history worldwide. Much is made of the natural benefits of herbs but it must be remembered that 'natural' does not necessarily mean appropriate to a particular case or beneficial in action, and some herbs are poisonous. There is also no evidence that the constituents of herbal supplements would not show up in a dope test. Their use in equine management is becoming increasingly popular, however, and herbal supplements for general health and specific problems are available in pre-packaged form. Some of the best known are:

Garlic

Beneficial to the circulatory and respiratory systems, helping in removal of waste products and pollutants; eases coughing; a natural antibiotic; also said to be fly repellent and good against worms.

Comfrey

Used to promote healing and to relieve pain and inflammation; also as a poultice. Toxic in very large quantities.

Yucca

A plant native to Mexico, yucca is a natural source of salicylic acid, used in aspirin, and is used as a feed additive to mitigate the effects of arthritis.

Commonly Used Additives

PROBIOTICS

The horse's digestive system depends upon the population of micro-organisms which break down food nutrients in the hind gut. Probiotic preparations consist of scientifically produced groups of live microflora (lactobacilli and streptococci) designed to stabilise and maintain the gut population. This is considered necessary to counteract: (a) the effects of illness or other invasive therapy, such as worming, and (b) the physiological products of stress, which can also seriously upset the balance. Probiotics may also protect against harmful microbes; they stimulate the immune system and may even have an anti-carcinogenic effect. The main purpose for their inclusion in the diet of endurance horses is to help the digestive system in coping with the effects of travel and competition stress. To be fully effective they must be fed on a continuous basis and the manager must decide whether the result warrants the cost in individual horses.

Some preparations also contain yeasts and enzymes.

YEASTS

Yeast cultures are known to have the effect of increasing growth without any increase in feed of youngstock. In the performance horse diet, their purpose is to aid the digestion of fibre and stabilise the activity of the hind gut, lessening the risk of upset.

ENZYMES

Enzymes occur naturally of course, but those included in supplements are intended to enhance digestibility of otherwise indigestible substances and thus maximise the absorption of nutrients from the feed.

CARBOHYDRATE BOOSTERS

The problem in longer-distance endurance rides is to provide an adequate supply of nutrients to maintain energy production throughout the competition, avoiding the effects of glycogen depletion and 'hitting the wall'. This is partly overcome by feeding a high-fat diet. However, cabohydrate boosters are increasing in popularity as a form of 'instant' energy. Commercially produced preparations contain mainly partially digested starch combined with simple sugars (fructose or glucose). These are given before, during and after the competition with the aim of providing immediately available energy and speeding recovery.

Carbo-boosters are a relatively new innovation and users should follow the manufacturer's recommendations for dosage.

SIMPLE SUGARS (GLUCOSE AND FRUCTOSE)

Giving glucose or fructose alone raises the blood sugar level which provides immediate extra energy but also stimulates a surge of insulin which removes the sugar from the blood and results in a subsequent reduction of available energy.

Appendix 3

Electrolytes

What are electrolytes?

Electrolytes are essential salts required for efficient muscle and nerve function and the maintenance of the correct fluid balances in the body.

The electrolytes of concern to endurance riders are:

sodium (Na+)
chloride (Cl–)
potassium (K+)
calcium (Ca++)
magnesium (Mg++)

Electrolyte particles are electrically charged and known as ions. Positively charged particles, such as sodium (Na+), are called cations, and negatively charged particles, such as chloride (Cl–), are called anions. They play a complex and vital role at cellular level in keeping the body systems functioning efficiently.

How are electrolytes lost?

The majority of fuel burned in energy production is converted to heat, with less than 25 per cent actually converted to movement. This heat must be removed from the horse's body to prevent it from literally cooking.

The horse produces large quantities of sweat – up to 21 pt (12 litres) per hour when travelling at 10–11 mph (17 kmph) – which evaporates from the skin surface and thus cools the horse. This is the horse's principal method of heat dissipation. Other methods are conduction, via water poured on to the horse, convection due to the effect of wind speeding up evaporation, and radiation, when the surrounding air is cooler than the horse's skin. The horse's sweat contains a higher (hypertonic) concentration of electrolytes than the normal (isotonic) concentration in body fluids; thus not only are electrolytes lost in sweat but the concentrations in the body become unbalanced. Research has shown that in prolonged, strenuous work, electrolytes are lost in far greater quantities than can be replaced during competition, even with periodic, balanced dosing.

Effects of electrolyte loss

Performance becomes impaired, with the loss of a minimal amount of electrolytes, long before signs of dehydration and associated illnesses become apparent. Reduced enthusiasm is the first thing a rider is likely to notice and if the situation is not corrected, the classic signs of dehydration follow.

Peak performance therefore depends upon:

a) minimising electrolyte loss by minimising sweating; and

b) sufficiently replacing losses before performance becomes impaired.

Some associated factors

The concentration of electrolytes is greater in the sweat of unfit horses than in fit horses. Fit horses also produce relatively less heat and therefore sweat less.

Increased heat and humidity increase sweating; wind has a cooling effect and also increases evaporation. Sponging or sloshing the body surface with water provides fluid for evaporation (as well as removing heat by conduction) and therefore reduces the need to sweat and the associated loss of electrolytes.

Harder and faster work both increase heat production and sweating.

Physiological factors, such as ratio of body mass:surface area, predominant muscle fibre type, skin thickness and amount of subcutaneous fat all affect ability to dissipate heat.

When to give electrolytes

An appreciable amount of electrolytes, especially potassium and calcium, can be replaced via food, particularly forage.

Some electrolytes are already available in the reservoir of digestible matter which is passing through the hind gut (caecum) on a continuous basis. The extent to which the working horse can call on these supplies needs further research. After a long journey prior to, or during or post-competition, there is likely to be an electrolyte loss and imbalance. Dehydration parameters (pinch test, mucous membranes, capillary refill) can be checked for variation from normal, to see if there is any clinical indication of dehydration.

Electrolytes cannot be stored in the body and any excess is excreted.

There is a case for giving an electrolyte dose prior to competition or early in an endurance ride, to minimise the risk of dehydration and imbalance later. This depends upon the effectiveness of the electrolyte dose in encouraging the horse to start drinking and thus replace lost fluid.

If a horse has already begun to drink well, electrolytes can safely be administered.

If a horse has begun to show signs of dehydration and is not drinking, **electrolytes must not be given** as they will not be absorbed and will increase the dehydration dangers by drawing fluid from the circulatory system into the gut.

WHAT TO GIVE

There are many commercial electrolyte preparations on the market and the principal caveat is to avoid those designed for ill horses in a state of acidosis as the effects of endurance competition normally result in a state of alkalosis.

Research suggests that most commercial preparations provide insufficient quantities of electrolytes to compensate adequately for the effect of losses on performance, even when the makers claim they are specially formulated.

Common salt added to the diet and provided via a salt lick gives a continuous supply of sodium. This can be maintained by giving salt in feeds or water during endurance competition. (Salts are generally more acceptable in feeds than in water.) A cheap electrolyte mix can be formulated using equal parts of sodium chloride (common salt) and potassium chloride (lite salt) with 0.5 part of calcium and magnesium carbonate (dolomite). This can be given by syringe, mixed with a suitable palatable base substance, at the rate of 1 oz (28 g) per dose, as required. For specific advice, consult your veterinary surgeon.

APPENDIX 4

Endurance Ride Checklist

RIDER

- crash hat and silk(s)
- riding boots
- chaps
- jodhpurs (two or three pairs)
- sweatshirts
- T-shirts
- underclothes (three changes)
- cotton and woollen socks
- neckerchiefs and handkerchiefs
- gloves (three pairs)
- waterproofs
- whip
- bum bag containing safety-pins, string, elasticated bandage, Band-aids, hoofpick, pocket knife, money for phone, food bars and electrolyte drink, other personal necessities, map, map carrier, compass
- non-riding clothes: tracksuit, clean T-shirt or sweatshirt, clean socks, trainers, handkerchief
- smart riding gear if needed for parade: black boots, fawn jodhpurs, jacket and shirt or clean competition shirt, stock, velvet cap or clean silk, gloves

HORSE

- bridle plus spare bits and hackamore if used
- saddle(s)
- saddle cloths and numnahs (min. three)
- girths (min. three) and sleeves, if needed
- stirrups (with cages if wearing trainers) and two sets leathers
- breastplate, crupper if needed
- Equiboot, Easyboot or Shoof brushing boots if worn (or for emergency use)
- other tack if used
- heart rate monitor, if used

Endurance Ride Checklist continues

CREW CAR/LORRY

spare tack as mentioned above
change of clothes for rider as above
quilted rug and/or jute rug with surcingle
anti-sweat rug (two)
woollen blanket(s)
New Zealand rug or rainsheet
cooler
travelling boots
leg bandages and gamgee
tail bandages
poll guard, if used
headcollar and leadrope(s)
water carriers and water buckets (min. three)
slosh bottles in crate
haynet
soaked sugar beet
oats/barley/coarse mix (according to taste)
carrots and apples
electrolytes, salt
stethoscope
spare shoes (hammer and rasp if you have them)
grooming kit: dandy brush, body brush, two sponges, sweat scraper, hoofpick, towels
fly repellent
torch
map of area
strong cord for repairs
food, drink and electrolyte and/or carbohydrate drink for rider and crew
first-aid kit (horse and human) containing antiseptic or antibiotic wound dressing, cotton wool, gauze dressings, poultice dressing, three or four 4 in (10 cm) wide elastic bandages, scissors, sticky tape, arnica ointment/tablets, petroleum jelly, wound ointment, headache/painkilling and indigestion tablets, Savlon, insect bite ceam, sun protection cream, lipsalve

STABLES/OVERNIGHT STAYS

mucking out tools
skip
bedding if not provided
feed: oats, barley, coarse mix, etc., soaked sugar beet, feed supplement, oil, carrots, electrolytes, alfalfa (optional), hay/haylage
spare buckets/manger
tack-cleaning kit and basic repair kit
any extra rugs
stable bandages
elastic leg bandages
ice-packs and leg wraps
Effol wash or similar
hot water bottle and cover or thermal heat pack
horse passport or vaccination certificate

Further Reading

Centred Riding, Sally Swift (Heinemann, 1985)

Endurance Riding, From Beginning to Winning, Lew Hollander and Patricia Ingram (Green Mansions Inc., 1989)

America's Long Distance Challenge, Karen Paulo (Penguin Books, 1990)

The Equine Athlete, Jo Hodges and Sarah Pilliner (Blackwell Scientific Publications, 1991)

Getting Horses Fit, Sarah Pilliner (Blackwell Scientific Publications, 1986)

Horse Nutrition and Feeding, Sarah Pilliner (Blackwell Scientific Publications, 1992)

Shoeing for Performance, Haydn Price and Rod Fisher (The Crowood Press, 1989)

The Tellington-Jones Equine Awareness Method, Linda Tellington-Jones and Ursula Bruns (Breakthrough Publications Inc., 1988)

INDEX

Page numbers in italics indicate illustrations